D1563602

A Celebration of Work

NORMAN E. BEST

Edited and with an

introduction by

William G. Robbins

University of Nebraska Press

Lincoln and London

Manufactured in the United
States of America

The paper in this book meets
the minimum require-
ments of American National
Standard for Infor-
mation Sciences – Permanence
of Paper for
Printed Library Materials,
ANSI Z39.48-1984.

Library of Congress
Cataloging in Publication Data
Best, Norman E., 1906–
A celebration of work / by
Norman E. Best; edited and with
an introduction
by William G. Robbins.
p. cm. Bibliography: p.
ISBN 0-8032-1212-7 (alk. paper)
1. Best, Norman E., 1906–
2. Trade-unions – United States –
Officials and employees –
Biography. 3. Labor and labor-
ing classes – United
States – Biography. I. Robbins,
William G., 1935–
II. Title.
HD6509.B47A3 1990
322'.2'0924—dc19
[B] 89-30401 CIP

My respect for Workers' contributions and my faith
in their even greater potentials
grew out of my experience with them over these many
years and many jobs in various
places. In a very real sense the book is dedicated to them
in that it is an attempt to give
workers a voice that too often has been denied to them.

Contents

ILLUSTRATIONS

MAPS OF JOB SITES

Acknowledgments

When one thinks of all the beauty and reality that goes with being, where do you begin to list the acknowledgments that make your work possible? My being begins with a friendly mother, always proud of her family, and an active father who had a high regard for his family and did his work with skill and pride.

Reaching back for family lodestones, I constantly recall the Sundays spent in the Methodist Church listening to the parables of Jesus and his disciples: Jesus, who understood the reciprocal benefits and the efficacy of the Golden Rule. This ideological lineage has stayed with me through all the changes in my work.

My role model and ideological lineage begin with Jesus and his emphasis on the Golden Rule formula that consideration for others is good for oneself and good for society. Later Jefferson extended the Golden Rule to a national political program for our young nation. However, as Jefferson's agrarian model was superseded by industry and industrial workers, Karl Marx gave the mantle of dignity and trust to industrial workers who were taking the place of Jefferson's farmers.

I was so impressed by Marx's respect for workers and their role in history that I decided to become one myself. That decision led me to feel the reality of the workers' world, which is what this book is all about. However, to persevere through the workers' reality I needed the sustaining rapport and support of our entire family.

My wife, Catherine, looked after all our needs while she kept all of us focused on the sensitive needs of each one personally and all of us together. In addition to looking after all of us, she had the appalling job of converting countless sheets of handwriting into legible typing—then retyping it more times than I can count. This process went on for ten long years as the dream began to develop into a manuscript. In addition to the above work, Catherine has provided a thrust for short, clear sentences with quality wordsmithing.

Michael, our oldest, encouraged me to go back to school after retirement and told me many times I should tell my story, since a worker's view of the workplace had not been told.

Peggy Jo, our older daughter, has set a model for me in the way she implemented her concern for people by working full time for the exploited farm workers on both coasts.

Elizabeth Ann, our younger daughter, expresses her feeling for people at close range to many who become her friends, yet still has time and concern for older Dad.

Our younger son, Rick, expressed his affection for people by going to prison rather than taking part or assisting in the killing during the Vietnam War. His rare perspective, combining an understanding of workers' day-to-day reality with an academic's analysis of political, economic, and social change, was very helpful throughout this long process.

In addition to the family, I am deeply indebted to a University of Washington logician, Cooper Harold Langford. He made ideas relate to each other with a positive clarity usually reserved for the sharp differences between numbers in mathematics. For me, this clarity remained a lasting model.

During the fall of 1977 I had several long, inconclusive discussions about labor unions with historian Beverly Heckart. She finally exclaimed that my forty-eight years in the workplace was a unique experience that should be told. From that vision, the book was born, and a laborious learning experience began. This led to pages of hand-lettered sheets that Catherine edited and converted to a typed rough draft which we revised again. Then, for confirmation or criticism, I turned to anthropologist Kathy Adams, who helped with this work for the first year. Later a friend, Barbara Yelland, gave the manuscript to Don Cummings, a gentle student of the English language. For several years Cummings reviewed the writing a few pages at a time while offering criticism and encouragement. These sustained contributions provided a day-to-day inspiration that kept the manuscript growing. When the strongest themes were developed, both Heckart and Cummings separately reviewed the completed manuscript. With a completed manuscript on hand my confidence in the book grew.

This faith withstood many friendly "yes, but" letters from publishers. Only Stan Weir (a publisher of small pocket books by workers) showed positive interest, yet the book was too big for him. However, because of his encouragement and the insight of David Frankel and Charles Harvey, the manuscript reached historian Joseph R. Conlin, who was intrigued by the book's unique treatment of work. Still it continued to draw dust until our older son, Michael, showed it to a friend, William G. Robbins, a West Coast historian. Once Robbins read the manuscript, things began to happen. Without asking for compensation, he volunteered to edit the book. All through the long review process he stayed with the editing. From a nearly forgotten manuscript he brought it to publishable form without losing any of the style and themes so dear to the author. So the once-dusty manuscript, now edited and enriched with notes by Robbins, was welcomed by the University of Nebraska Press. During this final review process I became deeply indebted to Joseph Conlin. From experience or insight he concluded that there was a missing story in the depression era. Because of his appeal for full treatment of the depression ideologies and their effects on me, a complete account took form, breaking through the bonds of my self-censorship and the hurts of the era. I am also indebted to historian Conlin for suggesting the title of the book.

That is the story of the background and the writing. Yet one more thank-you note is required. Late in the winter of 1983, a combination of cold, sunless winters, a pervasive infection, and a sort of burnout struck me hard. There was little energy left to my spirits. However, the healing power of the Arizona sun in Tempe and the companionship of people-oriented, antiwar activists brought about a long renewal process that allowed me the privilege of again sharing and working.

The following people made important contributions to that healing process: my longtime friend Anci Koppel, Mark Reader, Dick McGaw, Lillian Blahnik, Kelly and Sarah, Roger Axford, John Aguilar, Helen and Jim Simmons, Joe McCawley, Amy, J.B., Mazda, Jane, Phil, Pascual, Dawn, Steve, Umberto, Phil Kassell, and Gray Hale.

Editor's Introduction

WILLIAM G. ROBBINS

I first met Norman Best in the spring of 1967 when he was visiting his son Michael, then a graduate student in economics at the University of Oregon. Cramped into a small university-owned apartment one Saturday evening, a few budget-minded student friends and spouses had gathered for an evening of relaxation and political discussion. For one nearing the end of a Ph.D. program in history, the occasion made a lasting impression, largely because of the presence of Mike's father, Norman Best. Clad in a Filson jacket, worn by many outdoor workers in the Northwest, and with a six-pack of beer nearby, Norm shared with two or three of us the stories of his work experiences and his long involvement as a socially progressive union organizer and peace activist.

A Celebration of Work, written in the years since his retirement in 1972, adds emphasis to those impressions of more than twenty years: Norman Best is both an authentic and gifted storyteller. This memoir shows him to be a sensitive and perceptive person, fascinated by the broader meaning and creativity of the work process. He writes forcefully about his lifelong commitment to workplace democracy, to quality craftsmanship, and to the satisfaction that one experiences of having done the job well. His forty-eight years as a wage laborer and political activist ranged across the states of Idaho, Washington, Oregon, and Montana and included a stint in the San Francisco shipyards during the Second World War. Those experiences firmed up the convictions of his adolescent years in Idaho's northern Panhandle country: the interests of capital and labor were as likely to find common ground as oil and water.

Although the activities and events in this memoir are set in one part of the United States, *A Celebration of Work* raises questions that reach far beyond the confines of regional history. Trained on the job in a variety of crafts but especially as a machinist and highway engineer, Best carried with him values that he learned in the family home—the New Testament virtues of the Golden Rule and service to others. "The story of Jesus throwing the money changers out of the temple," he recalls, "was a powerful image." There was political activism, too, beginning with his childhood and adolescent years. He remembers family lore from the earliest days in Coeur d'Alene, Idaho, that spoke of the "proud élan" of the Wobblies—members of the Industrial Workers of the World—and their "opposition to the inhuman cruelty of the early logging camps."[1] His father, who was involved with the Nonpartisan League in northern Idaho, donated an automobile and his son's services to drive a congressional candidate through northern Idaho during the election campaign of 1920. Although the league candidates did not win, Best remembers the experience as a rewarding one.

*

Norman Best's life experiences embrace many of the broader currents of twentieth-century American history: political involvement, depression, war, union organization and the spread of industrial unionism, corruption in public office, membership in the Communist party, and the social turmoil and antiwar activism of the 1960s and early 1970s. Best's younger son, Rick, served time in a federal prison at Lompoc, near Santa Barbara, California, during the latter period, in his father's words, "making his strongest possible protest against the violence of a nation at war." Several months past the age of sixty-five and after wrestling with the question for some time, Best decided to retire from highway construction work; his purpose was a move to California with his wife, Catherine, to support their son who was serving time for draft resistance. That decision was a difficult one, according to Best: "It was not easy to turn away from a lifetime of concern for work, the reality that everything else revolved around."

The centerpiece of this memoir is the world of work—indeed, as the title suggests, its celebration. When he retired from highway engineering in 1972, Best concedes that the task no longer held the fascination it once did: "There was something wrong with the work, . . . and the job had lost its meaning." That view is more than the nostalgic yearnings for a bygone era; it is consistent with the findings of the most recent studies in labor history. The progressive rationalization of the work process in the twentieth century, the ever-increasing emphasis on greater productivity, and the narrow specialization of most occupational categories have reduced craftsmanship, widened the gulf between science and work (and between labor and end product), and produced widespread alienation among both blue- and white-collar workers. Those circumstances also have further reduced the laborer's control over the job process.[2] Along with that loss of autonomy, a progressive erosion of the worker's egalitarian moral code took place. It was not the machine that gradually came to dominate the workplace; rather, it was the capitalists' increasing ability to refine the science of work (that is, the science of managing the work of others).[3]

The conditions that prevailed when Norman Best retired were much different from the experiences of his early life. His youth was a time when the corporate world had not yet extended its hegemony over the workplace and where the ideas of Frederick Taylor, the father of scientific management, were only beginning to influence the way the job was done. Moreover, at that time it was largely in the industrial centers of the eastern United States that employers had made inroads toward rationalizing the work process.[4] In that respect, Best's life parallels the final stages in the transition from an artisan, craft-based economy to one in which the mode of production is centered on mechanization and automation. His story, therefore, provides a unique view of the social history of the working class in the United States and its relation to the evolution of modern capitalism.

If in the larger scheme of things that story has been one of overall retreat for trade unions from progressive political positions, especially in the last forty years, it is a tale that the more perceptive workers were aware of. Norman Best, whether as a representative of the machinists' union or as a publicly oriented highway engineer, was one of those who fought the capitalists' efforts to impose a production-based rationality on the work process.

This is not an achievment-model memoir to serve as grist for neoconservative labor historiography. Rather, it is a first-person account of a viewpoint and values that have been shunted aside in most histories of the workplace and of the working class, at least until recently. *A Celebration of Work* is a recollection, a memoir of a special kind, one that exhibits familiarity with academic scholarship yet never loses sight of the love for the values of craftsmanship and care for the way work is done. Norman Best clearly understands the growing constrictions that capitalism has imposed on the autonomy of labor during the course of his working life. His story provides a moving personal dimension to the struggle to maintain democracy at the work site and to keep corruption from public construction projects. That effort led him into radical politics, membership in the Communist party for a few years, and frequent changes in employment—the latter obviously a function of his activism on the job and political radicalism away from work.

For Norman Best there is no separation between the political and social worlds. The telling of this story is one in which politics—whether of the workplace, the union hall, the highway contracting system, or the ballot box—is center stage. Moreover, whether the workplace was in turmoil or peace, employment for wages was always inherently political, a refrain that runs throughout this memoir. They are all one of a piece. If the new social history of the 1960s and 1970s was inclined to fragment assessments of the working class, to break analysis into constituent segments that obscure the larger picture, to leave us without an image of the whole, Best's memoir does much to correct that tendency. There is no division in this account between home environment and occupation, between individual and community, between university life and blue-collar labor. The Golden Rule of doing good for others applied to the ethics of the workplace as well as to the Sunday-morning sermon.

*

The story begins in Coeur d'Alene, Idaho, a small town situated on the north shore of Coeur d'Alene Lake. The well-known mining district of the same name, the center of protracted industrial warfare and labor radicalism in the late 1880s and early 1890s, lay more than forty miles to the east. Although the mines continued to play an important part in the economy of northern Idaho, lumbering had surpassed mineral production as the region's chief enterprise by the time of the First World War. When Norman Best's parents moved to Coeur d'Alene in 1907, the town was the center of sawmilling and logging activity, the type of work that emphasized ingenuity and proficiency in a variety of skills. As the nearest urban enclave, Coeur d'Alene provided service, jobs, and entertainment for an extensive hinterland region. But whether the place of employment was in town or in the surrounding logging camps, as with other back-country areas, there was still a close association between the conception of work and its consequences, between thought and job processes.

Norman Best grew to maturity in that environment, one that placed a premium on experience, tradition, and the knowledge of a variety of occupational skills—the prerequisites of true craftsmanship. Work was purposive[5] and consequential activity, and workers themselves took great pride in the end result. The small-town repair shops in Coeur d'Alene also provided ample opportunity for inquisitive young people to learn the basics of machine skills and mechanical repair techniques through a variety of apprentice-journeyman relationships. It was there that Best learned carpentry and plumbing skills, acquired experience in small-factory production, and gained knowledge about automative mechanics and truck driving. He concluded early on that the purpose of the machine was to reduce the demands on human labor and to make the work task easier, an idea that was widely shared in the crafts. That view, of course, has changed dramatically during the course of the twentieth century; today the machine is more important to the employer, but primarily as an instrument to increase production (and profits) and to control the labor process.[6]

Because of its traditional setting and homogeneous population, northern Idaho was also a bastion of republican ideology, ideas and values that made the region fertile ground for the farmer-oriented Nonpartisan League.[7] That tradition, especially in the form of the ideas of Thomas Jefferson (the notion that freeholders were the proper repositories of political power), provided the intellectual foundation and an appreciation and explanation of Best's respect for "ordinary working people." Those values, modified by the social realities of the twentieth century, inspired relations with his fellow workers, served as a guide for egalitarian union organization, and provided a beacon when the dark forces of fascism were afoot in the land.

Readers will find *A Celebration of Work* the story of one person's lifelong commitment to social and economic democracy and integrity in the workplace. The memoir recounts Norman Best's persistent struggles against antisocial hierarchies that pitted worker against worker, conditions that corrupted the ethics of labor. But this is not a gloom-and-doom account, one that sees common people succumbing before the all-pervasive forces of modern capitalism. Through their collective ingenuity and strength, the author holds to the vision that rank-and-file citizens will yet build that cooperative commonwealth they have struggled so long to attain.

*

When I renewed my acquaintance with Norman Best in 1986, he still flashed that old sparkling sense of humor and the buoyant hope for the future that characterizes the struggle described in this memoir. Now eighty-two, he is walking, sometimes two miles a day, to maintain the proper meld (his favorite word) between physical exercise and rest to give him the strength to carry on his mental work. A contributor to the *Bulletin of Atomic Scientists* and *Monthly Review*, Best occasionally chides prominent labor historians, such as Jeremy Brecher, for their faulty analyses.

My association with this book originated in the late autumn of 1985 during a visit with my longtime friend (and Norman's son) Michael Best in Amherst, Massachusetts. I discussed the memoir that fall with the University of Nebraska Press, and the review process was initiated. In the interim, Norman has patiently and graciously accepted suggestions for reorganizing the manuscript and, at the urging of Joseph Conlin, carried through a major revision of chapter 6. The sense of community and shared affection in the revised version is, in my view, one of the more compelling sections of the narrative.

Otherwise, my involvement with the manuscript has been the conventional one of providing editorial consistency to the narrative and the customary attention that one should give to any publishable essay. The style, the choice of words, the metaphors, however, belong to the author. If my part in seeing this memoir to print has been time consuming, the task has been of the kind underscored in this story, where vocation and avocation are one. In the author's words: "It gave me a good feeling."

one

Introduction, 1972-1977

In the spring of 1972 I was working on a big construction job in a Seattle suburb. Several months past the magic retirement age of sixty-five, the years did not seem to bother me, yet there was something wrong. I had always enjoyed the creativity of construction labor, but now, working from little scribbled notes and vague verbal instructions rather than from a full set of blueprints, everything seemed confused and the job had lost its meaning. Besides all this, our younger son, Rick, was in a federal prison making his strongest possible protest against the violence of a nation at war. He was in the Lompoc federal prison, near Santa Barbara, California, twelve hundred miles from Seattle, a distance that made it difficult to give him maximum support.

If I retired, my wife, Catherine, and I could move to California and visit Rick the two times a week allowed by prison authorities. But as soon as a person requested retirement, it would set into motion civil-service procedures that could not be reversed. Moreover, it was not easy to turn away from a lifetime of concern for work, the reality that everything else revolved around. After wrestling with the dilemma for three months, I finally decided to sign the papers giving up my right to a job in return for a small retirement pension.

After my retirement, we moved to Santa Barbara and spent most of our time giving our son as much support as we could. In October of 1973 he was transferred to a halfway house in Seattle, where he served three months in a work-release program. The day after his discharge, he loaded up his old truck and headed for Amherst, Massachusetts, where his older brother, Michael, was teaching at the University of Massachusetts.

Mike had been urging me to come to Amherst and take some classes in economics at the university, so at Thanksgiving time, Catherine and I followed Rick to Massachusetts. It was exciting to be in that five-college area of New England. Amherst College and the University of Massachusetts are both located in Amherst, and Hampshire College is about three miles away. The old, prestigious women's colleges Smith and Mount Holyoke are not far away. The students of those five colleges had reciprocity for classes and library privileges, which made for an active college community.

*

The first opportunity to renew my schoolwork came when Rick brought me a catalog from Hampshire College for the January session. He recommended a class on China that required books written by William Hinton.[1] My first inclination was to reject the idea. I had already read most of the books and was concerned that the age differential between me and the other students might make for some tensions. After some thought and conversation, I took Rick's advice, enrolled in the course, and was pleasantly surprised to find that the young people simply accepted me as another student. And even though most of the students came from wealthy families, our objective of studying modern China placed us on common ground. After a few weeks I realized that in listening to the students talk about their reactions to Hinton's book *Fanshen* and in presenting my own responses, I was learning more about China in a few weeks than I had gained from months of individual reading. This first class was a rewarding experience and set the tone for many other courses that I took at the University of Massachusetts.

My first class at the University of Massachusetts was a course in political economy taught by my older son Mike that dealt with the relations between industry, banking, and the government. The first day was embarrassing because of the strange terminology and because I had never attended even an introductory economics course. I wanted to escape from the classroom, but that would have been too conspicuous and would only have added to my embarrassment. In spite of my negative reactions to that first meeting, after a few days I began to understand the material and became acquainted with some of the students. Soon I looked forward to both the lectures and the fellowship of the young people. At the last meeting Mike asked me to talk to the class about my experiences in the workplace and in the trade-union movement. Because the students were interested in what I had to say, that was a very rewarding session. This became the pattern for my continued studies in political economy and in my lectures where I was able to meld my own experience with classroom theory.

My next big experience took place in a class on labor history. In that class I assumed that my forty-eight years in the real world of labor would give me the proper prerequisites. I hoped to find some answers to why international unions can be so undemocratic and corrupt when the workers in the shop or on the factory floor are so meticulously honest and democratic.

The class was a disappointment. The struggles of the labor movement were atomized as the professor concentrated on unimportant details and a personalization of the labor struggle rather than dealing with the powerful deep-seated pressures that affect all unions. Many times I heard good men, with long records of courageous, unselfish work, sound like company agents when they left the shop and advanced up the hierarchy of union leadership. Why do good people with years of putting their necks out to support their fellow workers start speaking up for the companies when they become high union officers? I had hoped to hear some answers to that question in the class in labor history. Instead the historian didn't even address the problem, let alone comment or give an answer.

I complained to Mike about this so much that he finally said, "Dad, if you don't like the way they are teaching labor history, why don't you make up a syllabus of your own and offer it for a class?" It took some time to digest the idea, but eventually I followed his suggestion. Much of my syllabus derived from my own experiences in the labor movement, and I supplemented that with a study of the big pattern-setting strikes of the past. My proposal was accepted at Hampshire College for ten hours of lectures during January of 1977. Because of my concern about not having anything to say after the first day, I began to study labor history in earnest, concentrating on reading every available source about the big labor struggles—the railroad strike of 1877, the Homestead Steel struggle of 1892, and the Pullman railroad strike of 1894.

The Hampshire College officials said the class would be validated if six students signed up. Actually, twenty-one preregistered because of their interest in the paragraph I wrote for the catalog, and there was a daily attendance of about twenty-five. I was pleased with their interest and contributions. In spite of vast differences in our backgrounds—upper-class East Coast students versus retired working-class West Coast teacher—a fine rapport developed between us. In part because of the response of the students and my contacts with the administration, I was appointed Emeritus Fellow of Labor Relations for the spring semester at a handsome fee. In addition, the University of Massachusetts asked me to teach a three-hour course on the problems of democracy in the United States trade-union movement. Preparing for and teaching those classes is when my education really began.

*

As my study of labor history continued, I became excited at both the differences and the similarities in the long sweep of time as technological and political changes affected workers and their unions. During the heady days when thirteen colonies transformed themselves into a fledgling nation, most workers were either craftspeople or freeholding family farmers. Individually they could not change their colonial status within eighteenth-century mercantilism, but collectively under the impetus of Jefferson's philosophy of democracy, they stopped being instruments of England's commercial and governmental interest and became an independent nation. After that, decisions were made collectively by the citizens through the ballot box, which took the place of the concentrated autocratic power of nobility, royalty, and the East India Company.[2]

Jefferson considered the freeholding subsistence farmer to be the foundation of our new democratic government. He rightly felt that what was good for the freeholder was good for the nation. Jefferson's democratic principles have stood the test of time, although applying them has become increasingly difficult. As factories took the place of crafts and farm machines led to large specialized units, craftspeople and freeholding farmers gradually lost their independent way of making a living.

The owners of those factories began to represent a concentration of economic power that rivaled that of the old East India Company. For instance, when Andrew Carnegie and J. P. Morgan bought out over a hundred companies engaged in making steel and formed the United States Steel Corporation in 1901, they were able to dominate the entire steel industry. In the political arena those new concentrations of industrial strength had an influence comparable to the power of the nobility in England.

From my own early experiences of providing for a family through a job in a sawmill woodyard, I can understand how workers felt when they first toiled in factories after generations of laboring independently at a skilled craft or making a living from a subsistence farm. Individually, those workers could not resist the numbing exploitation of the factory any more than their ancestors had individually resisted the British government or the East India Company. Yet when industrial laborers joined collectively to resist the dehumanizing of their efforts to make a living, the government turned on them with federal troops and forced them back to work. For those first industrial workers, the early defeats were nearly as bad as if the English had won the War of Independence. The laboring people had lost their right to join together democratically to provide a better world for themselves and their families.[3] But the resistance to dehumanizing work, unemployment, and poverty went on. Finally, the Great Depression of the 1930s shifted the balance of political power away from corporate America to the people.

During the 1930s a political renaissance took place, reminiscent of the birth of our nation. The new revolution saw unemployed mill workers, out-of-work miners, bankrupt local businessmen, and family farmers elected to local, state, and federal offices. All of them were oriented toward working people and local businesses. With these new representatives in public office and Franklin D. Roosevelt and his New Dealers in Washington, D.C., the political atmosphere tilted towards common people. Legislation was soon enacted giving workers the right to use their collective strength to negotiate with big business. When rank-and-file workers struck General Motors Corporation in the winter of 1936–37, for the first time in United States industrial history the legal and military force of the government was not used against labor. When GM and the workers reached an agreement, industrial unionism was born in the United States.[4]

That unique configuration of increasing political influence for working people, coupled with a negative public image of industry, did not last long.[5] The United States came out of the Second World War with a miraculous record of production as workers of both sexes flocked to big defense plants (often planned and built with federal money). The unlimited demands of the war stimulated an output far beyond anything history had ever known. That effort continued through the four years of war, with unemployment virtually nonexistent. The inflation of wages and prices was kept from skyrocketing by government controls.[6]

Despite the violence to humanity around the world, the war brought prosperity to American companies and jobs to workers. Because the destruction of the war had missed the United States, our industry remained intact, geared to high production, and facing a world waiting to be rebuilt. With peace came an end to wage and price controls. Prices shot up and the big new unions born during the depression struck for wages to keep up with the spiraling cost of goods. Business leaders feared the new powerful unions that they were not able to control.[7]

Besides the problems business faced with unions, the war had created new power relationships around the world. After four years of facing the German war machine on the eastern front, the Soviet Union had finally prevailed against Hitler. Despite unparalleled losses of millions of young men, the Russian army was now astride all of Eastern Europe and remained in charge of all the invasion routes used by Hitler's armies. This new postwar power of the Soviet state created concern among many United States industrialists, a concern that added to their fear of the collective voice of workers in industry.

The industrialists responded by using their political and economic influence to neutralize both the Soviet state and the new industrial unions. Through access to the media, they were able to fuse people's alarms over Russian military power with an artificially created fear of the big industrial unions. They claimed that workers who collectively bargained to humanize the workplace were somehow part of a Russian plot that threatened the system of free enterprise.[8] The growth of the big industrial unions, in fact, simply reflected the workers' application of Jeffersonian democracy to collectively *regain* the control over work-

two

Through 1926

Coeur d'Alene, Idaho, is a small town of about eight thousand people on the northern shore of beautiful Coeur d'Alene Lake in the foothills of the Rocky Mountains. Because of the beauty of the terrain and the lake, the area has become a tourist and resort center. When I grew up there between 1907 and 1926, Coeur d'Alene was a sawmill town. It was a natural location for lumber manufacturing, because the hills to the east were covered with valuable timber and the rivers and the lake provided easy transport for logs.

My mother and father were from Wisconsin. My mother's family tree bore such names as Houlihan and Hepburn, people who traced their ancestry to Ireland and Scotland. Family lore has it that some of those people settled in Pennsylvania before the Revolutionary War. My father's people came from England and Ireland. The Borden branch of his family were Quakers who settled in what is now New Jersey under a charter from the king of England. The Bests came later from Ireland.

My mother's father, Charles Hepburn, ran the only store in Prairie Farm, Wisconsin, a small town located in the north-central part of the state, an area noted for its family farms and dairies. Besides being the only storekeeper, my grandfather is remembered as being the only active Democrat in town. My mother, the oldest of a large family of four girls and two boys, taught school in a neighboring town before she married my father. The two of them moved to Coeur d'Alene in 1907.

My father's father and his brother were orphaned by the time of the Civil War. Their father, a Northerner living in Texas when the war broke out, enlisted in the Northern army. His wife, also a Northern woman, left the hostile South with two small boys and the family dog in a horse-drawn wagon and returned north. Years later my grandfather and his brother acquired both farm and timberland in central Wisconsin, where they developed a showcase farm. They bred their own horses, both for heavy farm use and for fast, high-stepping carriage work. My father grew up on the farm with his five brothers and one sister. There they learned the art of teaching horses to pull and travel so they could get their crops grown, harvested, and hauled to market. My grandfather was active in building roads and was a leader in obtaining the first road grader for the county. With that machine he pioneered the concept of good drainage, ditches, and gently crowned roads to provide all-weather wagon travel.

In addition to caring for his own farm and the community's road system, my grandfather helped organize the Farmers' Equity. That was an early post–Civil War organization devoted to protecting the farmer's interests in achieving fair railroad freight rates, reasonable bank loans, and marketing prices sufficient to keep up the family farm.[1]

My father was very proud of *his* father's innovative accomplishments on the farm and in the community, and he liked to talk about their fine horses. By breeding the best coach horses with fast Thoroughbreds, his father developed coach horses that also had the necessary endurance to make good time on the long eighteen-mile hauls to the railroad at Wheeler and the longer thirty-mile trip to Menominee. Taking those excursions with his father was a big thing for Dad. As a teenager, he often made the long trips to Wheeler or Menominee with a heavy wagon loaded with produce. For that work, my grandfather bred another strain of horses by crossing heavy Belgians with regular workhorses. In many ways, the twenty- and thirty-mile trips with the horses seemed to hold more adventure than the much longer trips of today.

Traveling about the country made it easier for my father to go to school in Menominee. At that time it was quite unusual for the young men of Prairie Farm to go beyond the village grammar school, but Dad helped work his way through the Stout Institute in Menominee by milking cows morning and night. He considered Stout to be sort of an advanced high school and vocational-agricultural institute, not a college as it presently is listed in Menominee.

Before he graduated from Stout Institute, his mother died and not long after that his father remarried. The farm didn't seem to be the same to the boys, so one by one they left to seek other work. Dad and three of his brothers headed west. The oldest brother and my father worked in the woods, using their skilled horsemanship to skid heavy logs to a loading site and then to haul them on heavy wagons to a lake or stream. From there they would be floated downstream to a sawmill. The two younger brothers became engineers for the Great Northern Railroad; they worked out of Hillyard, a suburb of Spokane, Washington.[2]

I grew up listening to those four brothers tell of their accomplishments, their failures and successes as railroad firemen and engineers, and the problems of hauling heavy logs up steep hills—with horses for motive power and a prayer for brakes on the downhill hazards.

The stories about the accomplishments of these workers were the highlights of weekends during my early school days. Here, too, I heard about the Industrial Workers of the World (IWW). The brothers described the crowded, bug-ridden bunkhouses and the IWW's first successes in cleaning them up. The IWW succeeded in getting better living conditions with new, less-crowded bunkhouses and vermin-free blankets and hot water. Those were great accomplishments brought about by the unity and determination of the loggers in their collective action through the IWW.

The brothers who were employed on the railroad became engineers during the early part of the First World War, when there were so many jobs and so few workers that the engine crew labored sixteen- to twenty-hour days. Cleburn, the oldest brother, became a grievance man for the engineers' union, which tried to protect the men from such long, hazardous days by limiting the hours of work. Out of those efforts came a federal law restricting train crews to sixteen-hour days, followed by eight hours of rest. Those accounts told of workers' solving problems and the pride they took in their accomplishments.

*

After being raised on those stories about different jobs, I was excited to find after-school work during the third or fourth grade delivering groceries in Coeur d'Alene. Several of the grocery stores and meat markets jointly owned and operated a delivery service. After school I would hurry downtown to find the horse-drawn delivery wagon, or the bobsled that was used in the winter. I would help make the pickups in the stores and markets and ride around with the driver to deliver the orders to the customers. The grocery boxes were cleverly made out of wood with little hinges, so that after delivering the contents, the bottom would fold up and the sides and ends would collapse so that it would lay flat and solid when we returned it to the wagon.

It shocks me to compare the efficiency of this old-fashioned collective delivery system and its reusable boxes with the waste and pollution of today's shopping. Now each shopper drives two tons of advanced machinery to a supermarket, tramping through the store and carrying home wasteful bags and cartons. The old ways seem strangely efficient and so protective of the environment. That youthful apprenticeship was fun and interesting, a sharp contrast to the lack of work that prevails for many grade-school students today. As time passed, the exhilaration of the work turned to disappointment when I received the meager pay of fifty cents for a week's work. I wasn't doing the job for money, yet I felt an injustice in the pay for my work and decided to look in other directions for a job.

My next two jobs were miserable in both pay and work—picking strawberries and then cherries at about three cents per pound. Thankfully they didn't last too long, because the job was very monotonous and the picking so poor that I earned very little pay.

I have pleasant memories of my next job for two reasons—the nature of the work and the pay. I was in seventh or eighth grade when someone introduced me to the job of caddying at the Hayden Lake Golf Course, seven miles from home. The work was a pleasure, carrying the clubs around the beautiful course, and the pay was stupendous—a dollar and fifty cents for eighteen holes. If you were lucky you could get a thirty-six-hole day and earn three dollars. The only problem was the seven-mile walk to the course and the return home at night. Sometimes we would ride out on the fisherman's special, the early-morning electric interurban train, but I still have vivid thoughts about the long walk home at night.

In the political arena one of my earliest recollections is the sawmill whistles blowing loud and clear on my birthday, celebrating the armistice of the First World War. That was a great day.

Jobs were scarce after the war ended, but Dad had to have an income to support his growing family so he tried several selling jobs. At one time he traveled around the country on a bicycle, trying to sell a metal plunger, an effective tool for washing clothes at that time. Later he bought a 1917 Chevrolet car so that he could travel farther on his sales trips. He didn't sell many of the hand-powered washing machines, but he did get acquainted with many farmers. He learned that they were having hard times because of the low prices they received for their products and the high cost of everything they had to buy. Merchants or dealers set the prices paid to farmers for their produce and also what farmers had to pay for their supplies.

Because that arrangement did not seem fair, farmers formed an organization called the Nonpartisan League. League members hoped to cure some of the problems with two programs: (1) they encouraged farmers to cooperate in marketing by withholding their produce until they could get a fair price and still have something left over to keep the family farm together; and (2) they worked to elect their own people to office in the hope that this would influence the government to help the farmer get a price consistent with the costs of production. Such a price is called parity. Dad became very active in helping the farmers on both of those programs.

As I recall it, in the campaign of 1920 the league ran candidates for federal and state offices. Because most men had not learned to drive a car at that time, Dad lent his vehicle—with me as the driver—to the congressional candidate for a trip through the northern three counties of Idaho. That was a fantastic experience for me.

Although I wasn't a very experienced driver, we had no serious mishaps. Usually we stayed overnight at the candidate's farm home, where there was a lot of political talk about Congress and farm prices. The first night it seemed to me I was awake all night listening to one freight train after another traversing the prairie below the host's home. Dad also was a friend of the candidate for governor of Idaho, so we made many trips during the campaign. Most days were spent driving up to farmhouses, where the men would get out and talk about the campaign. Although our candidates did not win, that was a wonderful and rewarding experience for me.

Dad was an admirer of President Wilson, especially in regard to his efforts to prevent future wars. He believed that Wilson had good intentions but lacked the support to accomplish anything lasting in avoiding conflicts. He was disappointed with the Versailles treaty and with the failure of the League of Nations; he felt that little had been accomplished to avoid another war.

That home atmosphere got me into my first political confrontation at school. We were studying the programs enacted to prevent a second world war and the history teacher asked me to enumerate the steps that were taken in the postwar era to prevent another conflict. Instead of quoting from the textbook, I cited Dad as my authority and said nothing had been done to eliminate another war. That caused quite a furor in the class and I suppose was my first witness against the war forces.

My first full-time job was in the summer of 1922 when I was fifteen years old. My Uncle Warrie offered me a job as his helper to build a new wing on a large house. The prospect of working for my favorite uncle, who had a gift for getting along with young people, delighted me. When he told me that he was going to pay me two dollars a day, I was astounded and protested that it was too much money. He replied: "If you aren't worth two dollars a day, I don't want you." Warrie was a capable craftsman who knew how to use the carpenter's square that made it possible to cut lumber so that ridge boards, gables, and valley boards went together like magic. I believed that it would be a privilege to be initiated into the mysteries and skills of building houses.

On my first day, Uncle Warrie marked a rafter to cut and showed me how to start the saw, how to steady it with my thumb, and then to draw it back and push it away so it would stay on the mark. I tried to imitate his technique, but the saw whipped fore and back and vibrated noisily, so I pushed harder in order to cut through the two-by-four. Uncle Warrie interrupted me: "Don't fight the saw. Just take it easy—run it fore and back lightly and smoothly and the saw will do the work for you." I slacked off on the downward pressure and tried to move the saw with a light touch, but most of the time the tip of the saw vibrated with a loud, complaining noise. Eventually a smoother, quiet stroke emerged and I was elated at being introduced to the joy of learning a skill and the satisfaction of seeing a tool doing productive and beautiful work. Uncle Warrie cautioned me not to use the rafters I had cut as a pattern because that would mean an accumulation of error away from the original pattern, advice that I learned to apply to other jobs. He also taught me how to start shingles, to set the overlap, space, and nail the shingles, and something about putting in the metal gutters and ridge boards. Although most of the numbers on the carpenter's square still remain a mystery to me, that job was the highlight of my early work experience.

Later that same summer of 1922, one of Dad's close friends had quite a bit of remodeling work, an opportunity that gave me the chance to learn something of the plumber's trade. Most of our jobs involved hooking up water fronts in wood- and coal-burning ranges, installing hot-water tanks, and renewing drain or water systems. The boss showed me how to measure, cut, and thread pipe.

The standard tool for cutting pipe was a short, cradlelike device with a handle sixteen to twenty inches long. In the cradle were two sharp round cutting wheels. The handle was attached to a third sharp wheel; by turning a knob on the handle, the third wheel was forced into the pipe. Then you could swing the handle back and forth, and on each movement the three sharp wheels would do the cutting. By repeating the operation and then rotating the handle, the pipe was soon cut off. However, when cutting short pieces, this process could squeeze the pipe out of round. The boss told me to use the hacksaw in those cases. But the hacksaw was awkward and dull, so on one of the short pieces I used the cutter instead. That caused the boss to spend a miserable afternoon looking for a leak caused by my out-of-round cutting job. He didn't have to yell for me to feel the deep, painful ignominy of my faulty work. That incident is a fair example of the learning process in the workplace. Of course, one summer didn't make a plumber, but it was a good experience.

The next year, I got a job in a box factory and worked my way up to being a ripsawyer. That was a man's job even if it only paid boy's wages, and ripsawing, even on the night shift, put me in the sawyer hierarchy. With that went a certain acceptance that was very rewarding to a sixteen-year-old. The most experienced ripsawyer, Shorty, ran the machine on the day shift. It was his job and his saw. The machine itself was circular, with big, hooked teeth about an inch and a half long. It was powerful and sharp and could not be stalled. Although it didn't push at you like the oscillating cutoff saw, the saw required some skill and judgment to make it produce. Its spectrum of use was limited; it did not require the talent needed to handle a logger's ax or a falling or bucking saw, but it was amenable to the worker's rhythms and techniques. For that reason it was a challenging summer job for a young man.

Sometimes the order was to rip narrow slats, such as the ones used in cantaloupe crates. Because that put the guide less than two inches from the saw, we would cut out a pusher to shove the slat through the saw. The last piece cut was only a couple of inches from the saw and had to be pulled back by the left hand, a hazardous operation. One night I carelessly wiped two of my fingers on the saw, and it trimmed off a slice of both of them so fast it was painless. There was no reprimand for that, because the injury was slight and it was not unusual. The foreman sent me to the hospital to have my fingers bandaged. Although I came back to work the next night, the boss sent me home to stay until the fingers healed. He said working with the bandaged fingers could result in a real accident.

Shorty came into the box factory one night when we were ripping apple-box ends and showed me how to produce a lot more pieces with less energy and more safety. His gnarled hands and stumps of fingers spoke more eloquently than his words of the hazards of the saw. He wasn't telling me to be afraid of the saw, but he wanted me to pay it the respect it deserved. In a very real sense he initiated me into a part of manhood by accepting me as a fellow worker, an equal, because of the job I was doing.

Of course, the fact that I was running Shorty's saw on the night shift was not like a steady year-around job on the day shift. Yet, the fact that I handled it satisfactorily was meaningful; there was a kind of challenge to it. My recollections are not clear about being shifted to an apprentice millwright. On that job the boss put me downstairs, where all the line shafts, bearings, pulleys, and belts were keeping the machinery moving. It was rewarding to find that my nose was sensitive to saving us from a millwright's worst enemy, the hot box, a malfunction that would stop all the production upstairs. I learned to identify the smell of hot oil, and at the first whiff would alert the millwright. Usually a big application of the magic but expensive castor oil would save the bearing while other adjustments or realignments were made without stopping the line shafts or the big stationary steam engine.

Each day in the box factory was a great experience, and the job might have been more attractive except that it paid a boy's wages and I had to find work with higher pay because my father was bedridden with arthritis for almost two years. That left me the only wage earner for a family of six, and it was imperative for me to find a good-paying job.

*

In the late summer of 1924 I decided to apply for a job at the Winton Mill. Friends advised me to show up every morning at least one-half hour before starting time and wait around the saw deck to see if there were any openings. Showing up regularly at the early hour of 6:30, they told me, would be enough to convince the boss that I needed work badly. To walk the two or three miles to the mill meant leaving home between 5:30 and 6 A.M. So, after a big breakfast of eggs, pancakes, and bacon or ham, I would pick up my heavy lunch box and head for the mill. My mother got up before me, and breakfast was always ready when she called me for work. She also packed my lunch with tasty meat sandwiches, homemade desserts, and a pint of hot coffee in winter and lemonade in the summer.

Mr. Bronson, the superintendent, hired and fired and gave all the orders for the operation of the Winton Mill. The whole working world of the mill revolved around his beckoning finger or his dreaded order: "Go to the office and get your time." That was his procedure for hiring and firing.

There are no recollections of any conversation about asking for work, but one morning Mr. Bronson motioned for me to follow him through the mill into a vast woodyard. There he showed me several wagonloads of four-foot-long wood and told me to begin stacking it in the same manner. So that was a man's job at a man's pay! Those cartloads of wood had to be stacked in one long rambling pile after another. Piling wood soon became an inhuman rhythm—stoop and pick up a handful of four-foot edgings, raise and put them on the pile. No matter how I did it, there was no relief from the stooping, picking up, and stacking. That routine continued without a break from 7 to 11 A.M. and from noon until 4 P.M. Only one time in the seven months of piling wood did I go around behind the pile and sit down for a couple of minutes. No sooner had I done so when Mr. Bronson showed up and sharply told me to get back to work.

But it was a job and the work fulfilled basic needs, such as food, clothing, and shelter for my family. That gave me considerable self-esteem, and because I got the job on my own it added to my feeling of self-worth. That was especially true when the mill kept me on during the winter shutdown. The worst thing about the job was how slowly time passed. There was no satisfaction of work being done well. It was the kind of job that robs people of their personal resources.

My various schemes to lessen the boredom of the long days—different systems of stooping to pick up the wood—anything to add variety and introduce some skill to the routine, did little to help. Then I would dream about better things than the day-to-day reality of the job, about the power to persevere through adversity, about the power of the mind to reach out beyond the woodyard to another, better reality. For that, the Methodist Church offered some support.

Those long Sunday sermons—centered on the New Testament Gospels of Matthew, Mark, Luke, and John—made a lasting impression on me. The idea of service to others, following the Golden Rule, and laying down your nets to follow the man from Galilee, were central themes that stayed with me. During that period, I taught a boys' Sunday-school class and read or talked about the old stories from the New Testament that held up the virtues of concern for others. Although tithing was always held up as a model, I never went that far; a generous donation in the collection plate appeared adequate to me.

My conscience urged me to follow closely the New Testament models. Indeed, it was such that I finally told a young Methodist minister and his wife of my decision to dedicate myself to follow in their footsteps. That acknowledgment appears to have been the peak of the commitment, because it didn't interfere with my plans to attend a state university. That concern with ethics probably influenced my interest in the study of psychology and philosophy. The idea that in education you could learn from others without depriving them of what you gained was a persuasive concept. It was much superior to the idea of piling up material riches, much of it taken from others. The story of Jesus throwing the money changers out of the temple was a powerful image.

Regardless of those models, I was still confronted with the day-to-day job of making a substantial contribution to the necessities of food, clothing, and shelter for six people. That tempered my idealism, but it also gave me an incentive to look for a job that would combine good work and provide living necessities.

*

In the spring of 1925 I left the numbing impersonality of the woodyard and was introduced to the rewarding and sharing relationship that exists between an apprentice and a journeyman craftsman. That came about when my father found a job for me at the local Dodge Garage. My memories don't recall any farewell scene in departing the woodyard. There was no such courtesy as two weeks' notice before leaving that type of job. Actually, the attitude of the older men was to "get out while you have a chance." The job at the garage was a release from the tedious drudgery of the woodyard, so I hurried away and never again considered the mill as an option.

With the coming of spring, people were getting their cars out and my job was to fill the tanks with gas and check the oil and water. A small problem developed because I probably didn't show the proper enthusiasm for selling gas. Perhaps my attitude was simply not aggressive enough for me to be a successful salesman. At any rate, the boss soon took me off that job and put me back in the shop washing parts and helping the two mechanics. Getting my hands dirty in the grease and solvent in the shop didn't bother me. Having a chance to see what was inside a car motor and learning how it ran was a beautiful thing.

The job at the Dodge Garage didn't last long. The overhead at the small agency was quite high. Besides the owner—who was a man-about-town and a car salesman—there was an office man, a gas-pump worker who was also the handyman, and a shop foreman with a mechanic and apprentice mechanic working under his supervision. I was the apprentice mechanic and the last one hired, so when the push of spring and early summer work slowed, the owner laid me off.

After a short time I found another job at the City Garage, where there was no apprentice-journeyman, student-teacher relationship. That was a little hole-in-the-wall repair shop where an experienced mechanic had just quit. Because the elderly owner had no help, he hired me. The job was rather unusual for me. With only a few months' experience as an apprentice mechanic, the boss left me on my own with little or no supervision. The boss did the more difficult work. Most of the learning on that job meant doing it wrong the first time. Under an apprentice-journeyman relationship in a small shop like that, the journeyman mechanic would have directed and checked on me to avoid mistakes and save time. Learning by doing it the wrong way is a wasteful learning method.

However, there were some very rare and interesting experiences at the City Garage, especially driving and working on the Hicks and Seely stages. In those days, loggers would get off the train or the interurban stage at Coeur d'Alene to head for work in the woods. The Hicks and Seely stages transported them to the big logging camps back in the hills. The stage company had three seven-passenger automobiles and one locally made bus with an extended frame and a custom-made body. Some Monday mornings there would be more loggers heading for the camps than Hicks and Seely could carry in two stages. Therefore, one of the stage owners would hire me as a temporary, load the seven-passenger Studebaker with loggers, and order me to follow him to the camp.

Going east out of Coeur d'Alene we traveled along what is now Interstate 90 (see map 1 at the end of the book). For about three miles the road followed along the shore of Coeur d'Alene Lake, and then it rose and fell alternately in long, twisting turns above the beautiful lake. It was a spectacular road and considered quite hazardous for people who weren't used to driving. On the way to the Honeysuckle Logging Camp we turned away from the lake and crested the summit after seven winding miles of hilly road; then it was seven miles down the other side. In order to keep from burning out the brakes, we had to use the compression from the engine and shift gears expertly enough to avoid losing control of the car. At the bottom we followed the Little North Fork River for a couple of miles to Honeysuckle Logging Camp.

Besides the horse barns there were several small bunkhouses, with bunk beds along three sides of the room holding eight, ten, or perhaps a dozen loggers. There was also a big cook house. Because we usually got there just before noon, we had the privilege of eating with the loggers in the cook house. I had never seen so much food on one table at a time, except for Thanksgiving or Christmas: meat, potatoes, and vegetables and various kinds of pastries, including cookies, cakes, and pies.

The only disappointment about the job was that the trip didn't quite take the whole day and I had to work a couple of hours at the garage after returning to Coeur d'Alene. Work seemed to be an intrusion on the beautiful feelings of the trip, dominated by the view of the mountain road above Coeur d'Alene Lake and the vast scenery of the endless forest. The tall, stately Idaho white-pine trees, as straight as a ship's mast and usually over a hundred feet tall, stretched as far as you could see in any direction.

There wasn't much preventive maintenance done on stages in those days. On one occasion when we were heading up the long hill to Honeysuckle, the upper radiator hose broke on the stage that I was driving, spraying water over the distributor, which shorted out the spark-plug wires and disabled the stage in two ways: the radiator hose was broken and useless, and the electrical system was too wet to work.

All three stages were on the run that morning. Seely was ahead and

Hicks behind me, the inexperienced driver. When Hicks stopped and discovered the problem, he was so enraged that he swore and yanked all the wires out of the distributor. That disabled the stage more seriously yet, because each wire had to be in the proper hole to match the firing sequence of the cylinders. That sensitive timing was wiped out with one rage-filled jerk by my boss. Either he was mad at himself or the garage owner for not replacing the old hose; anyway, he and Seely crowded the loggers into the other two stages and they continued on to Honeysuckle. Hicks left me with the disabled stage, saying that he would tow me back on the return trip.

Standing around waiting for the boss to return seemed a waste of time to me. If I could expose the valve train to determine the order in which the valves were working, it might be possible to retime the distributor. After removing the valve-cover side plate to reveal the stems of the valves, I experimented by cranking the motor and removing a spark plug and using haywire to determine when the piston was at the top of the stroke. Then, removing the top from the distributor, it was possible to determine the direction the arm was rotating and to replace the remaining wires in the proper sequence. A popular firing order on six-cylinder engines was 1–5–3–2–4. If my analysis and work was correct, then all I would need was a radiator hose and some water, and we would be in business.

The road was used by a lot of fishermen, and the rocks caused many blowouts. A short investigation turned up a piece of discarded Model T inner tube and some haywire to use as a substitute radiator hose and clamp. Another search yielded an empty one-pound coffee can, and after many trips to a nearby creek, the big radiator was full. I got in the stage, tried the motor, and it ran as smoothly as ever.

I savored the drive home, which was much too short. Besides the good feeling of accomplishment in repairing the stage, the driving experience was enjoyable. Hicks and Seely were astonished when they found neither stage nor driver where they had left me; they couldn't believe that I had repaired the stage and driven it home.

It would be very difficult for a young person to get that kind of experience today. In the first place, a public-transit driver would have to be at least twenty-one years old (I was eighteen). Although radiator hoses still burst on hot days on long mountain grades, there aren't any small pieces of inner tubes lying around. And even if there were, the cooling systems of modern engines create too much pressure for an old inner tube to work. Everything is so specialized today that only a trained mechanic with special parts would be allowed to work on a stage motor. My experience was part of the frontier era, when there was lots of challenging work for young men.

The drive east from Coeur d'Alene on I–90 today misses the high ridges that presented such interesting challenges for me. Now travelers follow a straight, flat, high-speed interstate highway carved out of rock along the lake, and an impressive bridge carries them across Blue Creek Bay that saves many miles of travel. However, these interstate drivers miss the challenge and accomplishment of driving the high-climbing roads that existed in the summer of 1925. The old route that tested cars and drivers alike is still there, but the meaningful work and the apprentice-journeyman experience has been lost for most of today's young people.

*

Because the owner lacked interest in the City Garage, most of the drivers turned to better-equipped shops. Business declined; I was laid off and had to look for another job.

A custom machine shop in Coeur d'Alene, Diamond Drill Contracting Company, manufactured drill-boring equipment and contracted to do diamond-drill work for mining companies, skyscraper foundations, and bridge footings. Shortly after, I went to see the master machinist, Mr. Michener, and asked him for a job as an apprentice. He said he didn't need anyone, but I told him about my experience as an apprentice mechanic, certain that it would make a good impression on an old machinist like Mr. Michener. He remarked: "My goodness, I wish you hadn't told me about your garage experience, because I will have to teach you to unlearn that before you can learn to be a machinist." The reply shook me, but I continued to express my desire to learn the machinist's trade. Something about me evidently impressed him, because he told me to come to work.

The machine shop was a large, poorly lighted building in which a half-dozen men were working on metal cutting machines. My first assignments were very simple: using hand tools, such as a hacksaw, a file, and a hammer and chisel—the most elementary metalworking tools. But they were a foundation for understanding how the more complex machines worked. I recall one job of cutting countless teeth by hand in the end of a large piece of steel pipe, a tedious task, but under a master machinist's supervision it enabled me to develop a smooth, effective technique for working metal by hand.

In order to cut through steel, hacksaw blades are nearly as hard and brittle as glass, and they break very easily. Mr. Michener told me that he didn't want me to break more than three or four blades a day, which meant learning to do the job smoothly. Metalworking machines with a fore-and-back stroke are designed to pick the tool up on the return stroke, because metal tools are designed to cut only in one direction. The boss showed me how that worked with elementary hand tools. Another basic hand tool is the file, which cuts much like a saw but is broad and heavy and also should be picked up slightly on the return stroke. I also spent enough time with a hammer and chisel and learned to keep my eye on the cutting edge of the chisel without looking at the hammer. Michener's teaching of the fundamentals was so rich that it provided me with effective techniques that carried over to many difficult jobs for years to come.

After serving time on this elementary and manual work, he showed me the simple production lathe that had preset stops for the routine job of turning out diamond drill bits. Then the boss introduced me to the milling machine and the intricacies of cutting gears. At first, he made the setups while I watched, but later he let me make them by myself. That job was the opposite of the sawmill, where an endless amount of material had to be routinely picked up or piled. Each setup task was a challenge.

The main work of the milling machine was to cut teeth on round disks of steel, making them into working gears for the drilling machines. It was necessary to solve some complex problems in setting up the machine so that the teeth would be the proper size. When the setup was proven, I would start the machine and wait for it to finish cutting a tooth. A complicated set of disks allowed me to turn the gear to the correct position for the next tooth. Although it was a long process, I was very happy with the job and sat on a big homemade stool while watching the cutter work.

One day my job was to cut the teeth on a wide-faced gear—a time-consuming task. I was sitting on my stool watching the cutter work its way through the tough steel when a nearby machinist motioned to me. I ignored him at first but eventually took the few steps to his machine to see what he wanted. He related a dull story that didn't interest me, but I gave him my attention out of a desire to be polite. While impatiently waiting for him to finish the story, Michener, the boss, walked by. Even though I was only six or eight feet from my machine, which was working fine, he flew into a rage and shouted, "You're fired, go to the office and get your time." Once those terrible words were uttered, my career as a machinist was over.

When told of the boss's order, the office woman said, "I can't understand it. Mr. Michener has been so pleased with your work that you have become his pet." Although I considered her statement authentic, it gave me no relief. There was no union to arbitrate, no medicine for my injured pride. It was more than fifty years later before I was able to first share that ignominy with anyone.

The job was important to me, and beyond that the firing was an alienating experience because it was senseless. My observations had not shown me that it was imperative to stay at the machine, with all my faculties addressed to the job at hand. Probably the boss was frustrated about other things, and certainly firing me contributed to his control over the crew (although it probably cost him some respect). But the effect remained. The scar lasted through years of work, even when talking, listening, and consulting was germane and essential to my work.

A chance to go back to the job at the Diamond Drill Contracting Company happened when my father went to see Michener the night after he had fired me. He told my father that I could come back to work. My recollection is that my pride had been hurt so badly that I refused. The shop was an intimate family affair, and the patriarch had cast me out with such disgrace that it was impossible to face up to going back.

It was only after retirement from many successful projects that it was possible to talk about the firing. However, there was never any personal bitterness toward Michener. His whole world revolved around that machine shop. If he had not fired me, the challenge of working metal might have limited my world to that same shop. Many times when working around machinery, I was able to proceed with a job by recalling some of the lessons Michener taught me. Time has convinced me that he was a rare teacher, and it has alleviated the pain of being fired.

*

With the resilience of youth, I began looking for another job. In a few days the county road foreman, one of my father's many friends, offered me a job on a road-building crew at Fighting Creek, eighteen miles south of Coeur d'Alene. At that time there seemed little significance about the new work; I would never have guessed that it would be only the first of countless road jobs in the mountainous regions of Oregon, Washington, Montana, and Idaho for the next four or five decades.

Fighting Creek was simply a spot on the county road where there was a sharp turn around a little hill, followed by a short stretch that was not high enough to be clear of the spring runoff. It was a simple job for the county to take material out of the cut and to haul it to the nearby fill. That task accomplished two things: it straightened out a sharp curve, and it got the adjoining area out of water and mud.

The Fighting Creek job is of special interest to me, because it was one of the few times I had the opportunity to work with local farmers who made up the road-building crew using horse-powered equipment. That was not rich farming country; in most cases it provided a subsistence or a very modest living. Many of them worked at logging, cutting cordwood, or similar jobs to supplement their living. I was the only town person and knew nothing about the work at first. The crew was friendly and seemed to enjoy the labor, which for most of them meant handling their four-horse teams in such a way as to get a good day's work done and yet to protect the animals from injury.

The equipment for the job was rudimentary but effective. In construction language it would be called a horse and Fresno outfit. A Fresno is a giant version of a scoop shovel (like a snow shovel), designed to be pulled by several horses. In order for a person to control a Fresno, a long, trailing steel handle (called a Johnson bar) was attached to the back of it. There were chains attached to the sides of the Fresno, and those were fastened to the harness. Thus, by lifting up on the Johnson bar, the front of the Fresno, or bit, would dig into soft earth. As the horses walked along, the Fresno would fill up with earth, just as a hand shovel would when pushed into the ground. Here the resemblance to a hand shovel stopped. If the Johnson bar was lifted too high, the front of the Fresno would catch in the earth and the bar would be forced violently up in the air. If your hold on the bar was not secure, the handle would fly up in the air, bruising any part of your body that was in the way. It took considerable skill to load a Fresno.

Because a loaded Fresno was a hard pull for the horses, teamsters limited pulling distances to about six hundred feet. For longer hauls, earth would be loaded on wagons or trucks. A Fresno-like machine mounted on wagon wheels, called a wheeler, was used in building rail-

1. A four-horse Fresno traveling empty on its runners. Courtesy of the Farm Security Administration, the Library of Congress.

2. A crew prepares to load a Fresno of the type used by the author on his first road-building job. Courtesy of the Smithsonian Institution.

BUCK SCRAPERS.

For 4 horses,	**340 lb.,**	**34 cubic feet,**	**price**	**$28.00**
For 2 „	**230 lb.,**	**16 „**	**„**	**$21.00**

3. A drawing of a Fresno rigged for pulling by two horses. Note the hauling capacity of sixteen cubic feet compared with the capacity of today's monster scrapers at thirty to forty cubic yards. Courtesy of the Smithsonian Institution.

4. A Fresno being pulled by a Caterpillar tractor. Courtesy of Caterpillar Inc.

roads, but I never saw one in highway building. Historically the Fresno is important, because it was used to build many miles of roads and was the forerunner of the rubber-tired, self-loading monsters used on highway construction today.

My job at Fighting Creek was to dump the Fresno, which meant lifting the Johnson bar until the front edge of the Fresno bit into the ground, at which point it would tip and empty its load. As each teamster came up on the new piece of highway, I would lift the handle and dump the load and then get ready for the next one and decide where to place it. Moving dirt with a Fresno was not easy; the teamster walked along behind the horses all day long in a big circle, loading up, hauling out to the fill, dumping the load, and going back for another. That made for a long, arduous day, yet there were no complaints; those men were good to work with. On that job the horses established the rhythm of work, so they were allowed to set their own pace and were rested sufficiently to last the day. In some ways the horses were treated with more consideration than the workers in the woodyard.

After a few days dumping Fresnos, the foreman put me on the big breaker plow, pulled by one of the steadiest and strongest four-horse teams. With the slow, steady pull of the horses under the fine control of the teamster, the plow responded magically to the slightest pressure on the handles to open up the highway cut. After a while it occurred to me why the job was called plow shaking. Handling the big, heavy equipment and learning to be a plow shaker was fun, especially when I discovered that a slight gentle shake at the right time would easily control the plow.

The Fighting Creek job didn't last long. When it was finished, most of the teamsters went home to take care of their farms, and the county sent me to a job on the Trent road, eighteen miles northwest of Coeur d'Alene. The Trent construction job is of special interest to me for two reasons: I was doing the work myself, and the equipment represented the next step in the evolution of the Fresno into big construction machines. The job involved improving the vertical alignment of the county road, cutting down on the top of a hill and carrying the earth to the bottom, thereby improving the sight distance for motorists and making the road safer.

There were no horses on that job; I worked alone most of the time with a small Caterpiller tractor and a tumble bug, an improved Fresno adapted to being pulled by a tractor. Instead of being operated with a

5. A Caterpillar tractor pulling a tumble bug, the first step in mechanization of the Fresno. Courtesy of Caterpillar Inc.

long handle, it was set in a metal frame with adjustable stops that were controlled with a rope reaching to the tractor. The difficult and sometimes treacherous Johnson bar, with its long steel handle, had been eliminated in the tumble bug. Two big, heavy lugs of steel on a frame controlled the loading and the unloading of the mechanical adaptions that produced the tumble bug. As the tractor was substituted for horses, it became feasible to attach a heavy, unflexible steel bar to the tractor; therefore, by simple evolution, the hazardous Johnson bar was eliminated as well as the man to operate it. That is a small example of the way machinery evolved and displaced both animals and men.

When that job was finished, the county had completed its construction program for 1926. I was laid off again but was pleased with the road-building experience and accepted the layoff as a part of the completion of construction jobs.

*

Temporary work lasted me for a few weeks and then my father found me a job driving a truck for the Interstate Telephone Company's line-

6. The evolution of the Fresno continues: a rubber-tired tractor pulls a modern scraper that loads Fresno-style. Courtesy of Caterpillar Inc.

7. Today's two-wheel tractors and self-loading scrapers carry a load as big as that carried by forty Fresnos. Courtesy of Caterpillar Inc.

construction crew. The company used a big truck to haul a crew of six men and all the heavy equipment needed in the building of telephone lines. Inside the canvas-covered truck there were numerous coils of rope and wire, buckets of hardware, and racks of linemen's heavy safety belts and climbing spikes, called hooks. Outside there were several racks of long-handled shovels for digging the deep holes. It surprised me when they trusted me to operate the big truck with the crew and all the equipment, as I was not quite twenty years old.

The crew was building telephone lines through the rural areas of northern Idaho. In those days the long-distance lines consisted of cedar poles with crossarms and insulators to secure the copper wire. The Interstate Telephone Company's lines—or lead as the linemen called them—were rather simple, consisting of only four pairs of wires on one crossarm for each pole. Because that kind of lead didn't take long to build, the crew moved through the country fairly fast. In the days of slow highways and cars, it wasn't considered practical to drive many miles to and from work each day, so the telephone company furnished a large tent for the crew to live in.

The boss would locate a farm family to feed us and to allow us to pitch the tent in one of their fields. The tent lacked the companionship of a home and family, and the crew was deprived in a cultural way because they missed the company of women. The all-male company in the evenings was broken only by an occasional visit to a bootlegger, a speakeasy, or a home-brew parlor. Because the moving about interrupted friendships, only superficial relationships with women had a chance to develop. Some of the linemen had no home to visit, even on weekends, so their world revolved around the job and places where a little companionship was available. Conversations about women and visits to the different joints took up most of the evenings in the tent. Only the boss, who spent his nights at home, was exempt from the tent life.

In such an environment, we were a team nurturing each other as we worked on the challenges of building telephone leads wherever we were sent. The elements challenged us. The dry summer days were good, but rain made the poles slick and treacherous to climb. Rocky ground provided for difficult digging, but soft loam was easy. We raised the cedar telephone poles by our own muscle; no one was exempt from that work. Then we walked through the brush, pulling the wires out to pole after pole, each of which had to be climbed to lay up the wires on the crossarms. That, too, was hard work, but the rewards of climbing up the poles with the sharp hooks carried a satisfaction that was close to fun.

With the wires on the crossarm, the linemen and the boss climbed up every fourth or fifth pole to signal to us at the truck when the sag, or tension, was right. We then cut up leftover lengths of wire, tossed them into a bonfire to heat and then to cool so that they would be soft and bend easily around the insulators to secure the telephone wires. Only the linemen secured the wires to the insulators and arranged them in the proper order.

Although tough lifting and digging jobs were difficult for me, it was pleasant to learn that I had toughened up enough to withstand the arduous job of digging the postholes. Even though that part of the work was not to my liking, it gave me a lot of satisfaction to complete a hole and walk down the line past the four other men and start a new one. At the digging job and the work of standing poles upright, we were all equals. Only after the poles were in place did the linemen become the aristocracy of the crew, as they did all the "hiking" (pole climbing).

Hugh Casey, the foreman of this tough, free-spirited crew, was one of the finest people I ever worked for. The job required an unusual combination of individual skill and teamwork. That may have allowed the work process to sort out people in an evolutionary way so that a person with unusual talents and an understanding of people stayed with the job and became a natural leader. That job-developed leadership was made possible because the nature of the work made it difficult for an externally trained efficiency expert to look over the shoulder of a lineman and give advice on how to do it faster as he climbed the pole.

Casey's mastery of difficult and hazardous line construction was matched by his respect for the dignity of his fellow men. He did not let his interest in the progress of the work corrode his own humanity. Casey trusted us, gave us lots of leeway in learning to do our job, yet always seemed to have advice, demonstrations, or a helping hand when we needed it. That rare relationship between workers and the boss was enhanced by the nature of our shared learning experiences.

Working for Hugh was more than just a good job and a great experience. We shared so much. I had the feeling that my quitting work would be in some respects a rejection of Hugh's goodness. He is the only boss who ever evoked those feelings. For on-the-job rapport, only a few experiences with fellow workers ever matched the good sharing with Hugh Casey.

For all those reasons it was not easy to say, "I quit," and walk away. But a powerful urge to learn and be part of a university experience prevailed, and I tried to explain to Casey why it was necessary for me to look for still another world of learning and work. My brother Gus had graduated from high school and was able to take my place as a wage earner to keep the family afloat.

There has always been a lingering feeling that I let Casey down, and it is difficult to understand why one should still feel bad about it. Maybe it was because he accepted me as a person, as his truck driver, and as a potential apprentice lineman at some later time. My continuing shame at leaving Casey probably stemmed from the feeling of abandoning a relationship that would be difficult to find anywhere else. In spite of mixed emotions, I decided it was time to carry out my dream of going to college, or the dream itself would be in jeopardy.

three

1926–1930

The standard formula for going to college among my friends was to work a year, save five hundred dollars, and then enroll at the University of Idaho, ninety miles south of Coeur d'Alene. But with my limited resources, it was necessary for me to live in a city large enough to offer night-shift work on industrial jobs. I had never been to Seattle, but it seemed the place to go. While looking for a job and a place to live, my father's brother Cleburn would put me up.

I remember sitting in my 1914-model Ford bug, ready to leave Coeur d'Alene, and saying good-bye to my mother and father. Dad had given me an old leather suitcase that held my spare clothes, and just before my departure he brought out a typewriter and put it on the seat beside me. With that, I put the car in gear and headed for Seattle.

There were few official highway signs in 1926. Local chambers of commerce would put up big signs recommending routes through their towns. Although there was no road map in the car, my route would be west across Washington to Seattle. At one point there was a fork in the road. One route went west with a little stick of a sign pointing to the next town; on the other there was a big billboard that advertised a southerly route as the shortest and best road to the coast. I followed the latter advice and by evening was about 150 miles from Coeur d'Alene on the road to Portland and realized that I should have ignored the misleading billboard. On the second day I took a county road going north and west up to the shortest Seattle route. After spending the night in Ellensburg, my travels took me through the Cascade Mountains, around Lake Washington, and to my uncle's house at about three in the afternoon. The trip that took me three long days of driving in a 1914 Ford—doing a little roadside repair work en route—is driven easily now in one day. But I was in Seattle looking for a job to pay my way through school, and that was what counted.

There were still two months, August and September, to establish a financial footing for going to school. A steady job on a night shift would permit me to attend classes during the day. My first choice would be to work on the swing shift as an apprentice machinist. I had a letter of recommendation from Mr. Michener, despite the fact that he had fired me, and presented that at the Issacson Iron Works. At first it seemed that the company had brushed me off with little consideration, but as I got acquainted with apprentice programs in most machine shops, it became obvious that apprentices didn't look for jobs until they had finished the program. The fact that I was an unemployed apprentice was nearly three strikes against me. In retrospect, they probably didn't seriously consider me for an opening because I was alone and without support from a working machinist, an employer, or a friend in the industry.

With the passing of the days, there was an urgency to find steady work. Through some contact, I found a job riding a bicycle delivering messages for the Western Union Telegraph Company on the night shift from about five until midnight. It wasn't much, but it was steady work and the hours allowed me to go to school during the day.

After a while, riding the bicycle seemed rather a kid's job; furthermore, pedaling the old one-speed bike to the apartments on top of Seattle's First Hill was very strenuous work. I began to envy the motorcycle messengers as they straddled their powerful machines that ate up Seattle's steep hills. After inquiring at the main office at Western Union about a motorbike job they said yes, but I needed to buy my own bike.

Although without any experience on a motorcycle, I imagined that it would be just like riding a bicycle except that the motor would do the work. That turned out to be quite a fallacious assumption.

Because my savings did not permit purchasing a bike, I got in touch with my dad and explained the problem. Through a friend who lent money to needy college students, Dad sent me $150, which made it possible for me to buy a motorcycle from another Western Union rider. After transacting the business in the alley behind the office, I walked in to the delivery clerk and asked for a route of telegrams to deliver. He handed me a large stack and told me to put them in order for delivery. Because most of the addresses were strange, the route clerk tabulated my telegrams and told me to take off.

My only planning for the job was a small paper map put out by a real-estate company. The map had street names on the back and a pivoting arrow on the front to help locate them. That map and its arrow on a somewhat rainproof paper saved the day for me. With my metal book full of telegrams, I walked out to my motorcycle to start my new career as a motor messenger. The cycle was a 61-cubic-inch Harley-Davidson, by today's standards a big bike. My weight was only about 130 pounds, so it took a strenuous kick on my part to get it started. It was a typical Seattle night—dark and rainy. I turned out of the alley up James Street, one of the steepest hills in Seattle. In those days the steep hills were paved with red brick, an added hazard because they were very slick when wet.

So there I was, trying to learn to ride a motorcycle on one of Seattle's steepest, most slippery streets. I was terrified with the noise and power and began to realize that every street intersection carried the potential of a collision with a car. To add to my problems was my uncertainty about directions, and the light on the motorcycle was so poor that it hardly showed on the wet pavement. That made it necessary to stop under the street lights to consult the little map to find my way. Although I struggled through the night until the job was finished, there was a new appreciation for the quiet bicycle in the relative safety of the heavy but slower traffic.

That was a discouraging experience, but the boredom of piling wood at the Winton Mill was too keen a memory for me to give up. It was not a time for looking back, but to learn the streets of Seattle and to learn to ride the big Harley. Each night I learned more about the geography of Seattle and about riding a motorcycle. Although never as good as the other fine riders, the miles and the nights piled up and I was able to get by.

The major concern of all working bikers was to reduce the risk of automobile and bike collisions. Being hit by a car was every rider's fear. We had our own code that grew out of spending fifty hours or more a week on the streets in all kinds of weather. In Seattle, being out in the weather meant that you rode a lot on dark, wet streets with the rain in your face. When the conditions were favorable, we rode like the wind, but all the time we had to be poised to avoid trouble. It was of little consequence to have the right-of-way and be driving at a legal speed if you were crunched by a car.

The effort to avoid running into cars at intersections provided me with an unusual example of how learning processes and skills can develop. All night long I kept a constant watch for a flicker of light at each intersection ahead that would indicate an approaching automobile. While straining my eyes at that task, it was necessary to tip my head back and look past my nose for any possible sign of car lights. It was as if I were a puppet, because it seemed involuntary. But that position made me certain of being more aware of oncoming vehicles. One day in a psychology class we learned that in the upper part of the eye there are a greater number of cells that are sensitive to variations in the intensity of light. With that information, it seemed to me that there was some sort of learning process that was taking place deep within my senses.

My closest friend and co-worker, Kenneth Murdock, was a beautiful rider—a Hugh Casey of the working bikers. Both he and Casey had a dedication to their work, a sense of understanding and tolerance for their fellow laborers, and a grasp of the unity of the work process and its results. Every now and then people like Hugh Casey and Kenny Murdock show up, and working with them is a rare privilege. My warmest person-to-person relationship on the Western Union job was the few times Murdock and I ate together in a little beanery in the Western Union alley. Because we faced the same reality and respected each other, it was easy and good to share a few minutes.

Kenny was a fearless rider, but he didn't trust many bikers enough to sit behind them as a passenger. One night he needed a ride downtown from the university district. There were a lot of bikers around, but he asked me for a lift. His trust in my riding ability meant that he accepted me as an accomplished rider, at least in safely avoiding cars on Seattle's dark, wet streets. For nearly four years, traversing Seattle's streets by night was my working world. All that for a few daytime hours in the classroom and the library at the university. Those were the experiences I had been working and waiting for; it was nice to be a part of that world.

My first course was a five-hour class in psychology. I savored every minute of those lectures—given by Mr. Smith, the department head—and the opportunity to study and learn some of the mysteries of that noble subject. In addition to the course in psychology, a class on the study of logic taught by Harold Cooper Langford attracted me. Although my previous work lacked the proper prerequisites, Professor Langford approved my petition to be admitted to his course. That class turned out to be one of the most valuable of all my university experience; each day he examined the complex theorems of logic and patiently illustrated their relationships in easy, understandable language. Langford illustrated his concepts by applying them to everyday problems, such as testing the validity of the editorials in the daily newspapers. We found that many editorials were inconsistent and did not support the editor's conclusions.

One day Professor Langford showed me a magazine article about the Sacco-Vanzetti trial and said: "This is just what I said at the time of the trial." The article included some post-trial information on an aborted mail-truck robbery for which one of the defendants had been sent to prison.[1] But the gist of Langford's argument went beyond questions of evidence; he insisted that even if you accepted the state's claim of evidence, it did not follow that Sacco and Vanzetti were guilty of the Braintree [Massachusetts] robbery for which they were executed. Langford's analysis made a lasting impression on me. In addition to the lesson in the application of logic to important decisions, it was flattering that he made the effort to analyze that historically significant trial for me. Friends of Langford later told me that he had resigned from the Harvard faculty in protest because the president of the university had been part of a blue-ribbon commission which ruled that the state of Massachusetts had given Sacco and Vanzetti a fair trial.

I also studied the philosophy of ethics under Professor Savory, a handsome man who possessed a pleased and proud bearing as he delivered his lectures. Savory was the epitome of the traditional classical philosopher whose presence commanded respect—even if the rigor of his logic did not always match his demeanor.

*

During the summer of 1928, there was a welcome change from the hazards of riding a motorcycle through Seattle's busy streets. My father sent me word that he had found a job for me: driving a truck for the Idaho Highway Department. When I first arrived at the road camp about thirty-five miles east of Coeur d'Alene on U.S. 10 (now Interstate 90), the boss showed me an old First World War surplus truck with solid-rubber tires and steel wheels. He warned me that driving the old truck was complicated by its habit of burning out or throwing bearings, mechanical breakdowns that had held up the crew for several days the previous season.

The days were long, because the old truck was slow, especially going uphill. During the month of August I worked sixteen hours a day for thirty days, but the old truck motor kept running so everybody was happy. The best thing about driving the truck was the feeling of safety from my high seat behind the wheel, surrounded by a massive steel frame. That was in stark contrast to riding a motorcycle through Seattle's busy and often rain-soaked streets, where a minor accident could result in serious damage to the motorcycle as well as to the unprotected rider.

Hauling hot asphalt to the oiling site was my contribution to the process of turning a dusty, graveled road into a paved highway. Preparing the existing road for the asphalt was done with a large First World War surplus tractor and a road grader equipped with giant teeth that loosened the top three or four inches of the roadbed. The loosened gravel and soil was processed into a smooth, loose bed of gravel ready for the application of hot asphalt. A tractor-pulled grader then turned the gravel and asphalt over and over until it was well mixed. When that substance was well blended, an experienced grader operator (blade man) spread the mix over the roadbed in a thin, smooth layer. When properly done, the procedure produced a dust-free, smoothly paved road. That process was very popular during the 1920s and 1930s because it was economical and could be done with equipment owned by local road departments.

Through all the busy 1928 oiling season, I kept the old truck running without crowding it to where it would burn out a bearing or otherwise delay the oiling process. The summer of 1929 found me back driving the truck through the busy oiling season, again without a breakdown, as we continued the process of converting the Cataldo section of U.S. 10 into a paved roadway. After two seasons of keeping the old truck going and delivering the asphalt, I was accepted as a good truck driver on road construction.

After that second summer of work in northern Idaho, there followed a successful year at the university. For the first time in my university studies, there appeared to be a meld between my classroom effort and my search for work that allowed a maximum of personal development and challenge. That blend of study and work took place in an upper-division class in modern philosophy taught by Professor Blake. For some time I felt out of place among the four or five accomplished students in the class, but when I delivered my paper comparing the work of several modern philosophers, it gave me a new reality. Applying Langford's tools of logic to the problems of understanding and evaluating the views of the philosophers in the paper, I was able to combine all the elements of my best experiences. It was a shared search for truth and for an effective implementation of the ethics of the New Testament and the Greek and modern philosophers. The effort challenged all the resources of mind, body, and soul. That hour in Professor Blake's class was a culmination of years of seeking work that followed the traditions of the New Testament, a search that led me to the realities of the university.

I can still savor the euphoria of giving my paper, but my pursuit of a career in philosophy was abruptly stopped when word came that the bank where my family (and I) did business had closed. Its failure ended my career at the University of Washington. For four years I had straddled a motorcycle for eight hours a night, six days a week, for the privilege of studying at the university. The long nights, even with the heady daytime challenges, had worn me out. It was time to find a better job and to recoup our losses.

Spring was in the air and work would be opening up in the foothills of northern Idaho, so I headed home to share the depression with my parents, brothers, and sister. My hope was to find a job in northern Idaho other than riding a motorcycle—work that would give me a reprieve from the Seattle experience—and to refresh my body and soul and save money to return to the university and complete my interrupted studies. I took with me from Seattle the aura of my successful work in Professor Blake's class. Those recollections were strong enough to sustain my dream of studying and teaching in a university.

My success in keeping the old oil truck going during the summers of 1928 and 1929 gave me an inside track to driving a big dump truck on a job hauling gravel on the road around Kellogg, Idaho, a mining town a few miles east of Cataldo.[2] By the middle of the summer of 1930 the project was finished and I was out of work.

With fall and winter approaching, I needed a steady job. Thanks to the efforts of a schoolmate, Phil Fordyce, my unemployment didn't last long. Earlier in the summer I had the opportunity to put Phil in touch with a job driving a truck north of Coeur d'Alene. Because Phil wasn't much of a truck driver, he didn't last long, but he was experienced at highway surveying and got a better job as a rodman on a highway-location crew working out of Coeur d'Alene. When Phil found that I was out of work, he put in a word for me with his boss. Within a few days I was hired on the survey crew.

Surveying in North Idaho and Oregon: The 1930s

It was great to have a job again, even though it was temporary work that would be good until my return to the university. At the time I had no idea that, except for a ten-year interlude I would spend more than thirty years learning about surveying techniques. For the moment, however, it was nice to be told to come to work at eight o'clock in the morning.

The workers reported to the same office that I had been dispatched to as a truck driver, but this time we traveled in a station wagon with four or five young men and the boss. There were no college-trained engineers on the crew, not unusual for those times. The boss was Hugh Cochran, who had started out as a rear flagman, like myself, some twenty or thirty years earlier and had gradually worked his way up to the top job, that of resident engineer. He was in charge of the field crew with responsibility for locating a new highway up Mica Hill, a route that was to take the place of the existing narrow and treacherous road with sharp curves (map 1). Cochran was one of the finest people and one of the best engineers that I have ever had the privilege of working with. Like Hugh Casey, he respected us as individuals, but Cochran was more sociable.

We drove about seven or eight miles out to Mica Hill, where the fellows unloaded a variety of strange equipment and took off into the brush with it. Cochran handed me a range pole, an eight-foot wooden rod about an inch in diameter with contrasting white and red sections in one-foot units. Cochran walked to the shoulder of the road, where two stakes with large numbers on them had been driven into the ground. Between the two stakes he showed me another stake whose top was even with the surface. On the top of the stake (called a hub) was a heavy galvanized tack.

Cochran showed me how to place the pointed end of the range pole and how to hold it straight, or, as he called it, plumb. Then he pointed to a clearing where, barely visible, one of the crew was operating an instrument on a sturdy tripod. Cochran told me that my job was to keep an eye on the person with the tripod at all times; when he raised his arm, my task was to put the range pole on the tack and hold it as plumb as possible. When he raised both arms, I could relax until he raised his arm for another sighting or until he was through with that setup. Then he would signal me to come to the point where he had been while he moved ahead to a new spot. That process is characteristic of surveying or field engineering jobs. It isn't hard work, but it requires acute attention so the progress of the crew is not delayed. Even though my position was the most menial on the entire crew, it was exciting to be out in the woods with people my own age and to work with unfamiliar equipment and tools that I was eager to learn about.

We were running a preliminary line, a series of straight lines connected by measured angles (called a P line). The location engineer establishes the P line as he looks over the terrain and chooses the most favorable area for a new highway; it becomes the foundation map for the adjacent terrain. Our job was to measure the horizontal distances, the angles, the direction, and the elevation of the hills and canyons in order to make a contour map of the area. With a contour map an experienced engineer can project a center line for a highway. Projecting the route in the most economical location in mountainous terrain usually is considered the senior job in highway-location work. It would be twenty-six years later (1956) in the Cascade Mountains of Washington before I would be doing that task myself. In the meantime, it was good to be the rear flagman on Cochran's location crew on Mica Hill.

At first I wasn't in a position to learn much about what the rest of the crew did or the equipment they used. But just being with them and the boss was a new dimension of work experience. Cochran exuded an aura of confidence about his duties, and he treated the rest of the crew with the same friendliness that he had exhibited when he explained my simple job to me.

The basic equipment on the job was a sensitive and sophisticated instrument called a transit, a tool mounted on a solid tripod with telescoping legs. Phil Kuster, a young man who seemed to be positively brilliant, operated the transit. Eventually, it was explained to me that the instrument was used to measure the angles between the straight lines or tangents of the preliminary or P line. Although my job did not give me a chance to look through the transit that summer, I began to learn about the hundred-foot steel tape used to measure distances and the long wooden rod used to measure elevations. The experienced workers taught me how to mark the conventional surveyor's stakes and how to drive them into the ground, a task that was the next step above the rear flagman. That summer I did the most routine work, yet the mysteries and variety of what we were doing impressed me, as did the camaraderie among the members of the crew.

Later in the summer the Highway Department transferred me to the crew of Chester Adams, a young graduate engineer from Washington State College in Pullman, who was assigned to a location job at Port Hill, Idaho, one hundred miles north of Coeur d'Alene on the Canadian border (map 2). Port Hill is on the banks of the Kootenai at the foot of a hill leading down from the high country to the south. Like many of the roads of the 1920s, the hill coming into town was so steep that a car or truck needed chains to negotiate it after a rain or a light snow. Our job was to do the field surveying that would eliminate the steep hill by locating an all-weather highway with gentle curves and safe grades.

Port Hill was a tiny community of perhaps a dozen families. Its major business was a customs station staffed with a few border patrolmen. There was also a ferry across the Kootenai River and a general store with a gas pump. Because our arrival in town was notice that a new road would be forthcoming, we were met with friendly faces. The little money we spent around town was immediately appreciated, but more than that, the people looked ahead to the time when our road would become a reality.

I learned a lot about surveying on that job and also took part in some troublesome personal relations between Adams and the crew. The first time, those abrasive situations developed over Adams's solution to our housing problem. He found an abandoned commercial building on the Canadian line where the rent was cheap and decided to use it for a combination office and bunkhouse. It was so filthy that I could not face trying to live in such a place; in addition to the dirt, the prospect of all of us staying in one big room after work and on weekends was very unpleasant. Pat Gallagher, the head chainman, felt much the same way, so we scouted around for another place and found a clean cabin with two beds that rented for five dollars a month. We promptly moved in.

When Adams learned that we had rented a place of our own, he was upset and made some remarks that we thought we were too good to live with him and Ray Kindler, the youngest member of the crew. Pat and I, however, felt that facing Adams's displeasure was preferable to living in the old dirty building. But because it was going to be the office where we would work part of the time, we did help clean it up. Adams did much better finding a place to eat. Money was becoming scarce in 1930, and the owner of the general store invited the four of us to eat with his family for a very reasonable price.

With a place to stay and eat and an office established, we were ready to go to work. Using a small, hand-held instrument that measured slopes and grades, Adams flagged a route down the hill, locating areas where the slope was appropriate for a standard 5 percent grade. We cut a preliminary line through the underbrush and small trees in preparation for establishing a completed line with gentle curves and grades that would provide safe, year-around travel to and from Port Hill.

When we began measuring out the stations and staking the preliminary line, Adams promoted me to rear chainman, a job that required me to let the hundred-foot tape slide through my hand until the head chainman stopped or until the hundred-foot marker at the end was close. About two steps from the end I would call, "Chain." At that point, it was time to grasp the leather thongs on the end of the chain and lift it to a point level with the end held by the head chainman if the terrain allowed. Then I would drop the plumb-bob string over the chain and brace my feet before the head chainman tightened it. It was my job to be secure enough to hold the plumb bob firm, no matter how tight the head chainman pulled. When he slacked off, it was my task to call out, "Holding one hundred on station so and so." After he had called the correct station, I would drop the chain and hurry to the next spot before the head chainman moved forward. No matter how quick the head chainman moved, my responsibility was to get to the next chaining point before the end of the chain.

That summer we pushed hard all day in what was called a highball operation. In spite of the pressure to hurry, there was free time between the various operations. After I stopped the chain at the hundred-foot end, there would be a short pause while the head chainman got line from the transitman. When we had the line measured and staked as far as the transitman could see, we would have a few minutes to relax while the instrument was moved and made ready to go again. Running a transit line is quite a team effort; while each person is working, another man—or sometimes the rest of the crew—is waiting. Although each member tries to do his job as smoothly and quickly as possible, there are always pauses here and there to break up the push to get the job done. With that kind of rhythm, I enjoyed the challenge of learning to match my skill and muscles against the ever-changing terrain. I had a good feeling for the work and the way we pushed ahead with the line.

One night in the engineering office at Port Hill I studied the diagram of a standard vernier system used on transits and discovered how to read the angles consistently and reliably. I used that system in my thirty years of surveying and found its principled analysis sufficient to solve the problems of many makes and styles of transits. When my boss at Port Hill offered to show me how to read the angles, it was good to tell him that I already had learned the same from his little handbook of surveying. That combination of book learning and experience always impressed me.

*

In the spring of 1931, Chester Adams notified me that we were moving to Santa, Idaho, on a major highway-construction job (map 3). That was exciting news. The previous fall we had worked one hundred miles north of Coeur d'Alene; now we were going nearly as far south.

Santa, a back-country community on the St. Maries River with a population of fifteen or twenty people, boasted a general store with gas pumps, a post office, and a rustic, family-owned and -operated hotel. There were no roads east of Santa for about one hundred miles. An old route running north and south, built for horse and wagon traffic, provided a fair-weather connection to neighboring towns. Because the road was impassable for cars during the long winter months, an engineering crew was sent to Santa to lay out about six miles of all-weather road. It wouldn't be paved but would have a gravel surface with gentle curves and grades so the snow and rain wouldn't make it impassable. The roads and bridges were also to be built wide enough for two cars to pass safely.

It was a pleasant surprise when Adams assigned me the job of making the layout on a 196-foot timber bridge over Crystal Creek. He had decided that my experience was sufficient to prepare me for building the bridge. That introduced me to a complete road-construction job, from the initial survey to the completion of six miles of modern rural highway. I felt the pressure to avoid errors in setting control points and elevations for the contractor and observed for the first time the duality of responsibility and motives between the contractor and the state engineers. That was exacerbated by the shrewd practices of the contractor.

Under the contract system of highway construction, the engineering crew makes all the layout for cutting and fitting bridge material, in this case the massive wooden timbers. That responsibility was a heavy burden, but it was also a challenge and an unusual opportunity. My first task was to establish control points, which consisted of driving heavy stakes at the various locations where the contractor would drive pilings for the bridge. There were nine rows of pilings with six or seven pilings in each row. These rows are called bents. Because the bridge was on a curve, my job was more complicated.

The Jay Company was the general contractor. The bridge construction was subcontracted to a master bridge carpenter. He hired some local unemployed loggers and told them to cut trees in the nearby forest. The loggers soon showed up with beautiful pilings: straight, slim, and slightly tapered, true enough for ship masts. In addition to the pilings, they hauled in a load of timbers long enough to build a pile driver, a tall structure resembling a guillotine, about fifty feet high. It had to be large enough to hold up a forty-foot piling and still have some space for a fifteen-hundred-pound hammer to fall on the piling and drive it into the ground.

My job was to make sure there was a substantial survey stake in the ground at the right place for each piling; then the pile driver had to be pushed and maneuvered into place. That was done with man and horse-

8. Crystal Creek bridge, Santa, Idaho, 1931. Courtesy of the author.

power since there was no mechanical equipment on the job; the carpenter foreman, the loggers, and two big horses did all of the lifting and moving. When the pile driver was in place, the mammoth hammer was fastened to the timbers. A long wire rope, attached to the hammer, ran through a pulley on top of the pile driver and down through another at the bottom and out to the harness on the two horses.

Getting the hammer within a foot or two of the top of the pile driver was a very delicate and hazardous operation. If the horses continued to pull without stopping, it would wreck the whole pile driver and possibly injure some workers. It was an impressive scene to watch the precision of the old logger teamster; when he said, "Whoa," the big horses stopped in midstride and held the hammer there while a worker high up on the leads put a block under the hammer. That drama was played out at the start of each piling, yet the well-trained horses and the logger never let the crew down. The carpenter foreman and the men working on the leads were very jittery when the first few pilings were started, but as the horses and logger teamster played out their steady and precise stops, the hazardous operation became less formidable. We were privileged to see this ultimate ballet combining the power and skill of men and horses. In a less-dramatic way, the other local loggers and the bridge-building foreman matched the skill of the teamster and his horses. The men were proud of their skills, a pride that stemmed from their determination and ability to produce a high-quality bridge.

My next big job was to calculate where the top of the pilings should be cut so that the completed structure would match the grade of the new highway. The arithmetic of calculating the slope of the bridge deck to match the curve of the road was elementary, yet it was imperative that the elevation of the pilings be precise. At that time I was alone as inspector and layout man, so it was imperative to check and double-check my arithmetic before giving a reading to the bridge crew so they could cut the piling at the right elevation. I shuddered each time their sharp saws cut into the piling and hoped they were not too low. That would have been disastrous. Next, large timbers called caps were secured on the pilings. Then long wooden beams were hoisted into place that reached from one row of pilings to the next. The deck and handrails came last. The result was a sturdy, safe, usable bridge. For the person doing the layout, the difficult, troubling work was done once the pilings had been cut off. With no contractor to annoy the craftsmen with flimsy shortcuts, the rest of the work was almost relaxing.

My next assignment was to do the layout for a small timber structure, called a cattle pass, just large enough to allow cattle to move safely under the highway. On that job, I had my first confrontation with an astute and aggressive contractor, whom I will call Jay. The little structure consisted of two framed abutments with laminated two-by-twelves reaching from one abutment or bent to the next. The blueprints required that approximately every tenth deck timber be seated into a notch on top of the cap, a time-consuming job. Jay objected to the slow work, suggested a shortcut, and tried to convince me that his labor-saving procedure was also the proper way to do the job. Although admitting to youth and inexperience, I was not going to build the structure contrary to the plans unless he could get the resident engineer to agree. Jay laughed and said, "OK, kid, you got me this time, but watch out because I'll get you next time."

Although I had some admiration for the frank way Jay spoke out, it was also apparent that he was one of the shrewdest contractors in the road-building game. He may have been right in that instance, but the plans didn't show it, hence my resistance. In our next confrontation, Jay had his way, but that was a landmark in my experience and an education for me. On that occasion the resident engineer gave in to Jay, and the testing lab proved me correct.

The second confrontation grew out of an assignment to design a concrete mix and supervise its placement in small concrete headers installed on the ends of metal culverts. The resident engineer gave me some manuals on concrete that required careful study. On that job Jay was using gravel made for surfacing, rather than for concrete. My screening tests showed it to have a poor module ratio, because it didn't meet the uniform grading requirements of concrete aggregate. But I allowed the cement finisher to use it by making adjustments in the water-cement ratio, an adjustment that required more cement to compensate for the inferior aggregate. We also carefully measured out the water to meet the designed water-cement ratio.

When we were pouring our first header, the cement finisher complained that the mix was harsh and unworkable and wanted to add more water. I told him that with the inferior grade aggregate he would have to add more cement before adding more water. During the conversation, Chet Adams and Jay arrived on the scene. When Jay asked about "the holdup," I restated the problem of the poor aggregate. He objected to adding the expensive cement and turned to Adams, who said: "Give him all the water he wants. It will be OK." With those instructions, the work proceeded.

Later I took a sample of the lean mix and sent it to the Highway Department laboratory at the University of Idaho. The material, which was supposed to stand up to two thousand pounds of pressure per square inch, broke at less than eight hundred pounds. The report from the laboratory had a big red stamp on it saying that it did not meet specifications. Adams was upset, but it was a good lesson for both of us, and it reinforced my feelings about the need to avoid inferior work. Although the substandard concrete did not jeopardize the safety of the public on the culvert headers, on a bridge the inferior mix would have been treacherous.

Jay made another assault on the Highway Department through his knowledge about specifications and his close contact with the actual work. Jay's superintendent and foreman watched every item carefully. When they found any condition not specifically spelled out in the plans, they would report to Jay and he would present a special bill for those items. He would claim that in order to finish the highway he had to do work that was not enumerated in the contract. Those bills for time, material, and a percentage for the contractor were known as force-account bills.

Because of the inability to anticipate *everything* hidden in roadway construction, there was money in every contract for contingencies; thus, there was a certain validity to Jay's extra bills. However, he was a consummate artist at padding them. For instance, he had rented a used but top-quality Thew-Lorain shovel for about $150 a month from the Scenic Better Road Highway District, one of the financiers of the job. When he billed the state for his force-account work, he charged around $12 an hour for the same shovel. Since the Scenic Better Road Highway District was paying about 60 percent of the costs for building the highway, Jay charged the district more for the two or three days' use of its own shovel than he reimbursed it for a month's use. That particular item was unusual, but it was representative of the continuous pressure from contractors for greater profits.

When the concrete-header job was finished, I worked in the office to help compute the final estimate for the job, a position that enabled me to learn more about the way the state's money was spent. The old bridge subcontractor, who had built a quality structure because that was a craftsman's way of working, received less than half the amount the state paid to Jay. In other words, Jay received more for handling the contract than the crew did for building the bridge. The same thing happened to the loggers that subcontracted the clearing and grubbing; they received only a fraction of what the state paid Jay for their work. Time has eroded my memory of the long list of force-account items, but one recollection stands out: when he drove up in his Franklin car and walked into the office in his tan camel-hair overcoat with briefcase in hand, we would say, "Here comes Jay with the keys to the state treasury."

There was a positive side to Jay's success as a contractor; he was very efficient at moving dirt, the centerpiece in converting rough terrain into the uniformity necessary for a modern highway. To do that work, he had assembled different types of equipment: a new Lima power shovel, the Thew-Lorain shovel, and two rented trucks. In addition, he had access to different types of dirt-moving scrapers, and he even had a subcontractor working with a horse and mule pulling Fresnos.

Besides getting all the equipment on the job, Jay hired some good men who were organized and avoided moving material more than once. Contractors can buy big, fast-moving machines, but it is difficult to find workers who possess the magic of knowing when to stop lowering cuts or raising embankments. Usually, when a contractor has the road close to grade, he asks the state engineer to send out a survey crew to confirm that the grade is in the right place.

On the Santa job, I was privileged to see the subcontractor's foreman and crew using horses, mules, and old-fashioned Fresnos to complete a grade without a prolonged process of repeated cutting and filling. When the foreman asked the resident engineer to set the grade elevation, Adams looked the grade over carefully and remarked: "This grade is so good it doesn't need blue tops.[1] You can hook up your outfit and get out of town." Those were words of acceptance. In three decades of road building in Oregon, Washington, Idaho, and Montana, that was the only time I had ever seen a quality grade built on a job without the engineering crew's putting out several sets of blue tops.

*

When the Santa road was finished, it was my good fortune to be assigned to construct a new route up Mica Hill about five or six miles south of Coeur d'Alene, the location of my first survey job in the summer of 1930. This time we were preparing to build the road that Cochran had located in 1930. My assignment was to measure the elevations along the center line and establish vertical controls, or bench marks, for the new highway. Surveyors call that "running levels." Just as we finished the level running, I came down with a severe sore throat and was off the job for a month. During the interim, a young unemployed mining engineer, T. Matt Hally—with a lot of good feelings towards people—had taken over. Because of my absence, I was demoted to rodman, working for Hally. As the winter wore on and the snow became deeper, field activity was shut down and the crew laid off.

Before the work opened up in the spring of 1932, the U.S. Bureau of Public Roads in Portland, Oregon, offered me a job. After talking the offer over with the resident engineer, I didn't receive much encouragement about when we would be called back to work in Idaho. The offer of a job in a romantic place like Oregon appealed to me, so I headed west.

The government officials at the U.S. Bureau of Public Roads in Portland gave me a bus ticket to Sisters. En route to that small town, there was lots of time to reflect on the romantic history of Oregon, a name associated with the long trek that thousands of settlers made from the Middle West over the Oregon Trail to lush, green valleys like the Willamette. Once in Sisters I learned that the job was on the eastern side of a big highway project through Oregon's Cascade Range (map 4).

I have always felt there is something personally fulfilling about being part of a big job. The challenges and satisfaction of accomplishment seem more rewarding on the larger projects. The Santiam Pass construction work required the location, design, and building of nearly fifty miles of road through the rugged Cascade Mountains. That section of the highway traversed a long, high ridge which led to Santiam Pass. As the new grade rose higher and higher, we were treated to a spectacular scene. Far below us lay picturesque Blue Lake. The rock massive of Mount Washington towered nearly five thousand feet above the valley floor, furnishing a background for the impressive lake. During the summer that view was our daily fare, at least when we had time to look around. Most of the time, however, we were too busy to admire the scenery, spectacular though it was.

Because of the magnitude of the project, one of the most capable and experienced engineers, C. R. Short, was in charge of all phases of the work during the summer of 1932. Short's unique combination of professional training, interest in practical details, and strength of character enabled him to get quality work out of a contractor. His ability and experience also extended to procedures for accurate and expeditious surveying through rough terrain.

Short's qualities became apparent when we started blue-topping the section of the project that rose above Suttle and Blue lakes on the eastern ramparts of the Santiam section of the Oregon Cascades. Short showed us his answer to the contractor's problems of fine grading and the survey crew's job of setting and resetting blue tops. He visited a small, portable sawmill, where he bought a load of substantial edgings. With those long stakes in the truck, we started setting elevations for the contractor. If we found a spot where the road was two feet below grade, we would use the long edgings to indicate the design grade for the new highway.

On most state highway jobs the survey crews are not furnished stakes long enough to follow that procedure, so when the roadway is too low for the short stakes to reach the required elevation, the crew simply writes on the stake the necessary amount to bring the fill up to grade. The contractor then brings in more dirt and, in trial-and-error fashion, the survey crew returns to set more elevations. Short's method, although slower and involving a lot of heavy pounding with big sledgehammers, eliminated resetting the stakes. It also had a subtle tendency to encourage high-quality work on the part of both the survey crew and the contractor's laborers.

C. R. Short also was unusual in that he stayed on the job until the contractor's crew got the grade up to specifications, a task that often creates friction between the contractor's need to sell the grade "as is" and the resident engineer's responsibility to see that the grade meets the specifications as indicated by the blue tops. Short did not delegate that responsibility; he accepted it himself and carried it out with unique success.

Because we set the blue tops every fifty feet, there was still an expanse of roadway between the stakes at the mercy of the contractor's and inspector's judgment. It was not easy to see minor errors below or above a straight line for the fifty feet, so Short would shed his dignity and lie down in the dirt to train his eye on the line of the grade. From that vantage point, the imperfections were clearly visible. That took time, cost the contractor money, and created tension between the company and the resident engineer. But Short resisted pressures from the contractor, and he had the administrative support of his superior. As a part of his procedure for handling arguments, he offered to have our crew set the blue tops every twenty-five feet. The contractor didn't want that, so he accepted Short's judgment and stayed with the work until it met the specifications for a first-class roadbed.

His persistence was one of the finest examples of an engineer's protecting the public interest that I have ever witnessed. It is very difficult for an engineer to force a contractor to carry out specifications when the contractor is interested only in the profit he makes. In Montana and Idaho engineers were assigned to inferior jobs in remote areas for attempting to do what Short accomplished.

On the Santiam job the U.S. Bureau of Public Roads classified me as a rodman, a title that covers a broad range of survey work. Anyone on the crew may do the work of using the level rod, but the title *rodman* usually refers to someone with a lot of experience in chaining, rodding, and all of the fieldwork except running the transit. Although my rating at Santa was the same, the day-to-day work was quite different; it involved no direct contact with the contractor and no personal responsibilities.

The transitman is in charge of the field crew in the absence of a party chief or resident engineer, hence daily assignments may be at his whim. His work requires a knowledge of surveying and trigonometry, experience with field procedures, and some skill at handling the very sophisticated instrument. Although my experience included the basics of survey mathematics and operation of the transit, I would not call myself a transitman because of a lack of experience. Monty, the transitman on the Santiam crew, had my respect, both as an individual and for his skill. My ability to run a transit, however, got me into some difficulty.

My problems occurred when Short offered me the opportunity to run in a long curve, one of the more intricate procedures in operating a transit. Although I did so without any difficulty and was happy with the accomplishment, as time went on it was apparent that Monty resented my success in running the transit. For the rest of the summer he gave me the most menial jobs. When a field-survey crew is driving blue tops, the heavy work of pounding with a sledgehammer is usually rotated with the lighter task of holding the rod. When Monty organized the day's activities, he gave me more than my share of sledgehammering. Although it was hard work, it enabled one to develop a certain proficiency with the hammer. That paid off on the way back to Idaho that fall when I was able to ring the bell on one of those carnival machines where you hit the plunger with a hammer.

On the Santiam everything came in gargantuan proportions. On the west side of the summit the giant Douglas-fir trees grew so thick that it took an entire construction season just to clear four or five miles of right-of-way. There were no roads in that remote area, and the terrain was so rough that it was not feasible to put in a rough logging road. So, all that magnificent timber had to be cut and burned on the spot in order to clear the right-of-way in preparation for the next summer's construction.

One of our jobs was to set stakes marking the clearing limits for the contractors. The first of those jobs on the west side of the pass was accessible only on foot, so we walked westward to the summit, where we found fifteen feet of hard-packed, high-country summer snow. In order to survey on the west side, we had to cross over the summit and proceed until we got out of the snow belt, where the clearing contractor could go to work. At the most westerly portion, we had to walk eight miles (map distance) to the job site and eight miles back at night. Because we took a winding route through the trees and snow, we actually walked at least ten miles.

The uphill climb on the return trip made a strong impression on me. It was the most physical exertion that I ever faced, and there was a lack of comradeship among the crew. For some reason there was a lot of jealousy and resentment, and that limited any cooperation on the long ten-mile trek to the truck high on the east side. In truth, it became an endurance contest, with the transitman leading the way. He was in good shape and set a strong pace. The rest of the crew was strung out single file, facing the tough climb with very little enthusiasm. If someone tired or slackened his pace, another person would pass him without a word. I didn't like the racing but accepted the challenge and pushed on for a leading position. My youth enabled me to get stronger with each passing day and eventually to the number 2 spot behind the transitman. My sympathy went out to the older man walking in the rear or number 4 spot, but at that time my response to that cutthroat competition was to hoard my strength and carefully stay a few steps behind the transitman. Today, my participation in that endurance contest seems shameful, but at that moment I was caught up in the antisocial competition to be tough.

After the clearing was completed, Short worked with us on some line changes in the vicinity of Hogg Rock[2] on the west side of Santiam Pass. We traversed a long talus slope where it was seemingly impossible to drive a stake or set up a transit. My job was head chainman on that work. Because the progress and accuracy of a survey line depend on the judgment and skill of the head chainman, Short spent most of the day with me. His supervision and coaching through the obstacle course along the slopes helped me solve similar problems later in my career.

Before that experience I had learned field-chaining procedures from observing other chainmen. Among other things, Short abandoned the range pole we had used in Idaho in favor of the more accurate string and plumb bob. It took a certain amount of skill to keep the plumb bob from swinging wildly and erratically around the vicinity of the tack. It had to be steadied, or the result would be inaccurate angular measurements by the transitman. Short demonstrated different ways to use the range pole as a rest to steady the plumb bob. He also told me that if the terrain required me to hold the plumb bob so high that it could not be steadied with the range pole, the setup should be moved to a better location. That helped improve my techniques and gave me confidence in using my own judgment.

That summer on the Santiam was memorable in many ways: the opportunity to spend an entire season amidst the scenic grandeur of the Oregon Cascades; doing meaningful work on a big job pushing Oregon's first all-weather road through the mountains; and the opportunity to work with C. R. Short, who demanded quality performance from contractors. Short had a mastery of the theory and practice of road building, personal integrity, and a commitment to high standards. For that he had my deep respect. From the time of the Santiam job in 1932 until I retired from highway work in 1972, his work served as a model for my own inspection procedures and my relations with contractors.

*

In the spring of 1933 the U.S. Bureau of Public Roads offered me work as a rodman–head chainman on a job at Mapleton, Oregon. The bright-green colors that dominate the Oregon valleys west of the Cascade Range had always attracted me, but the beautiful foliage west of the Coast Range was far beyond anything I had ever seen before.

The Mapleton job introduced me to a river culture where ocean tides, river currents, and boats were the focal points of the transportation system. The Bureau of Public Roads had adapted to river transport by acquiring two houseboats to serve as living quarters and as office space for the resident engineer. Our job was to improve the rough twenty miles of highway that followed the Siuslaw River between Mapleton and Florence. Because the existing roadbed was impassable, our task was to place a thick base course, or foundation of gravel, and top it off with a layer of crushed rock. It was a big job to inspect and place the thousands of tons of surfacing material required to complete the first road between Mapleton and Florence.

Because the road gravel was transported on barges propelled by an oceangoing tugboat, the skipper always timed his casting off with the rising tide, which, in turn, followed the rising moon. When the tide was in, the water was deep enough to enable the skipper to make a safe passage with the barges carrying the heavy gravel. So it was the rising moon and its effect on the ocean tides that set my daily work schedule. Since the moon rose approximately fifty-one minutes later each day, my hours of work followed in like fashion. Thus my working hours slowly traversed the night and the day. That was a new world for me, and it had a powerful fascination. It made me feel closer to nature and I learned something of the lore of the tides and the sea.

Another feature of the Siuslaw River culture was the way people used the waterways for transportation. And their boats were different from any I had ever seen before. They were wide, flat bottomed, and without seats and were powered by sturdy, economical one-cylinder engines. They were steered by a long, vertical lever about waist high that was attached to a rudder. Those were working boats. In the rainy coastal weather the seats were usually too wet for sitting; moreover they were in the way for hauling cargo. On Sunday morning, churchgoers would be standing up in the boats; if it was raining, people carried umbrellas for protection.

One Saturday night we went to a dance at a schoolhouse down the river. We rode in a big boat built for hauling heavy supplies and found dozens of similar craft tied up at the schoolhouse dock. Because there were several boats already tied up, late arrivals had to tie up and then walk across the other boats to get to the docks. Everyone in the community came to the dance in boats, including the children. The skipper of the big boat from Mapleton had trouble getting people to go home; it was almost four o'clock in the morning before his passengers left the dance for the trip up the river.

While I was enjoying the romance of the Siuslaw River culture, we ran into a bad problem on my part of the big surfacing job. The gravel deposits along the river that we used for the roadway's base course contained large rocks up to four inches in diameter, accompanied by adequate amounts of intermediate and fine sizes. Years of road-building knowledge and laboratory tests had developed formulas for determining the proper amounts of interlocking sizes of aggregate that are essential for a stable roadway. When the right mixture is present, it is called well-graded material. Those proportions are listed in the standard specifications and are included in the contract between the government and the contractor.

The base course at Mapleton had a big range of sizes, extending from a maximum of four-inch rocks through the intermediate sizes down to rock dust. When not handled properly during the loading or the unloading process, well-graded aggregate is susceptible to being divided into its separate components, a process called segregation. In its segregated form, the course rock by itself is no more stable than a pile of marbles, and the fine particles by themselves are little better than garden soil that blows away when dry and turns to mud when the rains hit.

On the Siuslaw the separating process took place as the contractor loaded the big barges. When the barges delivered the gravel to my area of work, it had obviously segregated, a fact that became apparent when the gravel was spread on the road. Instead of a well-graded stable base course on the road, we had long stretches of unstable fine material, and following that we had a long stretch of big three- and four-inch rocks that were so unstable that even the construction equipment often got stuck in the loose rocks. I reported the problem to the chief inspector and suggested that the barge-loading process be modified by building a movable conveyer belt or by moving the barge so the surfacing material would be dropped on the barge in small uniform lifts. I wasn't present at the confrontation between the resident engineer and the contractor, but none of those changes were made and we used segregated gravel all through the summer.

It was very disappointing to me to see the contractor get away with seriously compromising an expensive roadway surfacing. The material we used did not give travelers the quality roadbed that the specifications required (and that the public had paid for). The Siuslaw job was a classic example of the difficulties encountered in forcing a contractor to follow the procedures outlined in the standard specifications.

That problem is systemic, in my view, in that it is caused by the separation of power and objectives of the contract system. The contractor has the power to hire and fire and to direct the men doing the work. Theoretically the resident engineer has the power to shut the job down when the contractor violates the specifications, but that is rarely done. When the engineer demands that guidelines be followed, it creates a bureaucratic and often a legal furor. The resident engineer then earns a reputation for not getting along with the contractor; the consequences are assignment to insignificant projects or paper shuffling. The dynamics of controlling the job favor the contractor. Moreover, after each job, such as the Siuslaw, the standard specifications are adjusted to cover previous faults. In that way, the requirements grow lengthier, the paperwork increases, and more people are busy dealing with administrative tasks. Yet the technology of the construction industry changes even faster, so the paper blizzard never solves the problem of the contractor's de facto control of the job and his desire to cut costs and produce profits.

After all the disappointments with the base-course gravel, it was a pleasure to work with the smaller-size crushed rock for the top course. Because that mixture held considerable moisture, it did not separate while being loaded onto the barges.

Our last objective on the Siuslaw project was to produce a proper finish for the roadway that had settled unevenly. One of the most significant personal experiences of my road-building career was the way the head grader operator (blade man) and I solved the problem of fine-grading the finished roadway without blue tops. After the base and top courses were in place, part of my job on the grade involved doing the same work C. R. Short had done on the Santiam, except that we were working with crushed gravel. The trucks would drop extra gravel in the low spots and the blade man, who was a first-rate operator, would

cut off the spots that were too high. Between the two of us, we turned out an excellent gravel road and it was fun for me. In just one season I was using the experience gained from watching C. R. Short. The blade man and I agreed with each other on our eyeballing decisions, and both of us enjoyed the creative work of turning out a high-quality road.

Everything on the Siuslaw project was in stark contrast to the Santiam job. On that project, C. R. Short pulled out on the job every morning at eight o'clock and spent most of the day supervising the contractor's work. Because of Short's courage and commitment to quality, every detail was finished according to the standard specifications of the contract. By contrast, on the Siuslaw job the resident engineer never came out on the project, and major violations, such as the segregation of the base-course gravel, were allowed to continue.

Those contrasts in quality control indicate that an individual resident engineer can have an effect on the way the job is run. With the benefit of hindsight, it is obvious to me that C. R. Short was an outstanding exception to the general rule that the contract system places the day-to-day control of the job in the hands of the contractor. In most cases the contractor's economic, political, and social power gives him leverage over many aspects of the job and limits the influence of the resident engineer.

Despite the way the contractor and resident engineer compromised the quality of the base-course layer, I enjoyed the experience and fellowship of sharing the work of building the first road down the tidewater reaches of the Siuslaw. It was also a memorable experience to be on a job where one followed the moonrise to work as those sequential risings traversed the night and the day. I also shared the unique experience of being part of a river culture before it was decimated by highways and automobiles.

More Surveying: The 1930s

When my six-month appointment ended in the fall of 1933, I was laid off by the U.S. Bureau of Public Roads. Because most of the bureau's construction was in the Cascade and Rocky Mountains, it didn't have much winter fieldwork. Once back in Coeur d'Alene, Chester Adams offered me a job as a junior levelman on a big job north of Spirit Lake, Idaho (map 1). Although my payroll title was the lowest of the instrument categories, that was a substantial promotion over the previous positions of rodman or chainman. I worked regularly with the instruments, running either the level or the transit on twenty-five miles of location work and about ten miles of construction.

The surveyor's tripod level was the state of the art of modern technology. It combined a sensitive eighteen- to twenty-inch telescope with a base that incorporated a precise level tube with adjusting screws mounted on a heavy wooden tripod. An experienced crew could measure elevations over a course of ten or twenty miles within an error range of approximately one-tenth of a foot. The standard procedure for our class of work in the 1930s involved a wooden rod with numbers in feet, tenths, and hundredths of a foot. The numbering started at the

bottom of the rod and ran up to its full height of more than twelve or thirteen feet. The rodman would hold the rod plumb on a bench mark of known elevation, and the instrument man would read the rod and record the figure in the level book. That reading plus the elevation of the bench mark gave the height of the instrument.

From that location the rodman would move along, taking readings at regular distances. Those readings then were subtracted from the height of the instrument to determine the true elevation at that point. Two or three hundred feet, according to the degree of precision required, is as far as a rod can read; therefore, it is necessary to set a turning point or a temporary bench mark no more than two hundred feet from the instrument. The instrument man adjusts the level, reads the rod carefully, and records the figure. That reading subtracted from the instrument's elevation gives the elevation of the bench mark or turning point. The instrument man then picks up the level, swings the tripod over his shoulder, and goes ahead to repeat the procedure again.

When reading a rod through the powerful telescope, many times the levelman would be so close that the red-colored numbers below the reading would be out of the sighting area of the instrument, although the upper foot number would be visible. Because the rod is numbered from the bottom, to read it correctly the levelman must always look down the rod for the correct foot, otherwise the operator may accidentally record the upper foot number in the book. An error of that kind might nullify several days' work. An engineer named Frank Reddy taught me to take time to signal the rodman to raise the rod for the lower red or correct number. That procedure helps to eliminate mistakes and can save days of frustration.

Normally each day's work was checked by a process called completing the loop. At the beginning of the day the crew started out at a known elevation. In the morning the measurements were taken as the men moved through the terrain. In the afternoon the route was retraced with readings taken at different locations. At the end of the day the crew was back at the known elevation. All of the elevations and sightings for the day were added or subtracted and if the work was correct, the result was checked out with the known elevation. This process checked that each reading of the day was correct. On that job, however, the boss was in such a hurry that he decided not to close the loop each day. Instead, we ran a straight twenty-five miles to another known elevation.

Even with the best of habits and concern for accurate work, errors occurred. On one occasion when we closed in our twenty-five-mile level circuit on another U.S. government bench mark, the tension was so strong that the rodman, at my request, read the numbers while I held the rod. He was glad to oblige, and as it turned out we checked in OK. It was a great relief to have the month's work prove out.

I never grew tired of running the transit, a procedure that presents many challenges. Because of my understanding of trigonometry, I was able to utilize the potential of the instrument and to read the intricate vernier that measures angles in degrees, minutes, and seconds. It requires practice to place the transit base precisely over the survey and map control point and to make it level and in a stable position. A light touch is needed in handling the sensitive controls. In addition to mastering those techniques, there has to be a precise verbal and visual communication system with the field crew. There is always room to improve one's skill, touch, and dependability. The transit's basic function is to measure angles whose precise measurement can determine the direction, bearing, or azimuth of a highway, or it can be used to calculate a distance through the common laws of trigonometry.

During my fourteen months at Spirit Lake in 1933 and 1934, I served a basic apprenticeship in the use of the transit. That enabled me to get by on succeeding jobs where more experience allowed me to develop my own procedures. Those experiences also permitted me to acquire an affection for that versatile instrument.

We completed the transit and level work on the twenty-five miles of the Spirit Lake–to–Newport job in the early winter of 1934–35. Although I had been laid off until spring in previous situations, that winter the department sent me to Harrison, Idaho, on a small construction job as the third member of a select crew that included two resident engineers. It was an honor that I appreciated to be chosen for winter work rather than being among the unemployed. On that job, partly financed by federal-aid highway funds, it was made apparent to me that the state would not carry a field crew through the winter when the work was financed by state funds. But they were happy to keep their experienced people on a payroll when a job was financed at least partly by federal money.

I became aware of two things that winter: whiling away time is much more tedious than working, and on a crew of high-rated personnel, most of the men wanted to avoid responsible work in favor of the lowest classification, which in this case meant doing the physical task of driving stakes and rear chaining. It puzzled me that the higher-salaried people chose the lowest-paid work when it did not entail a loss of wages or prestige. It occurred to me later that in a situation where everyone knew how to do every position on the crew and the project was of rather minor significance, there was little challenge to any crew position. Given the fact that every one of the crew would be returning to positions of significant responsibility, the job of driving stakes was more relaxing work. After a few months at Harrison, I was happy to be sent to Coeur d'Alene on a rock-crushing and seal-coating job.

*

In the 1930s most of the state highways in northern Idaho were covered with a low type of oil seal called a road-mix pavement. After only a few years those highways developed cracks and became porous, which allowed the fall rains to penetrate the roadbed. With the winter's cold weather, the moisture would freeze, causing the road to heave and break up. It was possible to avoid the cracking by applying a heavy coat of hot asphalt and immediately covering that with a thin layer of rock chips. The hot asphalt makes the pavement watertight and the new layer of rock chips provides another surface to protect and strengthen the old pavement. That was known as putting on a seal coat.

The summer of 1935, my eighth year of highway work, was special in several ways. I was given the responsibility for looking after two small projects: the first, crushing seal-coat rock for seventy-five miles of state roads, and the second, applying the hot asphalt and seal-coat rock before the fall rains began. Those projects were small as highway jobs go, but it was a big assignment for me. I was there by myself representing the state of Idaho and responsible for the quality of work, the payments to the contractor, and protecting the public's interest. As luck would have it, some unconventional developments took place on both projects that provided the skilled workers and myself an opportunity to use our experiences to produce high-quality work in record-breaking time.

The jobs opened with the crushing of rock chips for the seal coating, work that was done through the conventional contract system. Under those arrangements, the plans, specifications, and estimates of the job are advertised in the press, the bids opened in public, and the contract awarded to the lowest qualified bidder.

When I arrived at the site near Naples, Idaho (map 2), the contractor was setting up a crusher and preparing to produce the rock chips. The chips are different from other crushed rock in that they do not contain the fine material that is usually required to make a cohesive, stable mixture for roadway resurfacing. That is because the heavy asphalt sealing oil acts as the binder that holds the chips together. Eliminating that fine material turned out to be a problem for the contractor, but eventually we arrived at an ideal mix.

The specifications called for something like 5 percent of the chips to pass through a number 10 screen (ten openings per inch), but screens much larger than the number 10 had to be used in order to eliminate the unwanted fine material. This produced rock chips that met the specifications, but they were unusually deficient in the intermediate-size chips. Later, when we were using the rock chips in the seal-coating work, we found that this unusual and unexpected deficiency in the intermediate chips proved to be an ideal mix. As far as that contract was concerned, the aberration in grading was not anticipated in the specifications, so the chips were legal and acceptable and the contract was completed with no other problems.

With the rock chips stockpiled and ready for use, the next step was to apply a thick layer of hot asphalt and cover it with a thin layer of chips. Ordinarily a contract would be let with an oiling contractor for that phase of the work, but due to the lateness of the season, the state opted for a negotiated agreement and the job was let to a man I will refer to as John, who turned out to be a very irresponsible contractor.

I was in charge of that part of the project, reporting to Dick Pearson, the district maintenance engineer (similar to my responsibility during the rock-crushing contract). It wasn't long before the state started the oiling process by ordering tank cars of heavy asphalt to be shipped at regular intervals to a siding adjacent to the work. John began assembling the necessary equipment and engaged a competent hauling subcontractor with a small fleet of Mack trucks, all driven by experienced drivers. We (the state) assembled the necessary signs and a crew to drive the pilot car and control the traffic. At long last we were ready to start the seal-coating job.

We were quite excited when the big day arrived and we could make the first application of hot asphalt. The old oil mat was brushed clean, the asphalt was heated to the proper temperature, and the distributor truck laid down a uniform coat of oil. Then the big gravel trucks, poised with their beds raised, started backing over the hot oil, spreading a thin layer of rock chips ahead of them. The drivers did a beautiful job of guiding the backward-moving vehicles in a straight, precise line, so that all the hot, messy asphalt was completely covered with a uniform layer of rock chips. It is difficult to back up and follow the hot asphalt precisely at a uniform rate of speed so that all the oil is covered evenly. But all the truck drivers were experienced at the work and performed skillfully.

My elation over this good progress soon dissolved, because walking on the newly spread chips was like crossing a layer of marbles or ball bearings. It didn't appear to me that those big chips would ever penetrate into the oil mat enough to produce a smooth, stable surface. When I told Dick Pearson the bad news, he urged patience and that we keep the pilot cars on for a few days longer, which would enable us to control the traffic while the new asphalt softened up the old oil mat. We did so and kept the traffic at a low rate of speed so that the chips were not kicked off the highway before they were firmly seated. After a few days it was evident that the boss had been right. The result was a very good seal and several years of service added to the old pavement at a very low cost.

After the euphoria of the first few days wore off, it was plain that we were having problems with all phases of the work. There were bottlenecks showing up here and there. The contractor appeared to be very incompetent, or at least unable to respond to the problems that developed. For instance, the power broom that swept the pavement ahead of the oil application was not able to keep up with the trucks. We obviously needed another power broom to take advantage of the capacity of the oil- and chip-spreading trucks, but John wasn't sensitive to that problem. Yet, it was plain to all the key workers that production could be doubled by the addition of one more power broom.

Because the contractor refused to rent another one, I got in touch with Dick Pearson and explained our problem. Due to the urgent need to get the job done before the fall rains, he convinced John that he should rent another power broom in order to expedite the work. The second broom soon appeared on the job and we nearly doubled our production. The demand for that second piece of equipment was worked out through consultations among the hauling contractor, the distributor-truck driver, and myself—all of us involved in the day-to-day operations of the job. John was too busy shooting the breeze in the local restaurants and bars to be very sensitive about details.

The district engineer had considerable influence with John because of the nature of the contract agreements. Each had to be renegotiated after the completion of about five units of work. If John cooperated, the contracts were extended; if he didn't, we could get someone else to continue the project in a few days. Because of that leverage, Pearson convinced John that he should listen to the subcontractor and myself. Our advice proved to be effective; John began to lean on us more and more, and the job progressed to a successful conclusion in an expeditious manner.

We were almost through when the cold, heavy, fall rains caught up with us near Plummer, Idaho (map 3), on October 10. We used extra hot oil and finished the last mile of the job in the rain. In general it is not good practice to seal-coat in the rain, although the oil and the rock chips appeared to stick to the road in this case. Whether that last shot was a success or not, we were elated to have won the race against the rain for more than seventy miles of good roads.

Looking back at that job and comparing it with other seal-coat work done by established contractors, two unusual features of the project made it a showpiece for seal-coating work on low-grade, road-mix pavements. The unusually sticky gravel source required a screen with large openings to get rid of the unwanted fine material, which, in turn eliminated the usual but unspecified intermediate-size rock chips. The absence of intermediate-size material left space on the hot asphalt for larger rocks to make contact with the oil. Therefore, most of them became firmly embedded in the old mat instead of being kicked off the road by the traffic. In addition, the negotiated agreement gave the state an unusual amount of de facto influence over the contractor. Thus, a somewhat weak contractor and a highly skilled crew gave workers an opportunity to apply their experiences to the management of the project. Those factors produced high-quality work in record-breaking time as we finished the seventy-five miles of seal coating in thirty-seven elapsed days.

Long after the work was completed, I made inspection trips over the project during the course of several years and was amazed to see that much of the route still had the white appearance usually associated with Portland-cement concrete. That quality makes night driving much safer because of the light-reflecting surface. All oil pavements look black, and the best seal-coated pavements don't usually lighten the color very much. But on parts of our job, the large rocks were so prevalent that their color became the dominant shade of the pavement. That is the only job in my experience where there was sufficient retention of the large rocks to produce that effect.

Several years later in Boise on state highway business, I mentioned the success of those big three-quarter-inch rocks to the state's materials engineer, Cliff Havelick. He told me the state never used large seal chips on any project. The lab tests and specifications on my earlier work, I said, would disprove his argument. Later he checked and learned to his surprise that my explanation was right. When he told me that it was the only such contract in the state of Idaho, it made me proud of our job—and a bit negative about an administration that wasn't aware of our success or the reasons for it.

*

With the seal-coat job finished, the Highway Department sent me to Rathdrum, Idaho, to be layout man and inspector on two reinforced concrete bridges. The building of those two bridges involved unique features that extended beyond the conventional experience that goes with bridge construction. My old friend Chet Adams told me that my job was to do all the layout and inspection on both bridge sites, except for the approval of the falsework.[1] He felt that he should accept that responsibility himself. Adams told me to put up a rough eight-by-eight shack within sight of both bridges for an office, to pick up the necessary surveying equipment, and to study the plans in preparation for the contractor when he arrived.

My first look at the detailed blueprints of the Rathdrum bridge challenged my self-confidence. The sheets appeared as a maze of lines, showing only two-dimensional views of complicated details of reinforced steel. However, with several days to give the plans my undivided attention, some order and shape slowly began to emerge. The general diagram of the bridge and the footing details were soon apparent, so I went to work laying out the essential lines.

The details of a bridge are shown on the blueprint in relation to a small number of centerlines. First there is the centerline of the highway, which is used to locate the centerline of the bridge. There is also a centerline for each pier. Because all dimensions on the bridge were related to the centerlines, my job was to establish convenient points in the ground where they would not be destroyed by the contractor or covered up by a pile of lumber or reinforcing steel. Adams assigned an older, experienced rodman, John Stark, to assist me. I did the transit work and helped John with the chaining; we made a good team.

There is no room for simple errors in arithmetic when doing work of this kind, and it was an ever-present concern for me. Since the Santa bridge job, however, I had spent several years responsibly using the surveyor's tools—the transit, the level, and the hundred-foot chain. Those experiences had added a little confidence and helped me to develop procedures for checking my work. Still, no matter how much time is spent in checking the arithmetic, there is no lasting relief from the heavy responsibility for correct measurements until the bridge stands there in its massive reality. The end result is a tribute to the dream of bridge engineers, the efforts of construction workers, and the collective activities of a society dedicated to producing those transportation necessities.

When John Stark and I finished making the basic layout and establishing the control points, the next job was to inspect the gravel and sand that would make up the aggregate for the concrete. There were no central premix plants in northern Idaho during the 1930s, but there were lots of sand and gravel deposits in the Rathdrum–Spirit Lake region. Therefore, the contractor set up his own crushing, screening, and washing plant.

There is a lot of magic in the making of concrete. The cement is made by grinding hard limestone and then adding natural substances, such as shale, clay, cement rock, and slag from a blast furnace. By itself, cement is no stronger than a child's mud pie, but when it is combined with the correct proportion of sand, gravel, and water, the mix develops a strength equal to that of the rocks themselves. For this to occur, the sand and the gravel have to be just right. The aggregate must be strong, clean, and it must contain a uniform variety of sizes so that the smaller-size material will fit into the spaces between the larger-size pieces, and the water content has to be held to a minimum. My job was to make preliminary screening tests on the contractor's sand and gravel to ensure that it fit the standard formulas to facilitate the magic transformation of the semiliquid mixture of aggregate and cement into concrete.

While we were doing the basic layout work and the preliminary inspection of the concrete aggregate, the contractor, whom I will refer to as Jim, and my boss, Chet Adams, became involved in a heated argument over the design of the falsework. The falsework has to support the heavy, wet concrete in place until it dries and becomes the stone-hard concrete of the new bridge. Adams thought the best way to prevent the forms from settling out of shape was to preload the supporting timbers by driving them deep into the ground with a pile driver.

When Adams proposed that to Jim, the contractor, he responded by saying he could support the falsework with sleepers, which meant simply laying large timbers on the ground for the needed support. Jim argued that the procedures and methods were the prerogative of the contractor and that Adams's authority was restricted to the evaluation of the results of the project. Jim then wrote a long letter to the Highway Department stating his position and said Adams was unduly interfering with the progress of the job. The contractor was correct because at that time there was little authority for the inspector to evaluate or approve falsework designs. Because there was some truth to Jim's claims as to the authority of the positions, Adams gave in to the pressure and allowed him to proceed with his falsework design.

While Jim and Adams were quarreling over the falsework, the bridge foreman, the carpenters, and I were building the heavy wooden forms that would make the semiliquid concrete conform to the engineer's plans. I cherished the rewarding work of seeing the bridge take shape from the lines and figures on the blueprints.

The peak of the drama in building a concrete bridge occurs when the deck is poured, usually the culmination of nearly a year's work. That process included the supporting beams that spanned the distance from pier to pier and the concrete roadway for the driving public. Once the pour begins, there is no way to stop until the beams and roadway are completed. The concrete starts to harden in an hour or so, and from then on there is no turning back. A breakdown or faltering for a few minutes can spell disaster; everything has to be planned carefully for the big day. In the mid-1930s that meant a dawn-to-dark workday, largely because the mixers could only put out a few cubic yards of concrete every hour.

We were fortunate at Rathdrum to have a mixer operator who understood the importance of the correct ratio of the water content in the mix. Because of his rare talent the concrete was uniform and homogenous throughout the pouring operation. But when the pour was completed, it was evident that Adams had been right about the falsework, because it had settled enough to spoil the gentle, curved arc of the bridge. All the fine work of the foreman and the carpenters was somewhat marred by the contractor's poorly designed falsework. There was no way to raise the structure to the gentle arc detailed in the plans without tearing it down and starting over. The contractor had not produced the quality bridge that had been promised, and the state was stuck with a serviceable but ugly duckling.

Because the falsework on the Rathdrum project had settled sufficiently to mar what should have been graceful lines, Adams was determined to avoid that defect on the Spirit Lake bridge. He was pleased that Ed Milldollar, the construction superintendent, planned to drive piling, the accepted practice in providing support for falsework. However, while Ed was waiting for a crane from another job, Jim showed up and overruled his plan to drive piling and ordered the installation of round timbers as sleepers to hold the falsework pillars. With the Rathdrum experience still fresh in his mind, Adams notified the contractor that the sleepers were not a satisfactory foundation for the falsework and refused to authorize the pouring of the concrete.

Jim again went over Adams's head and asked the Highway Department to approve his plan. In a few days a representative from the bridge department came out to the job and walked around in the forest of timbers and beams. He was impressed with the number and size of the upright members of the falsework and after a few minutes of visual inspection, without any calculations, he gave the contractor an OK to go ahead with the deck pour. I felt sorry for Adams, because he had been repudiated by the bridge-department representative. He made no comment about the decision but told me to go ahead and look after the concrete placement and hope for the best.

At daylight the next day the big deck pour began, the culmination of nearly a year's work of pouring footings and piers, building forms, and erecting falsework. It was also Jim's opportunity to prove that his economical falsework would support the heavy green concrete in the precise location required in the plans, an objective that all of us had worked hard to attain. About two hours into the pour—as the deep beams began to fill with the heavy, wet mud—disaster struck. The sleepers, which were the foundation supports for the big timbers, settled four or five inches into the ground and destroyed the beautiful lines and arc of the bridge.

Ed Milldollar ordered the men to start washing out the green mix before it started to harden. His years of experience and pride in his work would not let him continue with such a defective pour; moreover, he knew that it was imperative to get the green concrete out of the forms

while it was still in a semifluid state. With the wet concrete washed out of the forms, he would have a chance to beef up the falsework and jack the empty forms back into place. Just as the men were preparing to follow his instructions, Jim drove up, countermanded Ed's orders, and told the men to proceed with the pour.

Jim's decision led to further trouble. We did everything we could to bring the bridge up to grade by wedging underneath the forms and thickening the deck, but our efforts proved ineffective. Because it was long after dark when we left the site, the full extent of the disaster was not visible until the next day. There stood a sad sight! Instead of a gently rising arc, the lines of the bridge drooped between the abutment and the piers. I turned away with a feeling of pain. Even though, as individuals, we had no control over the faulty work, all of us felt some personal shame for our association with such an abortion.

The project was closed down and all hands were laid off, except for a man or two cleaning up around the site. For several months state- and federal-government officials examined the bridge and worked on a formal decision to present to the contractor. While those inspections were taking place, Jim tried desperately to get the state to accept our pour or to pay him for removing it. But he met with no success, and after several months he ordered Milldollar to remove the defective bridge. Ed got a crew together to tear down what we had worked on for so long.

He faced a momentous task; the concrete with its tons of reinforcing steel had to be chipped out piece by piece. Compressors, pavement-breaking hammers, and chisels were used to pry off small pieces one at a time. That tedious operation took a couple of months and cost about the same as the job of building the bridge in the first place. Milldollar didn't complain, but every day of hammering and chiseling must have reminded him that it all could have been avoided if Jim had allowed him to wash the green concrete out of the forms before it hardened.

Besides the tragedy of all the work and skill wasted on a defective bridge, a gross injustice was meted out to Adams. From the beginning he had personally condemned Jim's falsework plans and fought to change them. When the falsework settled as Adams predicted, the

Highway Department associated him with the failure of the work and arranged to have another resident engineer finish the bridge. The decision to replace Adams was unjust because if the Highway Department had supported him, the defective pour would have been avoided.

The rebuilding of the bridge was rather anticlimactic. Because Jim's ideas about falsework had been discredited, he stayed away from the job and allowed Milldollar to go ahead and drive piling for the falsework supports. The pilings, hammered into the ground until they refused to go any further, would support the heavy loads of forms and concrete with no measurable settling. That is what Adams and Milldollar had wanted to do from the beginning.

After we had completed the deck pours, all that remained was the job of making the forms for the massive yet intricate concrete guardrails. They had a wide base with gently radiating curves leading to a narrow central section with arched windows about fifteen inches high and six inches wide. The windowed wall was topped with a wide parapet. Most bridge carpenters shuddered at the prospect of building the forms for that maze of curves and windows, but our carpenter foreman, Jack Holloway, had proudly mastered all of those problems. He designed and built a form for the arch-topped windows that had a slight taper to it and an internal wedge that could be pulled out when the concrete had set. Jack was proud of his work, and our rails were the showpiece that topped off the bridge. The guardrails were massive enough to keep a car or truck on the bridge, a type of form work that went out of style after the Second World War. They were replaced with simple pipe rails; another piece of fine craftwork was lost in the process.

I worked on many projects where we created solid structures from flat, two-dimensional lines that represented an engineer's concept of a completed bridge, but at Spirit Lake it was my privilege to meet the creator of the plans, the chief bridge engineer from Boise. We walked around the site while he inspected the bridge to see how the reality of our creation compared with his line drawings. That was a rare experience for me. He didn't need a set of blueprints in his hands; they were a part of him. And he was pleased with our work. After the aborted deck pour was torn down, we had built a quality bridge according to the designer's plans.

Building that bridge illustrates some of the problems that are associated with the contract system. When push came to shove, Adams's plea for a proper falsework setting was not supported by the contractor or the bridge department. When the bridge failed, the Highway Department took Adams off the job, thus associating him with the faulty bridge. That was a bitter pill for Adams to swallow. But incidents like that led to changes in the standard specifications; a contractor now has to file falsework plans with the Highway Department. That procedure allows design engineers in the bridge department an opportunity to study and approve or reject the plans.

Yet day-to-day authority still lies with the contractor, who hires, fires, and gives orders to the workers. My area of direct responsibility—ensuring that the aggregate was of the proper mix—was something I was proud of. As a consequence we were able to produce unusually workable concrete that was stronger than the state's testing machines. However, the problem of the alien influence of a profit-hungry contractor was still unsolved.

Aside from the disappointment with the faulty deck pour, the strongest feelings that filter through the intervening years are the comradeship that developed among the working bridge builders. I admired their skill and courage in the rough, hard task of putting up the falsework and their artistry in putting the finishing touches on the forms and the concrete. They accepted my relatively minor technical contributions, and together we constructed a good-looking, substantial, and trustworthy bridge.

*

With the Rathdrum–Spirit Lake projects completed, D. M. Faires, the new resident engineer, and I were assigned to a job building a railroad bridge in Sandpoint, Idaho (map 2). The work was financed through a New Deal program designed to eliminate dangerous railroad crossings. The Idaho Highway Department was given the job of building the little bridge to carry Northern Pacific Railroad traffic over a Sandpoint street. It was a new and interesting experience to work with both railroad crews and a contractor to build a structure that was designed to support the big mainline engines, the long freight trains, and the fast passenger trains that passed through several times every day. Because the work had to be done without any appreciable interruption of the train schedules, the job presented additional challenges.

Before we could begin the project, we had to build a temporary bridge that would allow access to the foundations of the two massive abutments for the new structure. That problem was solved by the railroad's own bridge crew. They showed up one morning with a big steam-powered pile driver, a large crane equipped to hold pilings in place while they were hammered into the ground. That piece of equipment was a far cry from the primitive horse-powered gravity hammer used at Santa and a refinement infinitely beyond the pile driver used for the falsework at Spirit Lake.

The Northern Pacific Railroad did not hire out the job of driving the pilings on its many bridges. Its crews did the work themselves with their own state-of-the-art pile driver and hired their own crews. In this way the railroad crews had complete control over the foundation work of the bridges that supported their trains.

An interesting phenomenon took place when we drove the foundation pilings for the Church Street railroad bridge. The specifications called for the pilings to be driven until they developed sufficient resistance to indicate that they would support a load of approximately fifteen tons each. The pilings did nothing like that. They went into the ground so easily that the weight of the hammer—without any driving impact—pushed them down their full length of thirty-five feet. Then, when the hammer was lifted, they rose several feet. It was necessary to rest the hammer on the pilings for some time before they would stay down. When we tested their load-bearing ability, none of the pilings was satisfactory. I assumed that longer poles would have to be ordered to reach a firm supporting foundation. However, the resident engineer and the foreman of the bridge crew decided to let the pilings sit for a few days and then give them another test. On the delayed test, the pilings resisted driving sufficiently to indicate the proper load-bearing specifications. Faires said that after the pilings had set for a few days they appeared to develop a skin friction sufficient to hold them in place.

Although that appeared to be a reasonable explanation, my concern was that the pounding of mile-long freight trains would break the pilings loose. I would have followed the standard specifications and ordered longer pilings, or at least referred the problem to higher authority. However, as Faires and the bridge foreman were both satisfied with the delayed test of the floating pilings, we went ahead and used them. Time has proved Faires and the bridge foreman correct. The completed bridge has successfully carried the heavy freight and passenger trains with no observable settling. There is no reasonable explanation of why the pilings still carry the load, but I am happy that the two old-time bridge men knew what they were doing.

The Church Street project was unique in other ways. The contractor left the decisions to his superintendent, Brutus Williams, and the superintendent in turn accepted my suggestions for quality procedures. That was most apparent during the pour of the massive abutments that would support the entire slab over which the trains would travel. In those days, wet concrete "mud" was wheeled in buggies along falsework planks to a hopper, where it was dumped into tubes called elephant trunks. The hoppers and tubes kept the green mud from segregating and splattering around in the reinforcing steel. Most contractors had one or two sets of hoppers and tubes that could be moved around as the green concrete built up in the forms. In order to avoid moving the hoppers and tubes, they usually would allow the green mud to build up under the hopper until it left high, sloping piles. That encouraged the green mix to segregate—and curing slopes to develop in the abutment walls. Arguments over the buildups and when to move the hopper were inevitable.

On our first abutment-wall pour at Church Street it was different. When the superintendent was making up his equipment list for the big pour, I suggested that he rent five or six sets of hopper and delivery tubes—enough to reach all the way around the large abutment—so that a buggy of mud could be emptied into each one. That would keep the mud level and avoid the dangerous separation and sloping curing planes. To my surprise he agreed, saying, "That is a good idea, we'll do it that way." To complete the pouring plan, he arranged to have a man in rubber boots standing under each hopper to knead the green mud into place. With cooperative planning and the contractor's acceptance of my concrete design and water-cement ratio, we turned out an excellent concrete bridge. When the forms were removed, there were no rock pockets to patch, no sand streaks to indicate where separated water had run off, and no cold joints or sloping sheer planes. When the finishers completed a light touch of "stoning" the surface, the bridge looked as if it were made out of white marble.

When I drove past the bridge in the 1970s, the concrete looked just as good as the day it was built and showed no effects from all the years of winter and summer weather. The only change: the city of Sandpoint had painted the abutments to cover up the graffiti. The Church Street bridge stands today as a unique and impeccable example of quality concrete design and placement. It is also an outstanding example of a contractor's giving his job-trained superintendent the authority to fol-

9. The Church Street railroad bridge in Sandpoint, Idaho, carrying mainline Northern Pacific trains. Poured in 1937, the structural concrete was still flawless after fifty years. Courtesy of the author and Duane Davis.

low his instincts as a craftsman and to take the advice of the inspector in the building process.

I have no explanation for that seeming aberration on the part of the contractor. The scuttlebutt on the job held that the contractor cooperated with the big operators in turning in high bids that allowed the big companies to get projects at the price they wanted. For that favor, rumor had it, every few years they would arrange for the contractor to get a contract at a reasonable bid. Whether the gossip represented reality, there is no way of knowing. In the Church Street case, however, the public and the railroad got a quality bridge at a reasonable price. The structure stands there today with no upkeep expense, for all to see, as the trains roar by on the sturdy bridge and the cars pass underneath on their way to and from the beach.

The Great Depression

The Great Depression brought many changes in our economy and politics and in people's approaches to one another. For years it was my goal to work in order to return to the study of philosophy, but the agonies of the depression led me closer to the problems of industrial workers.

In that quest I became affiliated with the Communist Party of the U.S.A. and abandoned my college career in favor of helping working people build a democratic trade-union movement. Workers, in my view, were going to have to learn how to shape the ethics of society to their own interests. They had the potential to combine economically and politically to give the ethics of the New Testament priority over the acquisitive ethic of big business.

*

While I was learning highway-construction techniques, almost everyone in northern Idaho was suffering from unemployment and the miseries of the Great Depression. On one occasion in the early 1930s when employees punched out their time cards at the Blackwell Mill in Coeur d'Alene, they were handed notices saying the mill would close the next day. Many of them refused to believe it, but the mill did not reopen and the fine machines eventually were sold to junk dealers and the workers were left on the scrap heap of unemployment. Other sawmills were slower in shutting down, but it wasn't long before all of them were closed. The same occurred in the mining towns of Kellogg, Wallace, and Mullan (map 1).

With the sawmills and mines of northern Idaho closed, industrial owners abandoned any pretense of responsibility for the hard times. Left to shift for themselves, workers found leadership among their own people that produced, in turn, a shift in the balance of political power and in legislative priorities. That grass-roots phenomenon was the inspiration of many New Deal programs.[1]

The Works Progress Administration, commonly called the WPA, was designed by Franklin Roosevelt and his New Dealers to alleviate the dominant problem of unemployment. The program accomplished that by the direct and effective method of producing jobs and paying the unemployed to do a great variety of work. Projects of the WPA included the long-lasting construction of schoolhouses, water reservoirs, sewer systems, all-weather roads and parks, and cultural projects, such as the compilation and writing of local histories, play writing and production, and support for art and dance.[2] The WPA provided the catalyst for all that creative work by paying the wages of the design teams, the authors, the artists, and the researchers. Sponsoring public agencies, such as counties, cities, or the state, paid only for the materials that were produced by local labor, such as buildings, lumber, cement, and other physical goods.

A good example of coordinating local needs with a government program to provide jobs was the construction of a concrete water reservoir for the village of Rathdrum, Idaho. Because my employment during most of the depression was with the Idaho Highway Department and the U.S. Bureau of Public Roads, I didn't work directly on many WPA jobs. However, the Idaho Highway Department "loaned" me out to design the concrete mix and to supervise the construction of the reservoir. Because there was adequate sand and gravel nearby, the aggregate was very inexpensive. The village of Rathdrum also had to buy the cement, some reinforcing steel, the form lumber, and a few heavy valves and fittings. Since the WPA paid for all the labor, that was not an expense to Rathdrum taxpayers.

Watertight concrete must be uniform and of very high quality. I designed a mix and emphasized how imperative it was to control precisely the water content, the placement, the consolidation, and the curing of the concrete. The workers and the foreman seemed pleased with my advice, and with their enthusiastic cooperation we created a durable water reservoir at minimum cost to the village. The job also provided a few men with meaningful work and a subsistence paycheck.

Another WPA project was completed in my hometown of Coeur d'Alene. At that time the northern transcontinental highway that is now I–90 ran through the entire residential and business districts of towns. There was a need to get some of the downtown traffic out of that area. The WPA designed and executed a project, called the Gibbs By-Pass, that was built more efficiently than if the job had been done by the usual free-enterprise contract system. The design was developed by experienced local highway engineers, and local and unemployed small contractors were hired to plan, supervise, and execute the work.

A concrete pavement called Hassam was used on the Gibbs By-Pass project because it could be completed with the available equipment and personnel. The Hassam design used a large-size crushed rock that was cheaper to produce than the smaller-size aggregate required for the usual paving machine mix. Both the design and construction of the project were tailored to fit local needs, equipment, and personnel. Engineers, skilled craftsmen, and unskilled workers combined to use their talents to produce a durable and economic highway. In that way the New Deal's WPA project was superior in both design and execution to many of today's street-building projects. That was possible because the job was built without the alien influence of some contractor who would be motivated to skew both design and execution to increase his profits.

Many of the WPA projects have stood the test of time. During the summer of 1980 I noticed a homely little project that illustrated what refinement in design can do for the almost forgotten outdoor privy. The WPA produced a privy with so much detailed quality in design and workmanship that it was still in use forty-five years later, serving as witness to both a resourceful design team and skilled workers. Those structures were built in vacant warehouses by WPA workers and hauled out to homes without sewer connections. Through refinement in design and construction, they avoided much of the problem of odor and sanitation by a ventilation system that was flyproof. The building was set on a concrete base so that it could withstand the erosive power of the elements and wood-eating insects. Any professional architect would still be proud of creating such a refinement of design and a meld of available resources that included local labor and materials to solve a problem that still plagues our cities.

Another New Deal–sponsored agency, the Civilian Conservation Corps (CCC), was active in northern Idaho in the 1930s. That organization gave unemployed city youth an opportunity to live and work in the remote forests of the West, many of whom learned to handle heavy construction equipment that led to regular jobs.[3]

At the time the CCC was formed, there were very few roads in the national forests of northern Idaho. The CCC teams often built their own housing facilities—some of which were temporary—and then went to work to improve conditions in the forests by building roads. That provided access to the majestic evergreen mountain timberlands for the general public, and they allowed firefighters to get to the scene expeditiously with men and heavy equipment.

In my experiences after the Second World War in highway construction, I have heard many equipment operators credit the CCC for the opportunity they had to learn how to handle construction machinery. That particular New Deal organization made a good record in providing unemployed young men from the city with an interesting experience in northwestern forests, where they had an opportunity to learn difficult skills. At the same time, they made a worthwhile social contribution to the region through their own efforts and those of their fellow workers.

*

Massive political upheaval around the world accompanied those domestic problems of unemployment and poverty. Dominant (to me) among those dislocations was the coming to power in Germany of Adolf Hitler's war-oriented dictatorship in the winter of 1932–33. There was little that we in the United States could do about Hitler's agitation for war, but through the years I have a clear recollection of refusing to buy the superior German drafting tools. Instead, I proudly used my American-made ruling pen, manufactured by T. Altneider of Philadelphia.

The storm clouds of war, therefore, became an ever-present backdrop for the jarring problems of collapsing industry, unemployment, and poverty. Despite those troubles, I still held to my dream of returning to the study of philosophy at the University of Washington. So, when the Church Street bridge in Sandpoint was finished, I asked for a vacation and headed for Seattle.[4]

That trip to Seattle was much different from my pilgrimage of 1926, when I was still single and only two years out of high school. By 1937 I had been a full-time worker for seven years and had met a young woman, Catherine, who shared my dreams of returning to school. We were married and headed towards Seattle. Catherine was an experienced legal secretary and very proficient at shorthand and typing. She soon found a job and it looked as if we would stay awhile.

We lived with Ellen and Ben Mason, my friends from the 1920s, who were both members of the University of Washington faculty. After talking to them about my return to the study of philosophy, I realized that the concerns of Ellen and Ben had changed a lot since the 1920s. Instead of the world of academia, they were talking about the rise of fascism in Germany and the program of the Communist Party of the U.S.A. under the leadership of Chairman Earl Browder.[5] The party was concerned about the destruction of democracy in Germany, the rise to power of the expansion-oriented war program of Hitler, and the meaning all of this had for the United States.

Browder emphasized the need for Americans to become familiar with their own revolutionary heritage so that they would be willing to defend democracy from big-business interests who disliked the family farm and worker-oriented program of FDR's New Deal.[6] I could understand Ellen's and Ben's concern that democracy was threatened, even in the United States; my experiences in the small company towns of the Northwest had taught me that the lumber firm dominated the entire community—the town council, the police, the school board, and the churches. That corruption of democracy, I observed, was not an aberration but had been fully developed by Lincoln Steffens in his autobiography, a book that I had been reading in for several years. In every town that Steffens had traveled through in his nationwide reporting, he found that major industries had corrupted the democratic process to prevent legislatures from passing social legislation that would be a threat (or an expense) to their interests.[7]

In order to prevent that sort of industry control of government from developing fascistlike tendencies in the United States, Browder and my

10. Norm and Catherine Best. Courtesy of the author.

friends wanted to help people appreciate our political heritage and to apply that understanding to the support of the people-oriented government of FDR. We also believed that democracy could be reinforced in the United States through the growth of big industrial unions that would allow workers to defend democracy in politics and to introduce it to the work place.

I was impressed with both the theoretical and the practical aspects of the program. My friends invited me to a Marxist study club where a speaker gave a comprehensive analysis of our domestic problems and the growing threat of war, both from Germany and Japan. In those talks, the lecturer offered solutions that were in the tradition of the Golden Rule and Jeffersonian democracy. At those study meetings I began to identify my personal search for good work with the right of industrial laborers to meaningful employment at a wage that would allow them to grow as human beings. As industrial workers broadened their horizons, so our country would grow in stature. For the notion that an informed and organized working class is important to our society, I am indebted to the Marxist lecturers from the Communist party.

The study-club members believed that the process of building the big democratically based industrial unions could lead to the creation of an economic system where productive workers and farmers would be rewarded with a decent share of the wealth they produced. They also believed that if we were able to build strong industrial unions, those organizations would help to resist fascism in the United States and thus preserve our democratic traditions. Our membership believed that the need for unity in support of democracy in the United States was so urgent that it was essential to give up socialist programs in favor of immediate issues that carried strong unifying support. The idea of supporting New Deal reforms while building the big democratic industrial unions made sense to me. That approach, I thought, would lead the way to an extension of democracy in industry and the gradual building of socialism or some form of production for use.

The people in the study club were among the finest that I have ever known. Their outline of both long-range hopes and immediate work appealed to me, because that related to my religious experience and my need for creative work with an open-ended learning process. I didn't like the name, *Communist Party*, with its reputation for arbitrary one-sidedness, yet in my association with friends and activists in the Marxist study club, there was a sensitive concern for people and a commitment to democratic learning processes. We would learn by applying theory and practice to difficult social programs. The social, economic, and political relevance of giving a voice to industrial workers far outweighed my personal satisfaction with the study of philosophy. I felt compelled to join my friends in their effort to resist the gathering war clouds and to extend democracy to industry.

Catherine and I discussed this proposal, but she was not impressed and said so. Perhaps she was sensitive to any sort of dogma, because she had already gone through the wrenching process of leaving the Catholic church because of her skepticism about authoritative views. To my way of thinking, the only way we could learn about the party was to join and to work with them awhile and see how it turned out. If the decision turned sour, I promised to leave the party with her. In that way, I abandoned my long-standing dream of teaching philosophy, joined my friends in the Communist party, and plunged into my new goal of making a contribution to the growth of a strong democratic trade-union movement.

Those developments reminded me of the seminal changes that I had experienced over the years. During the long lonesome days of piling wood at the Winton Mill woodyard, I felt dedicated to Jesus's instructions to his disciples: "Lay down your nets and follow me." Yet, despite that personal decision, I went to the broader learning environment and stewardship of the University of Washington and fell in love with the study of philosophy. Now, after years of work on many jobs, I was changing to an even broader canvas; I was preparing to join the industrial work force, hopefully as a machinist. My plan was to work during the day repairing or creating new machines. At night, I would cooperate with my fellow workers to help build a democratic industrial society where depression from overproduction would not occur and where laborers would be treated with respect. That new lodestone integrated my dreams from church and university and united workday and time off into one whole: the effort to build a better world through strong democratic unions of working people. With that view as a guide, I believed that each day would bring us closer to a Jeffersonian vision of the future.

That is what I gained from my experience with the Communist party in Seattle, at least insofar as the party gave a new reality to my favorite visions of a people-oriented world. Those are the dreams that held me steady on the course of Jesus, Jefferson, and Marx. They held me steady in my growing fellowship with industrial workers.

Even today, I am very proud of the decision to join the party, especially because it brought me into closer contact with other workers. If I had continued on the highway job or had become an academician, I would have missed an association with workers that I still treasure. Joining the party changed every working day and every after-work hour for me. From that day, work had another important aspect: it was judged by its contribution to workers' culture, their organizations, and their ability to introduce their ethics to the workplace and the political arena. That was the ever-present reality of work; discussing that is what being in the party was about. All this was carried out in the best traditions of Jeffersonian democracy as expressed in the second paragraph of the Declaration of Independence.

People became more important in that view, and their problems were more readily blamed on the capitalist system. Joining the Communist party brought together the Golden Rule and the old Wobbly slogan, "One for All, All for One." Even though my job was still an elitist highway-engineering one, I was now working for the good of everyone. I was proud of that new reality.

Although my objectives had changed from teaching philosophy to helping industrial workers build democratic unions, I still needed a regular paycheck. Jobs were still scarce in 1937, so we went back to Coeur d'Alene and my good connections with the Idaho Highway Department. Luckily for me, a job was opening soon at Worley, Idaho, about thirty miles south of Coeur d'Alene on U.S. 95.

Although I had to go back to the same highway-surveying job, I was a different person. Gone were the dreams of teaching philosophy. Instead, I was dedicated to showing that the potential and ethics of workers are more trustworthy engines to motivate a society than corporate profits. I looked for books on Jefferson and his era, labor histories, and Communist-party literature on how to build progressive, democratic unions. In addition to this theory, I had the names of a couple of tradeunionists who were members of the CP, people who could help me learn about unions from the rank-and-file level. Shortly after returning to Coeur d'Alene, I phoned my close friend, Richard Roe, and reviewed the highlights of my month in Seattle that had culminated in my decision to join the party.

Richard was interested enough to take a week's leave and drive to Seattle to check out for himself my interpretations of the party program. When he returned to Coeur d'Alene, he was full of enthusiasm about his personal visits with the young academicians affiliated with the Communist party. He said Hitler's *Deutschland über alles* was a threat to world peace and added that the best way to defend the United States against both domestic and foreign fascism was to make people-oriented capitalism work in the United States. He agreed that the growth of farmer-labor cooperation with the support of New Deal reforms was the best program available.

Richard was dubious about the Communist party's commitment to democracy, but because of the rise to power of Hitler's fascism, the party was deeply committed to a United Front program with all democratic antiwar forces.[8]

In the meantime, I got in touch with the two people referred to me by the party in Seattle—Oscar Kenanen and Mike Dalquist. I was pleasantly surprised to find both men to be friendly radicals very close to the political and personal traditions of my father. Both had spent a lifetime handling lumber around the big Northwest sawmills in the days when most of that work was done by men and horses.

Oscar and Mike invited me to the next meeting of the party, which was to be held at Oscar's house. I looked forward to that first meeting with pleasant anticipation and was surprised at the social atmosphere of the gathering, which included the four families of Kenanen, Dalquist, Roe, and Catherine and me. The major subject was how to sign up sawmill workers into the International Woodworkers of America, an affiliate of the Congress of Industrial Organizations (IWA-CIO).[9]

That evening's discussion convinced me of the great changes that had taken place in the lumber industry since my long winter in the Winton Mill woodyard. Then there were no worker-controlled unions. In those days a worker could lose his job by a boss's jerk of the thumb and the dreaded command "You're fired. Go to the office and get your time." Now FDR's National Labor Relations Act (NLRA) had changed all that.[10] During the years following the First World War, both the lumber companies and the mine owners, through political and economic pressures, were able to discourage worker-controlled unions from organizing.

In lumber, the Industrial Workers of the World (IWW) was destroyed by a combination of political, legal, and vigilante actions.[11] In the place of the IWW, the big lumber companies organized their own union and gave it the patriotic name of Loyal Legion of Loggers and Lumbermen, commonly known as the 4L.[12] That company-controlled union was supported by local, state, and federal establishments. When I entered

the labor market in the 1920s, the only union in northern Idaho was the 4L. All that changed under the National Labor Relations Act, which made company-financed and -controlled unions illegal. That opened the door for both CIO and AFL unions to organize, negotiate, and sign contracts in the lumber industry.[13] Oscar's and Mike's information was valuable in bringing me up to date on lumber and union issues in the Coeur d'Alene area.

Through those meetings I learned about the many problems associated with building a worker-oriented democratic union to take the place of the old boss-dominated 4L company union. Yet, in some ways, procedural things that I observed at the meetings were more important. First among those was Oscar's patient search for a consensus on all problems, rather than simply seeking a majority vote. Oscar's effort was time consuming, but it encouraged people to be patient in reaching a collective decision. Under authoritarian conditions, that procedure also could be intimidating, but in a small meeting among equals, it encouraged compromise and lent respect to minority positions.

Overall, the open sincerity of the workers and their respect for each other impressed me, as did the friendly hospitality of Oscar Kenanen and his wife. A visit to their house always meant coffee and homemade sweet rolls and a friendly welcome.

*

While Mike and Oscar seemed to be making progress in organizing for the IWA, Richard and I made very little headway in building support for a union in the Highway Department. Our fellow workers refused to join a union primarily because the job circumstances were good; ours was not a repetitive, mind-numbing work process.

Each job on a survey crew was different; each was on a hierarchical ladder reaching from the beginner's menial work of flagman through the increased skills of marking and driving stakes, rear chaining, head chaining, and operating the transit. The party chief ranked next to the top job of resident engineer. Every person could look forward to learning about the next job in the hierarchy. The nature of the work was interesting and personalized; it allowed individuals to learn and grow with experience.

Our biggest grievance was directed toward politicians, who often hired and fired workers based on the successes of the Democrats or the Republicans at the ballot box. Those elections provided an opportunity to lay off established workers and hire their own supporters. Most of the experienced people hated the process of hiring and firing that went with the changing fortunes of each political party. Yet, in those days jobs were very scarce and the less-experienced employees usually owed their position to some politician to whom they looked for job security. Because so many people felt that way, we were unable to develop a majority in favor of joining a union and standing together to stop the political shuffling of jobs.

In a few days my own job was settled when the district engineer told me to go out to the Worley project as the transitman on a small highway-construction job. That was an exciting assignment because it was the first road job where I would be responsible for all the layout and surveying for the roadway, culverts, and one small bridge. When the Worley job was finished, the district engineer in Coeur d'Alene transferred me to Wallace to serve as the resident engineer's "office man." That transfer was a quantum leap ahead, in both my working day and in my social-political work.

Being the office man meant doing all the calculations and drawings and making the finished inked tracings from which the blueprints were produced. The job usually was reserved for someone with a special talent or experience in drafting. I wasn't much of a draftsman, but a friend told me that it was possible to learn to do passable work if I took my time and practiced making full, round letters and numbers.

Besides the challenge of turning out respectable maps, the terrain around Wallace presented other challenges to highway engineers. Twenty miles west of Wallace, the main east-west transcontinental highway that is now Interstate 90 entered the canyon of the South Fork of the Coeur d'Alene River. On each side of the river, steep, rough hills rose out of the valley floor. The earliest roads wound around the base of all the irregular hills, but those winding curves were not satisfactory for a modern highway. Hence, the Idaho highway engineers planned to build much of the new road out on the floodplain of the river. That, too, presented problems, because in the flood of 1933 the river had washed out many sections of the highway and the nearby railroad.

In addition to the problem of protecting the exposed highway from floodwaters, on one seven-mile stretch of road between Wallace and

Mullan where the river entered a narrow canyon, there was no flood-plain left. Instead, the steep hills rose directly up from the water's edge. That presented an intimidating obstacle to our objective of constructing a modern, wide highway with gentle curves. To make matters worse, one side of the canyon already was usurped by the Northern Pacific Railroad. All of those problems made the assignment at Wallace very rewarding; each day was filled with one challenge after another.

The field crew under Joe Bernardy, the transitman, surveyed the valley floor and the hillsides adjacent to the proposed location of the new highway. They turned in field books full of figures, angles, elevations, and distances. My job was to convert those notes into maps that would be visual aids to both the existing terrain and the details of the new highway. There are no 3-D drawings for highway blueprints; a combination of two-dimensional drawings shows all the details. These include a plan view of the terrain—that is, a view looking down as from an airplane—and a profile, or view from the side. The latter shows the elevations of the existing ground and of the new highway. A series of cross sections, usually about every fifty feet, gives a cross-sectional view of the new highway and the original ground.

My job was to make those drawings from Bernardy's field notes. When they were finished, I made up a detailed cost estimate of all the work that had to be done to build the highway. These estimates, drawings, and supporting data make up the plans, specifications, and estimates that contractors use in making a proposal to build a highway at a fixed cost for each unit of work. That would include cubic yards of dirt to move, lineal feet of culvert to be installed, and other details. The plans are also used by construction engineers when the proposed highway becomes a reality.

The work went well until I was preparing the final estimates on the east Wallace construction project. When a contractor was awarded a contract through the low-bidder process in the 1930s, a document known as the engineer's estimate was made up. It listed all the bid items and the unit bid by the contractors. The cost for each item, however, was increased above the design figures to allow for contingencies that were beyond the foresight of the location and design crews. That tactic allowed small overruns to be paid to the contractor without the special approval of a work order. However, in all cases the contractor was to be paid only for the actual quantities moved or used as shown by supporting data from the field crews.

I spent months of tedious work calculating, checking, and rechecking the quantities for the final estimate from the field crew's notes and from the inspector's and checker's records. When my work was finished, there were several boxes of records and supporting data to prove that the work was done by the contractor. When I showed the final estimate sheets to the resident engineer, he said, "Write down these figures." Then he took the engineer's estimate of maximum allowable quantities and read off a random list of figures, just a little less than the top figure in the engineer's estimate. But his numbers were considerably higher than my calculations from the actual work done. He made those adjustments through the entire list of bid items. When he was finished, he said, "Type those figures up, Norm."

Those words made an indelible impression on me. I continued to work in a daze as one option after another crossed my mind; I could refuse to type it, which would mean the end of my career as a state engineer. That, however, would not decrease the contractor's economic, political, and social power to corrupt the work process or anything else that stood in the way of his profits. The resident engineer's action was a direct repudiation of the integrity of all of our work. For months the field crews had recorded careful measurements of the contractor's activities. From those measurements I had carefully calculated and double-checked all the pay quantities. There were boxes filled with supporting data for the contractor's final estimate. All that work was ignored because the engineer's numbers made the contractor a present of public money.

Despite the brazen nature of his crime, there was no point in sending him to jail. That would only personalize an endemic problem, while the corrupting power of the contractor would continue in yet more subtle forms. But it was my intention to find work away from the contractor's alien influence and to attempt in the political arena to expose the contract system and return the organization of work to those who carried it out and who used the product.

The corruption of the engineer was a complex mix of structural and personal pressures. According to conventional wisdom, he was the boss of the road-construction job, but he had been around the road-building game long enough to know better. For his part, the contractor had signed his name to a tough list of plans, specifications, and estimates, agreeing that he would build the highway according to those documents. Furthermore, he had put up a financial bond for the amount of the contract as security that the road would be completed according to the specifications. The engineer, as the authorized representative of the state of Idaho, was being paid to enforce the terms of the contract.

In the real world, matters were more complex. District engineers were fired because they stood up to a contractor who was a friend of a powerful politician; resident engineers were transferred to the boondocks or a basement office with trivial tasks because they took their work too seriously. The Associated General Contractors and individual operators had made substantial contributions to both the Democratic and Republican parties. Therefore, beyond the paper specifications and nominal state authority was the awesome economic and political power of the contractor. The engineer didn't want to move his family around from year to year on those remote jobs, and he didn't want to be stuck in a cubbyhole office checking somebody else's arithmetic. Neither did he want to gain a reputation for turning out shoddy work that went to pieces in a season or two.

The engineer had a narrow line to walk between two contradictory realities, so he made his own peace and twisted state law to fit the realities of the contractor's world. In fact, he bribed the contractor into doing good work and to accept him as a reasonable engineer. Without condoning these procedures, it is still important to look at the real world involved in the low-bid contract system as it applied to heavy construction for public agencies.

During the late 1920s I worked with county and state highway crews on a number of projects. On the road oiling and resurfacing of the Coeur d'Alene–to–Kellogg section of U.S. 10, all of the work was done with equipment owned by the state of Idaho and with men hired by the state. Paper reports, inspectors, and bureaucratic empires overseeing the job were nonexistent. Skilled construction workers did what they had been doing for years, with only a foreman to look after the supervision.

Today, there are laws in many states making it illegal for public agencies to do even small projects with their own crews. The Associated General Contractors and their friends have convinced the public that the contract system is the most effective way to build major construction projects. That concept, in my view, is another naked emperor. The supporting arguments for the contract system debase the skilled workers of America. For years I have watched the latter turn out quality results and have shared their pride in developing more efficient procedures from the learning process of the workplace. I have been saddened by the corrosive, corrupting influence of the contractor on the resident engineers, the inspectors, and the workers alike.

On a more specific level, the corruption of the resident engineer gave impetus to my determination to seek political changes that would curtail the power of the contractor to dominate the construction process and to find work away from the contract system.

*

In addition to all this challenging work—building mainline roads through the mountains and steep canyons on my eight-to-five job—I was in the midst of the famous Coeur d'Alene mining district, where every year capitalists reaped profits in the millions of dollars from the rich underground veins of silver, lead, and zinc. Mines with such names as Sunshine, Hecla, Morning, Bunker Hill, and Sullivan were known worldwide. Most of the riches left the county, while miners lived in wretched poverty in shacks clinging to the steep canyon walls. Prostitution and liquor were always available, even when they were plainly illegal under state law. The local miners swapped stories about the judges and fire chiefs collecting fees from the operators of the houses of prostitution.

Around the turn of the century those mines had no safety equipment and the air was so bad that many miners had silicosis before they were thirty years old. The miserable working conditions, poor pay, and shack-town housing forced the miners to use their collective strength through the Western Federation of Miners to strike for better working conditions and pay. The mine owners resisted the miners' collective efforts to be human beings. Violence broke out (from whose hand was never determined). Federal troops were brought in, and all the union miners were rounded up and put in a big bull pen out on the river flats near Kellogg. The mining district was under military law for some time.[14]

Out of all those troubles came a mine-owner program of no jobs for union members unless they signed a contract repudiating the union.[15] Then, for the long haul, the mining companies established a central hiring office, whose chief officer was called the King. The King had files on union men from all over the mining districts of the United States. Before a miner could search for work in the district, he had to get a "rustling" card to show that he was free of any taint of unionism.

Without it there was no work in the Coeur d'Alenes. In the district folklore there were many stories of union men who were denied a rustling card—and even cases of sons and daughters and relatives of union men being denied the opportunity to search for work.

The King's domination was not broken until Franklin D. Roosevelt's National Labor Relations Act made such discrimination illegal. The removal of the King's authority made it possible for miners to form their own union in the best tradition of the old Western Federation of Miners. In a short period of time there were three locals of the International Union of Mine, Mill, and Smelter Workers, commonly known as Mine-Mill. That union turned out to be a very democratic organization controlled by and working for rank-and-file miners.[16]

In addition to its dramatic labor history, the Coeur d'Alene mining district had a unique ethnic background, with a strong contingent of Finnish people, who were polarized into right-wing and left-wing groups that had taken opposite sides in Finland's struggles during the First World War. Many of the latter group had been in the old miners' union in Michigan's Upper Peninsula. That was the background and the context in which we sought to learn about the new union: Mine-Mill.

Because we were strangers in Shoshone County (map 5), we asked Oscar Kenanen for the names of Finnish people he knew in the mining community. With that as a beginning we soon became acquainted with some union miners and a few business people with small shops, many of whom became lifelong friends. Most of us had been through the Great Depression and were ready for visions of a cooperative community. We had many long discussions about the need to strengthen the New Deal programs and to build strong democratic unions. We were helped by the fact that within a radius of twelve miles from Wallace there were three locals of Mine-Mill. Before long we had many friends who were active in the union in Shoshone County.

The Coeur d'Alene district is a world where miners work thousands of feet underground, carving out tunnels, sinking shafts, and raising stopes in bad air and constant danger. This is not as hazardous as coal mining, but it is still difficult work. Not from personal experience but from my years of association with miners, I gradually got a picture of the substance of their activities.

All of the mine tunnels (drifts) in the 1930s were seven feet high and five feet wide. Every eight hours a miner was expected to set up a monstrous pneumatic power machine, a big brother to the noisy pavement breakers one hears doing repair work in the cities of today. The miner inserted big drills into the machine that noisily *hammered* holes into the rock. In order to clear out all the rock in that five-by-seven space the miner had to drill five-foot holes nearly side by side along the roof, bottom, and both sides of the tunnel. Then he had to drill many slanted holes towards the center to clean it out first. When all the holes were drilled into the solid rock, the miner loaded them with a sensitive nitroglycerin exploder, filled them with dynamite, and then fired the powder, hoping in the process to move all the rock. For the next eight hours air pumps were used to remove some of the poisonous powder residue. Then eight hours were allotted to shoveling (mucking) out the shot rock and hauling it to the surface.

One miner, sometimes with a helper, did all the drilling and blasting. That work was done at miserably low wages, considering the dangerous conditions, the foul air, and the skill required to drill and blast out a clean tunnel.

Will Bixby, one of the union miners, and his wife, Edna, soon became close friends in a way that lasted. Will had been interested in production-for-use themes for a long time, so when I gave him the Browder program of strengthening democracy in the United States, he responded immediately. He was already working to strengthen the Kellogg local of Mine-Mill. In addition to being close friends, Will and Edna were our first recruits into the mining-district section of the Communist party. It was good working with Will. He taught me a lot about the trade-union movement, especially the organization he was active in. I had more reading in political and economic theory and he had more practical experience; together we made a good meld.

I am especially indebted to Will for his friendship and shared knowledge of the politics of the mining district and the reality of a miners' union working against a society dominated by mine owners with their fetish for profit. I believed that the program of the union and the party were similar in many aspects: to work collectively in the best Jeffersonian tradition to strengthen FDR's New Deal and to build strong democratic industrial unions. Both Will and I were convinced that out of those organizations we might be able to preserve and extend our democratic institutions so that an American drift toward fascism could be avoided.

On the basis of that simple program and with the help of many local people we recruited twenty-five or thirty people into the CP. Elated with our success in the isolated mining district, we asked the Northwest chairman of the party to stop on one of his auto trips from the East and talk to our members. He agreed and the meeting was set up in the

home of a Finnish family where the father and all the sons worked in the mines. The home, built by the boys and their father, had a large open dining and living room. It was constructed that way so they could entertain their many friends and have meetings of the many Finnish organizations.

When the Northwest chairman arrived, we proudly told him that gathering of thirty or forty people were the new members of the Communist party that we had recruited in the last year or so. I made it plain to him that those people were members of the mining district's new section of the CP. But when he started his talk, it was obvious that he was trying to recruit instead of welcoming them to the party. Perhaps his behavior can be explained by the fact that he had never seen a gathering of working miners, with a sprinkling of businessmen who owned their own one-person shops. For some reason he did not identify the élan of the working miners, mostly of Finnish descent, with his image of the party. He never once asked for feedback from the unique community of miners. So much for the understanding of some of the CP bureaucracy. In our eyes all the people present were in the best tradition of workers anywhere in the United States.

Shortly after that incident I received word that the district engineer wanted me to be the chief inspector on northern Idaho's first four-lane paving job, a route that extended from the Washington-Idaho state line eastward toward Coeur d'Alene (map 1). I looked forward to the responsibility of building a big section of paved highway.

We drove to Will's and Edna's place in Pine Creek to talk over the new turn of events and to evaluate our year's work in the mining camps. Their home had become the party headquarters for this part of the valley. They had a few books and some party literature and, more than that, a hearty welcome for anyone who dropped in. Through our work in the party we had met many fine people. We had effectively integrated our social and political time—studying, visiting, and even relaxing at Saturday night dances in the Finnish hall in the lower valley.

While we were living in Shoshone County, we also met the fine family of Mary and Joe Jensen and Joe's older brother, Paul. They were old-time party members and very unique people right out of the world of Jeffersonian subsistence freeholders. They had a small truck farm close to the tiny community of Enaville. On those few acres they raised strawberries, raspberries, corn, cherries, apples, and all kinds of vegetables. Berries and fruit, which were sold to working neighbors and small stores in the mining towns of Kellogg and Wallace, were their staple cash crop.

In the fall after the growing season was over, they hunted for deer and elk in the adjacent hills. Then, in the long winters, Joe trapped muskrats and mink in the many sloughs and lakes along the Coeur d'Alene River. They had a ready market in Seattle for the pelts. In the spring and part of the summer, both Mary and Joe worked together logging the rich white-pine trees growing on the steep hillsides bordering the river valley. Together they cut down trees and sawed them up into sixteen-foot lengths ready to be hauled to a neighboring sawmill and cut into valuable lumber. From all that varied hard work they earned enough to send their four sons through the University of Idaho. For recreation, Mary and Joe played the violin and piano for Saturday-night dances in the valley schoolhouses. The country-schoolhouse dances were a special treat for us as we would drive down from Wallace during the afternoon and spend the weekend with Mary and Joe and return on Sunday evening.

Through the years and distances separating us, that friendship has been nourished by common values, interests, and dreams. The durability of some of those friendships is demonstrated by an incident that took place over thirty years after we spent that time with Mary, Joe, and Paul. During the big peace mobilization of 1967 in San Francisco, our family decided that we would drive to Eugene, Oregon, where our older son and his family were living. From there we planned to travel with some of them to San Francisco and take part in the big peace march up Market Street and listen to Coretta King in Kezar Stadium. Because we needed economical housing, we called Mary and Joe for the address of one of their sons who lived in San Francisco. They were happy to give us his address and told us that we would be more than welcome. As it turned out, part of the family was able to participate in the big antiwar demonstration without having a hotel bill (and with the added adventure of meeting the son of our old friends from the 1930s).

Joe's brother, Paul, had a record of being a war resister going back to the First World War. Joe was not old enough to be drafted, but he and Paul were both card-carrying Wobblies. Because of their opposition to serving in the army during the war, they hung out deep in a remote section of central Idaho near the headwaters of the Clearwater River, living off the land and hunting and fishing until the war was over. Paul spent all of his working years as a proud woodsman, a Wobbly, and a member of the working class. He always had a good story for workers but little good to say about the capitalists. When the years caught up with him, he remembered that our younger son had been a war resister during the Vietnam War and had served time in the big house at Lompoc, California. Paul arranged to meet Rick during a visit we made to Mary's and Joe's; there he gave Rick both his bankroll of three hundred dollars and his bedroll. That was Paul's way of honoring a fellow war resister. Rick still cherishes those expressions of war resistance that spanned the generations. That is a poignant example of the antiwar heritage of a proud worker.

Looking back at that year in Shoshone County made me feel good about our work. We succeeded in helping to create a community of people with shared ideals of working with one another to build a better world (rather than each of us searching for personal riches). We were a community that rejected the capitalist ideology of personal good being obtained or measured by economic worth. In our search for an ever-broadening, caring, social community, we were practicing the Golden Rule seven days a week rather than just talking about it on Sunday. We integrated our work and our social life with the goal of making a political and economic system that was directed toward meeting people's needs. Despite our disappointments with the Northwest party leadership, I am still indebted to the organization for providing the structure that established a lasting community in northern Idaho in the 1930s.

*

Now it was off to the excitement and responsibility of a big, fast-moving Portland-cement (concrete) paving project to be built by the J. H. Collins Company. Shortly after arriving I learned that all the finishing was going to be done by *hand*. The only machine on the project was a big concrete mixer, called a paver. On those jobs, financed largely with federal money, the ingredients of sand and gravel are subject to easily monitored quality specifications. However, the fieldwork of adding water, mixing, consolidating, and converting all those ingredients into a safe, durable highway is left to a lot of decisions that are not subject to simple quantitative controls.

My job was to see to it that all the operations were done in a professional manner, so I stayed close to the paving and the finishing crews—watching, listening, and feeling the green mud as it came out of the mixer. When it felt right, I gave the operator the OK sign with a slight wave of the hand. If it was too dry and too stiff, I would raise my hand to my mouth as if taking a drink, and the mixer operator would add a little water. If it hit the ground and splattered like cow droppings, I would twist my hands as if wringing out a towel, and he would screw down the water gauge for the next batch.

Those cues were carefully coordinated with other quantitative evaluations, including the quick slump test that gave me a measure of the workability and water content of the material. Then I checked with the head finisher and our inspector, who was running a ten-foot-wide, long-handled straight edge over the pavement to determine whether the concrete had any bumps or hollows in it. If all was going well, my judgment was usually verified by the progress of the finishers toward building a durable, smooth-riding highway. Those activities kept me busy all day long, and it was a pleasure when we could walk over one thousand feet or more of day-old concrete and see that we had created a product that would provide years of safe driving for thousands of cars.

On the J. H. Collins job, everything went together smoothly, and I was very proud of my contribution to the finisher's work—the men who actually create the concrete pavement. As the chief concrete inspector, I was responsible for obtaining a good pavement, yet only the contractor could hire or fire the finishers. I couldn't show the finishers how and when to use the big bull floats to cut down the high spots, because I was not strong enough and hadn't served an apprenticeship as a cement finisher. But it was my job to see that the concete mud was beyond reproach. With that foundation to work on, I encouraged the contractor to support the finishers in their task. On the Collins project, everything went well, and we produced a job that we were proud of.

Two years later the Idaho Highway Department assigned John McLean and me to the next section of a four-lane concrete paving job in northern Idaho on U.S. 10 to the west of Coeur d'Alene. McLean was the resident engineer and I was the chief concrete inspector. A well-known contractor was the low bidder. I was very pleased with the equipment and the crew; this contractor had new, wide-based steel forms, a paving machine to do the consolidating and the rough finishing, and an excellent crew that had just finished a showpiece job a few miles away in Washington. It looked like a great start for another quality job.

At first it seemed that everything was going to work out well. The mixer operator responded to my signals and turned out an ideal mix. It was stiff enough to hold its own shape; it hit the ground with a soft, contained thud, and it was soft enough to be workable but firm enough to be homogenous. The finishers were pleased with the consistent mix, and I was enjoying the work. Because we had turned out an excellent, durable pavement with the same procedures on the Collins job, I was pleased.

When we were only a few days into the job, McLean told me that the contractor thought I wasn't giving the mix enough water, and so McLean was to take over and handle the water-content issue. There was little for me to say but "OK," which meant that the contractor was calling the signals on the water content and could manipulate the water-cement ratio in the direction of greater profits and lower quality. When more water was added, the contractor could push his machine faster through the soft mud. Despite his new machine and good forms, he was objecting to the same water content that Collins had used and worked by hand.

The contractor hadn't said anything to me about the water content of the mixture. Instead he quietly went to the resident engineer. If McLean had not been friendly with him and responsive to his suggestions, he could have taken his grievances to other high officials in the Highway Department or even to the governor's office. That is how many powerful contractors work. They build personal friendships over long periods of time; then, when the time is right, they call in the chips. According to my friends in the trade, this contractor had wined and dined McLean during the previous winter. Whether he influenced McLean is not as important as the built-in push of the contractors towards profits at the expense of quality work.

Years of scientific work and experience have gone into the design and construction of modern concrete pavement. Although my training taught me how to use that science and art to produce quality pavement, that job did not allow me to do so. Under the contract system, a contractor with sufficient economic, political, social, or personal power can nullify everything. This job was a clear demonstration.

The experience was demoralizing. I felt like quitting, but I didn't like the idea of that contractor's running me off the job by going over my head to the resident engineer. In many states, if a contractor is able to remove an inspector from the job, it usually means no similar assignments for that person. But concrete was my game and I had a proven record of quality bridges and pavement; I aimed to stay.

If McLean had consulted me, I would have explained the guidelines for the water-cement ratio. It would have been plain at that point that he was seriously concerned about quality and standards. But McLean simply deferred to the contractor's opinion and his desire for more water. It was plain that McLean had caved in and didn't want to talk about it.

McLean allowed the mix to be overwatered. As a consequence, the free water and cement separated from the rest of the mix and rose to the surface; within two years the cement peeled off and left ugly, rough-riding blotches all over the new highway. Those peeled sections were crude, and the new concrete was compromised with unsightly and rough-riding asphalt patches. A few miles away on the Collins job, where I had controlled the water, the concrete was as good as new.

Contractors have a record of producing faulty results, but laborers on the other hand have a record of producing work that demonstrates a mastery of their craft. Because both workers and highway users want a quality product, the contractor's authority could be limited through the exercise of democratic controls by workers and users.

By contrast with those disappointments, Catherine and I were happy with the birth of our first child on October 3, 1941. While we were still savoring the event, the disaster of Pearl Harbor struck. With the end of the construction season the district engineer, T. Matt Hally, drafted me to be his assistant in the preparation of budgets for strategic materials, such as gasoline, tires, and parts for essential equipment that had suddenly become scarce in the face of the need to build a global war machine. My job was to confer with city, county, and highway-district officials in Idaho's five northern counties and to develop a budget to maintain the highway system during wartime. On those trips I also made up shotgun estimates for the state's highway program. That assignment pleased me, because the work was usually done by high-ranking engineers.

To round out my duties, I often accompanied Hally on long trips around the district. On the drive back to Coeur d'Alene he would relax in the back seat and let me drive him home. That was heady work for a young man; if my job was carried out properly, a substantial advancement would soon be in order. However enticing the duty, it was still my goal to get away from the contractors' corrupting influence on the construction process. I wanted meaningful employment with workers to help build a society where quality counted and public benefit was the end rather than building substandard roads for a contractor's profit. The events at Pearl Harbor made highway construction even more meaningless. I was too old to be drafted and had too little liking for the destructive violence of war to enlist. Because of the demand for men in the West Coast shipyards, I decided to look for a meaningful job and be part of a workers' movement.

My only regret in leaving the Idaho Highway Department was telling Matt Hally of my decision. Matt was very special among district engineers in that he was a man first and a highway engineer second. He had a solid background in both theory and practice, and that may have helped him cut through many pretenses of authority. For that quality, he was loved by all his fellow workers and engineers. It was unpleasant telling him that I was leaving highway engineering to look for a job as a machinist. It brought back memories of my decision to tell Hugh Casey that I was quitting the telephone company to go to school.

When I told Hally about leaving for San Francisco, he was disappointed and seemed to resent my quitting, especially after all the breaks he had given me. Although he had the power to make me a resident engineer, that was no consideration for me. Being a resident engineer for a district supervisor who was a prince of a boss couldn't change the system. With mixed feelings, I left for San Francisco.

*

My objective was to look for a modern version of the Diamond Drill shop where I could help create useful machines and be part of a big, democratic trade union. We had considered moving to Seattle, because of the stimulation offered by the University of Washington, but San Francisco seemed more attractive. It was the intellectual capital of the West Coast, especially in the trade-union movement.

As I talked the move over with Catherine, it surprised me to find that she was even more ready to go to San Francisco. Because she also was attracted to the idea of living in the big, romantic city on the bay, we packed up the car and drove to the bay area in late February of 1942.

For some reason I went to Bethlehem Steel to ask for a job, perhaps because the new factorylike jobs repelled me. The machinists' union also recommended Bethlehem Steel because it was part of an old, established shipyard. The firm built navy destroyers and did repair work on all kinds of ships, both merchant marine and military. The new milling machines with elaborate dials and controls in the Bethlehem shop amazed me. They looked a lot more mysterious than the simple machine I had operated at Diamond Drill in Coeur d'Alene.

When I told the foreman that it would take time for me to get acquainted with the new machines, he was emphatic in stating that they had openings for qualified journeymen only. He was firm in saying that he expected me to handle all the work with no help from anyone. That was quite a hard-nosed attitude. He could have offered to let someone help me with the first setup, informing me about the elaborate, dialed controls that represented such an awesome sight to me. The foreman wasn't interested in anyone who needed a few days to get organized, so I decided against trying. But he offered me a job working as a bench and floor machinist, assembling and repairing machinery and doing all the handwork required to fit machine parts together. I accepted and he gave me a card to go to the office for a physical and signup of the employment papers.

Despite my disappointment in not making it on the milling machine, it was good to be a journeyman machinist. Once in the machine ship, I felt a beautiful glow of comradeship that seemed to flow from sharing the productive craftsmanship of the work. Almost every man in the big shop was a journeyman; an individual using the lowest-level tool, such as a file or wrench, or running one of the giant milling machines—all were classified as journeymen machinists. Production and quality came from the pride and skill of each worker.

It gave me a feeling of euphoria to be away from the frustrations of contractor corruption and shoddy work. It was exciting to be part of a large group of people building and repairing the machinery on the big ships. It also was a new experience for me to be part of a democratic union where decisions were made by the membership. I was proud to be a journeyman machinist. In San Francisco there was a saying: "When one of those proud, old-time machinists walks out of the shop, you can't tell by looking at him whether he works there or whether he owns the place."

seven

The Second World War

It was exciting to participate in the meetings of the machinists' union. The meetings of Local 68 of the International Association of Machinists were models of egalitatian democracy. Machinists could be very elitist, but in union meetings every member was treated with respect; the right to speak up and be heard was a cherished privilege.[1]

Many grievances arose over the way the wartime wage freeze worked.[2] The War Labor Board used Local 68 union contracts to set wage scales in the San Francisco Bay area. The wage level in the local's contracts were those established for the skilled craftsmen in area shops. Those were the apprentice-trained machinists who read blueprints, set up their own jobs, and sharpened and made their own special-purpose tools. The wages of all those men were frozen by an executive order enforced by the War Labor Board. However, as the work mounted, thousands of partly trained people entered the metal-trades industry. Many of those semitrained or untrained people, like myself, were getting paid Local 68's wage scale. Because of the local's high standards, thousands of inexperienced workers received a substantial pay increase, while the experienced old-timers received none. The work rules of the machinists' union aggravated the situation by requiring that all workers who used the tools of the trade had to be paid the journeyman rate. The only exceptions were the specialists who operated a repetitive machine where controls were built into the equipment or were set by another machinist.

In machinist-union shops, apprentice training was the only recognized route to journeymen's work and pay. The program was restricted to young men, and serving one's apprenticeship was the equivalent of professional training, a hallowed tradition in all union shops. There was also a classification in the machinists' union for menial jobs; those workers were called helpers, and they had no access to training. They assisted the machinists, fetched tools, and cleaned up the shop but did not use the tools of the trade. Those union work rules were a far cry from the reality of the modern assembly line, where the work process has been broken down into simple, dulling, and repetitive segments.

At each union meeting, two business agents reported to the membership on the previous week and asked for approval or guidance in pending negotiations. For years Local 68 had been a trend-setting union for the San Francisco area. It had a record for helping other unions through difficult times, and in their best moments, union members showed a concern for others and a pride in their work that was the core of the old Wobbly spirit. Being a member of the union was a big thing for me, because working at the machinist trade was a step ahead of watching a contractor turn out faulty concrete pavement.

About that time I began to change in other ways as well. Things that had been important in Idaho, such as payroll classification, promotions, and getting along with the contractor, were no longer a part of me. It felt good to be a proud member of Local 68 of the International Association of Machinists. Every afternoon I had to get down to the Bethlehem yard and work on a piece of steel, shaping it to fit as a component of a ship. Seeing those big blocks of iron grow into functioning machines had always interested me, and now I was working on a job where the process took place.

As my world changed, my priorities, interests, and perspectives also changed. It seemed to me that this process is what Marx must have meant when he said, "Man's consciousness is determined by his relationship to the mode of production." As my satisfaction with my new career developed, I wrote to my friend and former boss, T. Matt Hally, and told him about the euphoria of my work as a machinist. Hally never replied to my letter, perhaps because he considered me disloyal to highway engineering. I would have appreciated his approval for my move, but that was not a major concern; it was time for meaningful work among my fellow machinists.

*

Shortly after we arrived in San Francisco, a memorial service was held for Tom Mooney, the labor martyr.[3] I was indisposed with a sniffly nose, but my wife pushed me out the door to honor Mooney. The meeting was impressive; there were many important speakers, including the governor of California, Culbert Olson, who had pardoned Mooney and Warren Billings.[4] Every liberal politician in the state was there vying to do homage to a workers' hero. Besides those political figures, prominent labor leaders were there to speak a few words to honor Mooney.

Late in the program, one of the best-known leaders of the International Longshoremen and Warehousemen's Union, Harry Bridges, took the podium and was greeted with a standing ovation. After he had been speaking for a few minutes, I realized why the government was trying hard to deport him. He had a potent magnetism about him. Petty differences between people seemed to evaporate as he reviewed Mooney's work in the labor movement. It was one of the most inspiring speeches I have ever heard and one of the best illustrations of why Bridges has such lasting significance. He proved to be a caring person. As Bridges talked about the values of cooperative unity and concern for others, my mind wandered back through the highlights of waterfront history on the West Coast.

For years longshoremen's work rated very low in most job choices. One great problem arose out of the hiring system, called the shape-up. When workers wanted a job, they gathered in the dock area hoping that a boss would choose them. The system fostered corruption: kickbacks, favoritism, and various forms of toadyism for those who worked regularly. Those who were not chosen could only go home and hope for a better day. Many people thought those indignities were simply a part of the scroungy world of the waterfront. During the rough years of the 1930s, however, waterfront workers themselves decided to try for a better, more equitable world. They went on strike for a hiring hall where workers would be dispatched through a system of regular rotation. The waterfront employers' association resisted that move and enlisted power of the police, the business world, and the international offices of the International Longshoremen's Association.[5]

Although those bitter struggles lasted for years, they produced a brilliant leader from the ranks of the working longshoremen, Harry Bridges. Eventually the union won the hiring hall and a new, progressive rank-and-file-controlled organization, the International Longshoremen and Warehousemen's Union, with Harry Bridges as president. Under his leadership the dock workers' union led the way in bringing dignity and humane conditions to the waterfront. Longshoremen became a proud group of people; they pioneered in eliminating discrimination against minorities for reasons of race or political opinion and supported many landmark programs for workers.[6] The extent of their interests and confidence in themselves has been illustrated by their worldwide interests and the way they carried them out.

In order to keep abreast of international affairs and dockside technology they sent delegations of working longshoremen abroad to see for themselves what was happening. Invariably they would return with first-hand information. Those delegations were selected by vote of their fellow workers. All those changes were brought about by rank-and-file members and their working leaders, who had a dream of a better world and a faith that workers had what it took to bring it about. Here was a demonstration of the efficacy of the Golden Rule and a form of immortality of good works that laboring people could feel and observe for themselves. In Harry Bridges I found a modern role model in the best tradition of the New Testament and the workers who had impressed me—my father, Hugh Casey, and Matt Hally.

In addition to bringing dignity and justice to the waterfront, the success of Bridges and his fellow longshoremen set an example for other workers who lacked humane working conditions. The longshoremen's organization became a pattern-setting union.[7] Its members were able to improve their conditions, which allowed them and their families an opportunity to grow as human beings. Bridges was called a Communist for bringing democracy and dignity to the West Coast waterfront. The United States government brought him to trial four times in an attempt to deport him.[8] From that example of the way big business and big government resisted efforts to bring democracy to industry, I could see that my goal of achieving that objective was going to be a long, hard row to hoe.

*

After a few days of doing odd jobs for the shop superintendent at Bethlehem Steel, I was assigned to a crew of about ten machinists who did filing and fitting work. Although much of it was boring, there were peripheral benefits. During a lunch break, I supported an older machinist who was being roughed up in a political argument by several young men. The older man, Ernest Simmens, appreciated my support and we soon became close friends. Simmens had left his home in the German-Swiss border country to avoid the draft for the First World War. He was a strong trade-unionist in the Wobbly or socialist tradition and a master machinist who had spent his lifetime at the trade. He soon introduced me to its many secrets; he used a file to create machine parts with the finesse that a concert violinist uses his bow to create beautiful sounds. Watching him work and sharing his friendship was a sustaining experience for me.

One day the boss gave me a job cutting threads by hand in the cylinder heads of a large engine for a Dutch ship. That work was done with a small boltlike tool called a tap. The tap was tempered steel with cutting edges hard enough to cut matching threads in cast iron or steel. Because those taps were tempered so hard and were so small in diameter, they were very fragile and broke easily. If they were pulled out of line, they would break and leave a machinist with the difficult job of getting the pieces out of the hole. I worked on the tapping job for several weeks, and it was probably my best experience in that particular effort.

Besides gaining a lot of knowledge tapping holes, I had an opportunity to work with and observe the layout procedures used to transfer the engine-design specifications to the cylinder heads. Those layout markings and data were used by the machinists to produce the finished product. I was pleased to see that the same geometry and trigonometry used in highway and bridge layout work were used in the machine shop. That aroused my interest in the work because it combined highway techniques with my limited machine-shop experience to make a challenging job.

In addition to the layout work, another bonus was learning to operate a drill accurately to place holes in the precise position required on the blueprint for an engine head. The three-inch-diameter holes in the engine head had to be located very precisely so that they would match the base of the engine when the assembly bolts were installed. When a drill is started through tough iron or steel, it often drifts off to one side or another. Usually that meandering is tolerated. However, on this job it could not be allowed and the machinist showed me how to correct the deviations.

As soon as the drill started to bite into the cast iron of the engine head, he would check the position of the hole for an observable deviation from the blueprint location. Then he would chisel a groove on the opposite side of the partially completed hole and as the drill started up again, the cutting edge would slip into that groove. That would pull the drill towards the correct position. By that careful process of trial and error, precisely located holes were drilled. This is a classic example of the daily process of passing on knowledge of the workplace. Although that precision in drilling is rarely required, to know how to do it if necessary is what separates the master machinist from a journeyman. This is just one of the hundreds of techniques that an experienced machinist has in his bag of tricks. I have no doubt that in all of the books about machine-tool technique there is no such simple elegant solution to a rare but difficult problem.

After that job, work tapered off in our section, and in a few days we had nothing to do. We tried to while away the time by making tools out of old files, or we devised other work projects. I made a fine bearing scraper and a heavy-duty center punch, tools that are still in my possession and whose workmanship gives me great pride. There was a limit, however, to those make-work jobs. The man in charge was a petty fellow who had become a pompous martinet in lieu of being a qualified foreman. When I asked him for a job, he never gave me more than a grunt or a haughty, disdainful answer. It looked to me as if the Bethlehem Steel Corporation was simply hoarding men who were probably charged up to other projects. Those conditions made each night a long ordeal of hanging around trying to find little things to do.

During that period, my wife paid a visit to northern Idaho. The combination of a lonesome house and unproductive worknights was too much for me, so I hocked my watch for train fare to northern Idaho, to home country and friends. As soon as the train was under way, I began to relax. Getting away from that no-work night shift and the lonely house was like getting out of jail.

Everyone in northern Idaho was talking about the big naval base that was being built at Farragut (map 1). I hitched a ride out there one morning and found that my friend Chet Adams was the chief engineer of the construction work. He offered me a job as chief concrete inspector, and the next day I went to work for the navy on the immense project.

Although that was a prestigious job for me, it soon became apparent that neither the navy officer in charge nor my intervention could stop the subcontractor from debasing the concrete with garden dirt instead of clean, washed sand. It was impossible to remain on the job and lend credibility to that fiasco, so I returned to San Francisco in an effort to find meaningful work.

Back at Bethlehem Steel I was determined to avoid my previous experience in the machine shop of being denied work assignments. Because the big ships tied up at the regular repair docks had always fascinated me, that appeared to be a good place to look for a job. When the superintendent of the marine machinists learned that my experiences did not include work on a ship, he offered me a job as a helper. I resented that because in a union shop there is no way to advance from helper to machinist; moreover, a helper is not allowed to use the tools of the trade. It didn't seem to me that installing or repairing machinery on a ship could be much different from working on the same equipment elsewhere. I told the superintendent indignantly that I could install a piece of machinery according to plan as well as anyone. For some reason that convinced him to accept me as a journeyman; he signed me on as a marine machinist.

The next day, with my heavy toolbox in hand, the superintendent took me past dock after dock. Finally, at the last dock there lay the biggest ship I had ever seen and my next workplace: the *USS Pennsylvania*. That was all very exciting for me. The boss led me through long corridors and down one ship's stairway after another until we looked down into one of the main engine rooms. It was immense—seventy feet wide and fifty or sixty feet long. From 7 A.M. to 7 P.M. day after day, that was to be my working home. The ship was of First World War vintage, powered by direct-drive turbines, two of which were to be dismantled, inspected, overhauled, and reassembled for the rigors of ocean travel.

The most visible example of turbine power is the old windmill that once dotted the western plains. Winds turned the multiblade rotors sufficiently to draw water for the family farm. Today the most visible turbine power is the jet engine that powers the modern high-speed airplane. Between those two kinds of turbines were the immense direct-drive types that powered the thirty-five-thousand-ton *Pennsylvania.* Everything on the ship's engines was gargantuan. Rising out of the engine-room floor was a giant steel casting about ten feet high and fifteen to eighteen feet long. Our job was to remove the top half of the giant casting and to inspect the hundreds of turbine blades to make sure that they were ready for sea duty.

That job was a long way from the Coeur d'Alene box factory, the Dodge Garage, the City Garage, or even the Diamond Drill Contracting Company. But there was a lot of carryover from one machine to another. At Diamond Drill, Mr. Michener had taught me a lot of fundamentals that were useful throughout my working career. One day I was holding a big cold chisel for him while he hit it with a heavy sledgehammer. While he was pounding, he remarked that when you wanted to succeed with a tough hammering job you had to be sure that there was no cushion between your hammer and the tool.

I remembered that casual remark in the engine room of the *Pennsy* when two of the most-experienced machinists were frustrated by the refusal of the big turbine housing bolts to budge from their positions. One man held a steel bar on the end of the housing bolt while the other hit the bar with a twenty-nine-pound sledgehammer. Still the bolts didn't budge. Because the bar may have been absorbing some of the hammer's energy, I went upstairs to the ship's machine shop and found a short piece of steel shafting and gave it to the men and suggested they use it. At the first blow of the hammer the bolt jumped out of its hole. I was proud that a few casual words from Michener on a little job in Coeur d'Alene would provide an answer for a big turbine repair job on a battleship in a San Francisco shipyard.

At the shipyards much of my learning came from working with more-experienced people. One day I was trying to jack a heavy propeller shaft back into position so that the coupling bolts could be installed. As I put pressure on the coupling, the jack would slip out of place in the same manner that a car slips off a bumper jack. With only a grunt of explanation an older man showed me how to secure the jack safely so that it wouldn't fly out and hurt someone. That old Italian rigger had taught me a lot about safe procedure. There are many important methods and little tricks to be learned from associating with fellow workers. The old rigger's confident work set an example which helped me in many tight spots. That is what experience is all about.

The most unusual carryover of my previous experience took place on an important piece of equipment used to load the *Pennsy*'s big fourteen-inch guns. A machine called a ram, made up of heavy links of steel about the size of tracks on a Caterpillar tractor, was used to do that work. A complicated two-way clutch with a large lever extending up to the loading deck activated the ram and pushed the projectile into the gun. Every time the gun crew used it for a few minutes, the clutch would burn out. Our boss told us about the overheating problem and warned us that it might not be easy to fix since it had already been overhauled by the machine-shop crew. When we took the clutch apart, I was surprised to see that the disks were similar to those on my old Model T Ford, although the clutch was more complicated because it had to drive the ram in two directions: out and back in response to the direction that the gunner moved the big lever. My partner and I took the disks apart and then reassembled them.

When the gunnery crew ran the ram fore and aft at full speed for some time and it didn't heat up, everyone was happy. That job established us in the repair gangs, a group already with a reputation as sort of an elite crew on the waterfront. And it was a classic example of how my experiences on the job carried over to other work. The Model T Ford knowledge helped me fix a clutch that loaded the naval guns on a battleship. I have been told that the same clutch design is used today on most motorcycles, an indication of the diversity of application in a design.

After that success, my partner and I were assigned to several responsible jobs and trusted to do the work with very little supervision. We put new bearings in a training motor for one of the big turrets; we installed a couple of big machines in the main fire-control rooms; and we did a lot of work making the twin five-inch gun turrets poison-gas proof. I stayed on the *Pennsylvania* until the job was finished and the navy personnel began to take over.

Through all those months I worked twelve-hour shifts, seven days a week. At the end of those days, it was a long trip home on the crowded San Francisco streetcars. It was necessary to transfer on Market Street, get off the street car in the Twin Peaks tunnel, catch the elevator to the surface, and then wait for a bus for a ride partway home. After several months at that pace, I was worn out and weary and asked the boss if he had an eight-hour job. He said our next assignment was another twelve-hour day on a submarine. Although dearly wanting to work on that boat with all its fascinating machinery, I didn't want to face any more of the twelve-hour days with the long trips home at night. I had always worked hard on eight-hour days and never learned to slow down enough for the longer shifts.

With the help of a friend I found a forty-hour-week job that turned out to be a terrible mistake. The work was stupid; my task was to serve as a helper on a job bolting down complete gun units. We might as well have been installing washing machines. That was a letdown after all the challenging work on the *Pennsylvania*.

My next assignment was on a new twenty-two-hundred-ton destroyer still on the ways. Those fast ships were designed around immense high-pressure boilers and high-speed, double-reduction geared turbines that drove the twin-screw propeller shafts. Because of their location and the pressure to complete the work quickly, the boilers had to be installed while the shell of the ships were being assembled.

The navy didn't use the expeditious, high-speed welding techniques of the famous Victory ships.[9] Instead, each plate was secured to its adjoining plate by rows and rows of heavy rivets. The riveting process in the shell of the ship, which was like an elongated steel bell, was my first experience with noise that produced a pervasive, driving pain in the ear. I don't see how the riveters could stand it. In the midst of that numbing noise, my mind began to consider other job options. The best possibility was doing layout work in the Bethlehem Steel machine shop. That job combined the geometry and trigonometry that I had used in highway and bridge layout with machine-shop practice. It would be a challenging and fulfilling task.

For the moment, however, I regretted leaving the repair gang. But there was no way back, so my goal was to get in fifteen hundred hours of work, which would give me a week's vacation with pay. That would let me get away from the awful noise for a week and allow me to return to Spokane and Coeur d'Alene for a visit. While in Spokane I planned to check out the big aluminum rolling mill being built at Trentwood, Washington. When my fifteen hundred hours had accumulated, I asked for my week's vacation pay and, with my tools, we took off for Spokane.

*

Once in Spokane, I went to the office of Local 86 of the International Association of Machinists (IAM) and asked about a layout job. The secretary looked at my paid-up book from Local 68 in San Francisco and called the master mechanic at the Trentwood plant of the Aluminum

Corporation of America (ALCOA). They needed a layout man, so I drove to the mill to see the master mechanic, who asked about my experience. I told him about my apprenticeship at Diamond Drill, my experience at Union Iron Works, my job in the Bethlehem Steel shipyards, and a bit about my experience reading blueprints and doing layout work on highway bridges. After a friendly visit, he hired me as a layout man in the machine shop at the journeyman's pay of $1.20 per hour on the swing shift.

From the first day there was something good about the layout job at the rolling mill. As a machinist it was possible for me to use the skills of early craftwork and to meld those with the technical expertise gained from years of highway engineering. In short, most of the time I was able to control the quality of the work through my own efforts, skill, and experience. Nearly every night there were all kinds of interesting jobs coming into the machine shop from the forty-seven acres of equipment that had to be kept in running order for round-the-clock operations.

*

In addition to the meaningful job at the rolling mill, I also had a unique social experience in joining my fellow workers in a major, pattern-setting international union. Shortly after beginning at the rolling mill, there was an election to determine which union would represent the workers in the plant. The Aluminum Workers of America (a CIO affiliate) and a council of craft unions affiliated with the AFL were on the ballot. There was nothing but confusion when the AFL craft unions tried to explain how they would divide up jurisdiction among the production workers. Industrial labor just didn't fit into the old craft divisions, so uniting them into an effective, unified bargaining group would be next to impossible. Because of that confusion, almost all of the production workers voted CIO. And, since there was only about one craftsman for every ten industrial workers, the vote went to the Aluminum Workers of America (AWA).

The first local union president, W. O. "Bill" Allen, followed the pattern set by the international president, Nick Zonarich, when the latter visited the rolling mill. He acted more like an ALCOA agent than a union representative. Either that or he had a perverse idea of democracy, because I don't recall that he ever consulted with any of us about grievances after he was elected.

At one of the early union meetings Allen announced that he and

11. Norm Best talking with his son Mike and niece Carrie. Courtesy of the author.

ALCOA had arranged a small across-the-board increase in most of the pay classifications except those at the top. That unilateral action on his part—without consulting our executive board—was characteristic of his approach. It also illustrated the power of the company to act and then leave workers with an accomplished fact. A lot of questions were directed at Allen's irresponsibility. His only answer was that he didn't want to delay the raise by waiting for a meeting. That was not well received by the members, but it was hard to repudiate the raise. Although we never learned the circumstances surrounding that event, I presume there must have been some flexibility within the War Labor Board's determination of the prevailing scale or some small modification of it.

Some time later Allen appointed one chief shop steward for the entire mill. That appointee, accompanied by Allen, went around the mill settling grievances and establishing precedents without any consultation with other union committees or members. Soon there were complaints coming from all over the three-thousand-person mill because ALCOA was using precedents and patterns set by Allen and his chief shop steward in settling other grievances. When that was brought to my attention in the machine shop, I talked the problem over with other union activists, both in maintenance and production. The result of those talks was that a friend, Lloyd Brooten, and I drew up an organization chart that dealt with shop stewards and their responsibilities and relationships with the union. We divided the mill into seven departments. In order to establish unity between the crafts and production workers, we allowed a chief shop steward for each craft and one for each of the four divisions of the production workers. A basic part of the plan was that only those seven chief shop stewards had authority to negotiate grievances above the foreman level.

We presented the plan to the local union meeting and it was accepted almost unanimously. In order to give every worker an opportunity to vote, we decided to hold the election of the seven shop stewards at the mill. In that way, eighteen hundred people cast ballots. The company was notified about the chief shop stewards, and the union committee was in business.

In the past the company had its own way in settling grievances with Allen and his chief steward, but now all that was changed. The company still had its team—the assistant works manager, the industrial-relations chief, the personnel director, master mechanic, production superintendent and his assistant, and any special experts it could muster—but we could match them with our seven chief shop stewards. I was certain that we could rely on the workers' own knowledge and unity to remove injustices and to introduce as much humanity as possible in the operation of the plant. Our plan allowed for a maximum of worker input, participation, study, and decision making. As Thomas Jefferson looked to the vote of the agrarian freeholder to release human potential bottled up by the authoritarianism of royalty, we looked to the vote of the workers to help solve the problems of industry's autocratic power over the workplace.

All of the seven chief stewards were full-time workers in their departments. Collectively, they more than matched management's expertise. In fact, their contact with the workers was an authentic relationship, the kind not available to management. The committee's collective knowledge and expertise won many grievances and established precedents in our favor.

Negotiations of that kind usually center on a fair application of the company's own rules and regulations. That material is usually the result of some serious consideration on the part of management. However, when it is applied down in the plant, a lot of favoritism and inconsistencies may result.

Many of the grievances were about pay inequities. But the thrust of most of them was a request for the company's foremen to treat workers fairly and to open advancement to gentler or less-boring jobs to all workers equitably, rather than bestowing those privileges on the basis of whim.

For example, in the machine shop there were several people operating engine lathes at third-class pay. We asked the master mechanic to clarify the company's definition of a second-class machinist. He said that anyone doing rough work on a lathe would be considered a second-class machinist, so we simply applied that formula to the shop. Because quite a few people were doing that work at third-class pay, those machinists received a nice boost in wages. That kind of thing went on all around the mill. The company did not repudiate items agreed upon at meetings between the top management and the seven chief stewards. It appeared to us that decisions made in that way were far superior to those based only on some foreman's opinion. Of course, those negotiations could not affect any change in the wage scales set by the War Labor Board. But it was very rewarding to correct inequities, both in personal satisfaction and in pay to a large group of workers.

A democractically controlled union introduces a sense of fairness and a feeling of shared community. The chief shop stewards knew how their sections or departments worked, and each unit, in turn, was small enough so that the workers knew what the shop steward was able to accomplish. That created a sense of responsibility between the workers and the stewards.

The employees who were part of that process began to see the results of their input in the attitude of the foremen and the work procedures. As their contributions and work rhythms were respected, morale began to rise. We were very excited about our great experiment in industrial democracy. Looking back on it, I can see now that the implementation of the seven-steward system provided a good example for the introduction of democracy in the major pattern-setting plants of basic U.S. industries.

My part in conceiving the plan for a democratically elected chief-shop-steward committee was one of the highlights of all my years in the workplace. My confidence in fellow workers stemmed from my affiliation with radical political groups and from my personal pride in solving the problems encountered by skilled craftspeople and productive workers. That confidence in accomplishing difficult jobs was demonstrated and reinforced by construction workers building bridges—carving straight, smooth roads out of rough terrain and creating durable, usable concrete pavement when they were allowed to control the work. Probably the greatest pride in mastering difficult jobs came from the old IWW, the Wobblies that I encountered on various jobs. That pride and dedication gave them an élan that highlighted the potential of workers. It was also my belief that democratic committees and councils could be steppingstones to more democracy and fairness in the workplace if management did not use all its resources to prevent it.

General Motors personnel officer Thomas Fitzgerald cited the importance of management's monopoly on control of the work process:

Once the competence is shown [or believed to be shown] in, say, rearranging the work area, and after participation has become a conscious, officially sponsored activity, participators may well want to go on to the topic of job assignment, the allocation of rewards, or even the selection of leadership. In other words, management's present monopoly—on initiating participation, on the nomination of conferees and on the limitations of legitimate areas for review—can itself easily become a source of contention.[10]

Michael Best and William Connolly, critics of Fitzgerald, offer a different view in their book *The Politicized Economy*:

Meaningful work reform, Fitzgerald agrees, would involve job redesign, worker participation in the decision process, and worker access to the requisite information for intelligent participation. But inroads in these areas would in-

crease the power and indispensability of workers while decreasing managerial monopoly over information and power. Once this process is started, it could easily get out of hand. So it is best not to allow it to start. "History," Fitzgerald warns, "does not offer many examples of oligarchies that have abdicated with grace and goodwill."[11]

The success of our local democratic grievance procedure and its implications for management explain the international union's move during the next contract negotiations. A deal was worked out whereby the international won a union-shop contract which made union membership a condition of employment, with dues deducted from the worker's paycheck and sent to the international's office in Pittsburgh. In return, the international's negotiators agreed to abandon our seven-steward committee in favor of the old system of one chief shop steward. The deal accomplished two major things: the local union lost its powerful, elected, seven-steward system, and the international union won a financial windfall. To gain that kind of financial security, international unions have shown that they are willing to help the companies blunt the workers' nascent efforts toward industrial democracy. Those deals are endemic between United States labor unions and large corporations.

Another of the more blatant perversions of democracy by the international union and W. O. Allen involved contract negotiations during the war.[12] I was on the local negotiating committee, and we were instructed to draw up a tentative set of proposals to be presented at a union meeting for approval. Our committee met at the union hall and proceeded to draw up a list of improvements for the next contract. By that time Allen had been appointed an international representative. He came into our contract-committee meeting and told us that we were wasting our time; the international, he said, was doing the same thing in Pittsburgh and would send its proposal to us. I recall some of his language because it was new to me. When we received the international union's proposal, he said, we could "take the hay out of it and send it back to Pittsburgh." The committee accepted Allen's suggestion and waited for the Pittsburgh proposal.

We heard nothing for several months. Then one day our local president got word from the international to come to Pittsburgh for contract negotiations. He made the trip expecting to take part in the negotiations for a new contract. W. O. Allen met him at the train in Pittsburgh and invited him to a bar for a drink. Allen informed him that the real purpose of the trip was not to negotiate or vote on a new contract but to take part in the interpretation of a contract that international President Philip Murray had just signed. That still sounds far fetched to me to this day, even though I was a participant.

That incident was a fair example of the way the steelworkers' union and our international union operated. Only powerful rank-and-file pressure has forced modifications toward democratic responsibility.

By contrast with the miserable lack of ethics on the part of the international union officers, I found that most workers had a strict code of expectation and concern for one another:

1. They must be qualified—meaning that a person could produce the necessary product in a capable way.
2. The item or work must be produced in a graceful way with a minimum of effort. Running at a job, huffing or puffing, or being an eager beaver were considered second class.
3. Consideration for one's fellow workers was essential.
4. Patience—a cool head—when everything goes sour was necessary.
5. Toadying to the boss and ranking fellow workers was looked down on.
6. Ranking fellow workers to a boss was simply taboo.
7. Lending a hand, demonstrating by *doing*—not by *talking*.
8. Sticking one's neck out, to a boss, in support of a fellow worker in trouble was the epitome of a good guy.
9. Criticism of a fellow worker was something to be handled with consummate skill, usually to be associated with a quiet demonstration of a better procedure.
10. Expressed concern for fellow workers and their problems should be limited to areas of shared concern.
11. A willingness to accept the tough jobs with confidence was essential.

I have worked hard with other men in the five Pacific Northwest states from 1924 (at the age of seventeen) until I retired in 1972. All of my fellow workers, with practically no exceptions, followed the above ethic, and they took pride in being able to turn out a productive day's labor.

Respect for a boss is complicated and not susceptible to standards and stereotypes, but in general it parallels similar characteristics that are respected in a worker. In many skilled crafts the shift foreman immediately above the employee is expected to be a qualified journeyman in that craft. Above the position of shift foreman, however, familiarity with the trade becomes diluted.

My relationship with Bob Dix, the general foreman of the machine shop at Trentwood, illustrates some of those complexities. Usually my assignments came from the shift foreman, because layout men were not a part of administration. Sometimes I served as a technician between administration and the crew. At other times my job was simply that of an experienced repair machinist. As an interpreter of the plans or blueprints, sometimes my contacts were directly with the engineering department or jointly with a foreman and an engineer.

One assignment regarding a modification of a big machine called a scalper illustrates some of the problems of those relations. Bob Dix assigned me to the job, which involved a complicated modification on a big production mill, but without plans or blueprints. On the way to the scalper, Dix told me that he was embarrassed to show me the job, because he didn't know anything about it or the machinery for that matter. He said that he was part of the ALCOA family, and for reasons that he didn't understand, he was asked to accept the general foreman's job. There wasn't much for me to say. I wasn't old enough myself to feel superior. I told Dix of my respect for him for leveling with me, that no one person could be expected to know all facets of the work, that I was happy to work for him, and that it was our job—mine and the welders, floor men, machinists, etc.—to get the work done.

Dix had my respect for those confidences, because he was a first-rate general foreman. That information was never used against him. I probably told more intimate friends about his remarks than was necessary, but it did not reflect badly on him. In my opinion, and that was shared by most of my friends, he was an OK guy. He respected us as people, as workers, and as machinists. That qualified him as a boss and as a general foreman. Whether he had spent years working at the machinists' trade was not important to us.

During the latter part of the war our mill had caught up with the demand for airplane sheet metal so there were some layoffs in the plant. Without any notice to the union, one of our best welders, Lundburg, was laid off and another welder who bailed out on the tough jobs was kept on. The Lundburg case became important for two reasons: it illustrated that administrators often do not have authentic information like that available to workers, and it showed a lack of sensitivity on the part of a union steward in presenting issues that went beyond our collective decisions.

On the first issue, we had the company cold. Months earlier we had a job producing a heavy conical filter that was very difficult to fabricate. It involved making a heavy frame into a section of a cone. Then a light screen had to be welded to the massive frame. The welder assigned to

the job couldn't handle it; he burned big holes in the screen without making any welds to the frame. Another welder, Lundburg, was assigned to the job and reclaimed it; he built up the screen, got the frame hot, and welded the two together. When Lundburg was laid off months later and the other man kept on, the company claimed Lundburg wasn't a qualified welder.

It wasn't going to be hard to prove that ALCOA had laid off one of its most qualified men, a person who was needed for the difficult jobs. One of the most experienced machinists, an older man named Rusty, was chief steward at that time. Rusty won the grievance all right; but according to Rusty and others present, he carried out a vendetta against the general foreman, claiming that Dix was incompetent and not qualified for the job. As a result, Dix was fired and a lot of bad feelings were brought into union-management relations. It was my policy to concentrate on the crux of the issue—in this case, to get Lundburg back to work. As a matter of fact, it was not Dix's personal responsibility to judge the welders. That was a job for a shift foreman or lead man.

It was easy for the foreman to be poorly advised, but I was not concerned whether the foreman was an experienced machinist or not. All that mattered was that he treat us properly. Beyond that, the union was not concerned. A single grievance, corrected by the return to work of the qualified welder, was the center of the union's concern.

Looking back on that incident, I feel uneasy about my role. It would be unfortunate if Dix's leveling with me had anything to do with his being fired. I may have been insensitive about the ramifications of telling a few workers about Dix's disclosure of not being a machinist. At the time, that seemed to prove Dix to be a real person and that he should be respected for his role as a general foreman and for his integrity. However, my revealing the incident to Rusty probably added to his vendetta against Dix. I further suspect that Rusty's bitter attack on Dix probably involved some personal frustration with the man.

*

After the war the Trentwood rolling mill was sold to the Kaiser Aluminum Company, which hired Bob Dix as the master mechanic in charge of all the hiring for the machine shop. As a result, I had to ask him for a chance to work at my old job as layout man in the machine shop. It was ironic that Dix had been fired from his old job as machine-shop foreman because the union challenged his judgment in laying off Lundburg, yet now he had the authority to say, "Norm, we don't have a job for you." In effect he fired me before there was even a chance to go to work. Union contracts have no jurisdiction over who is hiring, so the company laid me off. I could have explained to Dix that I was not behind Rusty's vendetta against him, which was true. But any explanation of my union activities to a foreman would have compromised my integrity as a union member and shop steward. I took his no with some pain and began to look for another job.

It hurt to lose what seemed to me the best job I ever had. But an integral part of my responsibilities was my right as a union member to protest miscarriages of justice for fellow workers. I missed both the work and the fellowship at the mill and envied my comrades who got their jobs back. Our very success as union members had caused my unemployment. The experience taught me that losing a job was one of the hazards of being an elected shop steward. But my pride in that position gave me something that Bob Dix and Kaiser couldn't take away from me. Looking back over those long years, it is clear to me that giving up being a shop steward to keep my job was just not an option. It would have been contrary to everything that I believed in—everything that gave meaning to being a worker. No job, as desirable as it may be, is worth the price of ignoring or selling out a fellow worker.

*

Beyond the disappointment of losing my job in the rolling mill, I gained a valuable lesson from the rather unique features of the plant. Primary among those was the fact that the United States government owned the mill. Through the Defense Plant Corporation the concept of the operation was conceived, financed, and built to produce aluminum sheets for the needs and use of the nation's military aircraft. Simply put, it was built to produce aluminum for use, not for corporate profit.

The standard procedure during the Second World War was for a company to operate government plants through an agreement called a fixed-fee contract. Under that procedure the government paid the costs for operating the plant in addition to a negotiated fee to ALCOA for its management. That fixed-fee arrangement took the place of the highly criticized cost-plus contracts. Under the latter, the more money the company spent, the greater the profit.

One way in which that affected the working environment was in the process of grievances. I was surprised in my relations with the local ALCOA officials, who came to the mill from the firm's headquarters in Pittsburgh. They were very open about our grievances. As managers of the rolling mill, they seemed to be more intimately concerned with production than the national union representatives. Under wartime conditions there was no army of unemployed to choose replacements from. So the company apparently decided that it would listen to the workers, hoping that with progress on our grievances we would have more energy and incentive to make things work in the plant. Whatever the company's reasoning, with good labor relations we produced more aluminum every month than the designed capacity of the plant.

With management freed from the drive for profits and the value placed on workers in a zero-unemployment economy, both management and labor were able to combine efforts to get the job done. Although work in the rolling mill had a different objective from the New Deal WPA projects—production for national need (the war effort)—it shared the same approach, and that was the elimination of the profit motive and government intervention as a result of central planning. The 1930s depression is the most severe internal crisis the country has faced in this century, and fascism in Europe and Asia has been the most severe external crisis. The opportunity to participate in the successful efforts to overcome those crises were the high points of my working career. As I look at the crisis the nation faces in the coming years, I hope that what has worked in the past will be remembered.

Business Agent for the Machinists' Union, 1946–1952

Because of my union activity—protesting the firing of one of our best welders—I was not welcome back on my old job and had to settle for unemployment compensation for a few weeks. It also gave me time to think about the changes in my career since leaving the Idaho Highway Department. At that point it did not occur to me to look for a job as a highway engineer, but rather to stay in the machinist trade as a union member. At my wife's insistence, my membership in the machinists' union was current and my name in good standing. I was proud of being a machinist and looked forward to finding a job somewhere repairing or building machinery.

*

At the same time, another decision made in the depths of the depression did not stand the test of time. My association with the officials and bureaucracy of the Communist party was not working out. Apparently I was more a philosophical socialist than an apparatus person. During the war Earl Browder changed the Communist Party of the U.S.A. to the Communist Political Association. That change in policy carried powerful consequences; it meant that American Communists were abandoning their historical isolation and becoming part of the political scene. The party was throwing in its lot with coalitions of United States voters while retaining its right to express a socialist position.[1]

In the course of the Second World War, Browder wrote to Communist-party members in the trade-union movement and directed them to avoid pushing plans in union meetings that did not find support among their shopmates. That is, programs that did not receive support from fellow workers should be reconsidered. That concern for workers' opinions was contrary to the usual operation of democratic centralism. During the four years from 1937 to Pearl Harbor late in 1941, the Seattle officers of the party never recognized or implemented any of Browder's concepts. Everything coming from the Seattle bureaucracy was a one-way track. I never saw any consultation with members in the hinterland, such as the small towns and mining camps in northern Idaho. The district's method was to send messages through young, unemployed urban people, or simply to send them over to check on us.

At a chance meeting in a little Seattle café, I challenged the procedures of the Seattle office. The district chairman told me that they (the district officials) decided who would report on northern Idaho. From other developments, I learned that the district bureaucracy probably never even consulted with the leaders of the University Marxist Club in Seattle about their reaction to the Molotov-Ribbentrop Pact of 1939, a Soviet foreign-policy venture which was a disaster.[2] On the other hand, many historians will agree that the foreign policies of the Soviet Union, as developed by Maxim M. Litvinov from 1933 to 1939, will be considered the Soviet Union's finest hour. During all those years Litvinov called out for Allied unity against Hitler. His motto was "War and peace are indivisible." He continually called on the Allies to unite and stop Hitler before Germany became too strong.

The signing of the Molotov-Ribbentrop Pact of 1939 took place only because the Allies had not acted on the Soviet Union's plea to the Western powers to unite with the Soviet Union to stop Hitler. The Molotov pact may have gained a little time for the Soviet Union, but it did not portend peace.[3] It did mean that Germany's war plans would continue. However, the Seattle office of the Communist party sent a big pack of leaflets to northern Idaho hailing the Molotov pact as a step toward peace. My response to the leaflets was to burn them, and I did just that.

When the Second World War ended, my difficulties with the one-way messages coming from the party's district office increased. Because I was an industrial worker, it made me uncomfortable that other people were telling us what to do, especially those who were not wage laborers or who were not in touch with the ways and ethics of workers. I decided to end my affiliation with the Communist party early in 1946. My decision was reinforced when a young man came to Spokane and told me to introduce a resolution in my union requesting that the United States government bring the marines home from a seaport in China. I told him that such a resolution had no reality to me or my fellow workers. The young man told me that my opinion didn't matter, he was giving me an order. That was the *only* time anyone from the party had given me an order, and to ensure that it would be the last, I told him in strong words what he could do with his order. With that verbal explosion, my affiliation and contacts with the party were history.

Later a group of Seattle party leaders called on me about continuing my affiliation, ignoring my recent confrontation and decision to leave. They advised me to sign the non-Communist affidavits and to continue my membership in the Communist party, but to reduce my contacts to a few responsible leaders. Their proposal was beyond the pale of anything in my world. I told them that duplicity of that kind was out of the question. Those sordid forms of contact provide a miserable picture of what was at one time a hope to work for a Christian cooperative commonwealth with fellow workers. It was easy to leave the party.

The heady days of Roosevelt's New Deal were gone. Our hopes for avoiding war were not fulfilled. Earl Browder's cooperation with the New Deal and the work Communist party members had done to build the big industrial unions was history. Browder had been expelled from the party because of his ideas of constructive cooperation with capitalism. Now the cold war was emerging and the McCarthy-Taft-Hartley era was a reality. Through all of those changes my goal of bringing democracy to industry had not changed; rather, the Communist party had changed. That may have only been my perception of a change. Browder was probably a deviation from the policy of democratic centralism that was reasserting itself. That top-down organizational structure that ignored the daily reality of work was intolerable to me. We parted company. I stayed with my fellow workers, and the party as an organization became irrelevant.

Those incidents were not aberrations of Communist-party policy. Instead, they flow from an elitist view, one that abridges Jeffersonian democracy. The party did that through a policy called democratic centralism, a device which denies members the First Amendment's rights of protest and review once a decision has been made. That limitation of grass-roots protest to a previously made decision isolates the Communist party from important feedback from rank-and-file members. The system denies membership the right to dissent. It took me some time to find that out, because during the war years I was too busy being a union member and building and repairing machinery to even think about the party.

That abridgement of Jeffersonian democracy disqualified the Communist party for political leadership; it also denied its own leadership the essential flow of information from workers' reality and ethics. Workers need the help of scholars and scientists who have the time and talent to study economics and politics, but those intellectuals should be free of any entangling monopoly on wisdom. Their research should grow out of workers' reality and ethics, and the Christian sharing of unionism. The results of scholarship should come out as educational research, not authority from a bureacracy or a multimillion-dollar corporation.

My old affiliation with the Communist party continued to cause trouble for me. Some time after my association with the party ended (probably in 1947 or 1948), the FBI phoned me at the office of the machinists' union and asked me to come to the local federal building to talk. The agent delivered a subtle threat of harassment by reminding me that he was offering me the opportunity to come to the privacy of the federal building. Otherwise, he said, I might be embarrassed if they came to the union office to interview me.

On the way to the courthouse, I decided not to talk about people like myself who had worked with the Communist party during the depression or after. Despite that determination not to embarrass a lot of good people, I didn't feel like refusing to talk at all. In that frame of mind, I met with the two men who identified themselves as FBI agents. They had learned about my leaving the party and hoped that they would have my cooperation. They showed me a picture of a young man on wide, courthouselike steps, but I had no idea who the man was and told them so.

Next they asked about my acquaintances in the party. My contacts included only a couple of people who, in fact, were open representatives for the party. Therefore, I mentioned those people with a clear conscience, because their job was to represent the party openly. Actually, membership was such a loose and unchecked affair that only a financial secretary could distinguish between party members and those who were interested visitors. Anyway, that information seemed to satisfy the agents and the meeting was over, with no confrontation and no damage done.

The FBI didn't contact me again until 1955, nearly eight years later. That meeting, in the little mountain hamlet of Lincoln, Montana, was vexing for me. I was proud of joining the Communist party in the 1930s and of my effort to join with others to develop a program that would allow industrial workers and farmers to share the fruits of their labor. We also took satisfaction in our efforts to expose Germany's and Japan's thrust towards war. My participation in those struggles was done within the tenets of the New Testament, especially the Golden Rule, and the principles of Jeffersonian democracy. The latter, to my way of thinking, would help relieve the miseries of the Great Depression. I was proud of that work and happy to talk to anyone about it. Yet the media had created a monster stereotype of Communists and their fellow travelers as being disloyal Americans who were working as agents of a foreign power. Because of that, I was afraid to speak to my neighbors about my membership in the party.

It was in Lincoln that the FBI agents asked me to rejoin the party and to work for them. I brushed that off quickly and the visit was over. My wife did even better; she simply told them that she didn't want to talk and didn't say a word to them about anything. My major recollection of that visit was the problem of explaining to our neighbors why two FBI agents had visited with us.

A year later in Phillipsburg, Montana, the FBI phrased its proposal in starker terms. If I did not rejoin the party and work for the FBI, it threatened to get me fired from my job with the Montana Highway Department. With two sons, two daughters, and a wife to support and with highway work slow, that threat was very real. However, the idea of becoming a stool pigeon for the FBI was repulsive, so I smiled and told the agents that jobs like mine were a dime a dozen! With that emphatic answer, they left. The idea of having to move to some distant construction site and start all over again was not a pleasant thought. Yet, I was proud of my unquestioning refusal of their proposal, and apparently the agents believed me because that was the last of their threats.

*

Because of being laid off at the rolling mill, my membership in the United Steelworkers of America automatically ended. Eventually, I landed a mechanic's job under the jurisdiction of Local 86 of the International Association of Machinists. I waited for my United Steelworkers image to wear off and then went to a meeting of the machinists' union.

The purpose of that meeting, it turned out, was to nominate local officers for the ensuing year. Before the nominations took place, a bitter argument broke out between a machinist at the Diamond Drill Contracting Company and the business agent for the union. The machinist took the position that the business agent was responsible for Diamond Drill employees' losing one hundred dollars a year. That argument grew out of a War Labor Board decision that granted the ironmolders' union an additional five cents an hour because of the extremely dirty nature of the job, one that involved considerable expense in replacing clothing and in cleaning up after a day's work. When the molders received their raise, the machine shops, which also had molders working for them, gave their machinists the same increase. For years the machinists and molders had been working at the same wage rate. However, workers in machine shops without foundries received no raise.

At the time the argument arose, the jurisdiction of the War Labor Board no longer applied; thereafter, negotiations would be between workers and the company, without any government restrictions. As the long bitter dispute wore on, I was reminded of an article by the Dutch syndicalist Anton Pannekoek,[4] on how companies resisted unions and then kept them divided and quarreling among themselves. It seemed to me that it was time to forget the old argument and get on with the new business of negotiating a good contract for 1947. Because no one did anything to end the disagreement, I decided to put in my nickel's worth and told the fellows that it was time to stop quarreling about the nickel an hour and move on to the business of getting thirty-five cents an hour for everyone. That met with the approval of the members, so the argument stopped and we went on with the business of nominating officers.

When it came time to nominate someone for business agent, a somewhat inebriated machinist sitting in front of me got up and said: "I want to nominate that fellow in back who put up the argument for the thirty-five-cent raise." He didn't even know my name; in fact, hardly anybody in the hall knew me. Two machinists that I had worked with at the Diamond Drill shop in Coeur d'Alene twenty years earlier told the audience they knew me. So I was nominated for business agent of the machinists' union.

After the meeting, the business agent for the heavy-duty mechanics introduced me to the internal power struggle between the machinists and the mechanics in Local 86. In larger cities, mechanics and machinists have separate, autonomous local unions, both chartered by the Grand Lodge of the International Association of Machinists. But in a city the size of Spokane, the expenses of two locals—offices, officers, and other overhead—were too high; therefore, to save money the two groups were united into one local. That marriage of convenience, however, did not dissolve the differences in philosophy between the two crafts.

The mechanics' business agent told me that his group didn't like the other nominee because he represented a segment of the traditional school of thought on labor matters, one that emphasized the clublike atmosphere of the union and supported the general idea of getting along with the companies. Members who were not friendly to the mechanics also supported that argument. The mechanics' business agent didn't ask me for anything. He simply said that they felt more comfortable with my expressed idea of uniting together in a struggle for better conditions for all working members. He went on to say that if I wanted to work at the job of business agent for the machinists, the mechanics would support me. I told him that the nomination and the chance to represent the men was an honor. That was the extent of my campaign, and I was elected by a large majority and proceeded to go to work as the machinists' business agent.

I began the new job with a sense of buoyant good feelings. That position, as a representative for the workers, was in a very real sense the fulfillment of years, maybe even a lifetime, of effort and dreams. My grandfather had organized the Farmers' Equity in Wisconsin in the post–Civil War days; my father had organized for the Nonpartisan League in Idaho and Montana during the 1920s; and now, because of my talk in favor of unity labor struggles, the union machinists and mechanics had elected me to be their organizer, spokesperson, and business agent. All else seemed preliminary or preparation for that work. I was determined not to sell the men out. Together we would make a powerful team. That was my job, working full time for pay, at a task that grew out of years of struggle.

My first big job as business agent dealt with the machinists' negotiations for a new contract with Associated Industries, the employers' organization of local machine shops in Spokane. The machinists were the elite of the skilled crafts and were nearly all apprentice trained. Serving an apprenticeship is very meaningful to a machinist; it is the equivalent of a diploma or an advanced degree. There was very little turnover in Associated Industries shops, and in some cases men would spend their entire working life in the same place.

The jobs were mostly custom, whether it was a new machine or a repair task. There was very little production work, or the repetitive type that characterizes the manufacturing industry. The men operated powerful, sophisticated machines—lathes, milling machines, drill presses, and all the incidental equipment in the shop, which was not automatic or programmed, but under the constant manual control of the machinists. Despite the high degree of skill required, the wages of Associated Industries machinists were lower than skilled crafts in local shops not controlled by Associated Industries. I do not have the figures, but the differential was and still is substantial.

*

Shortly after my swearing in as business agent, I called a series of meetings for all the machinists working in the shops covered by the contract. At each meeting, all sections of the contract were opened for deliberation and all proposals were discussed. There was no limit to changes any member could propose. Although many proposals were very idealistic, a consensus was required before an idea would be accepted by the membership. After considerable discussion and usually much voting and amending, an item would become part of the union's proposal to be submitted to the companies. It usually took several meetings to go through the contract in that fashion.

The president of the local usually presided at meetings and the secretary took notes. As business agent, I sat with the secretary but took a very passive part in the discussions, because it was the members' prerogative to develop their own consensus about their needs. My job, after those matters were decided, was to support those proposals to the limit, or at least until the members were satisfied or decided to reach an agreement with the companies.

There was a feeling of urgency about the negotiations that was exceptional. Besides the old grievances about machinists' pay being lower than wages for comparable or less-skilled crafts, there was a bitter feeling that the 1946 negotiations had been handled badly by the business agent and the Grand Lodge. With that background, I was determined to support the union's proposal until the men made a decision to settle.

Rather early in the negotiations we received an offer of a fourteen-and-a-half-cent increase. The membership turned it down unanimously and took a strike vote at the largest meeting ever held in the local. The vote to strike, unless our proposals were met, was practically unanimous.

A few days later Joe McBreen, the union's general vice-president for the ten western states, was in the office waiting for me upon my arrival at eight o'clock. That was my first meeting with such a high officer in the union, because his appointees—known as Grand Lodge representatives—usually took care of all the Grand Lodge business. My experience with international representatives of the steelworkers' union made me wary of high-ranking officials, so I decided to keep the discussion to noncontroversial items.

McBreen opened the conversation with congratulations for getting the fourteen-and-a-half-cent offer and reminded me that this was the pattern set on the coast. After those preliminary remarks, he asked my reasons for turning it down. In order to avoid arguments over such issues as reducing the old differences in pay and other discrepancies, I simply answered that the fellows wanted more money. He asked if we thought we were better than the locals on the coast. My response was to say that the men rejected the offer because they wanted more money. That was the important fact to me; as their representative, they had my support without reservation. The discussion went on for some time, with the general vice-president repeatedly asking me why we turned down the offer. I gave the same answer: "The men want more money." Finally, in exasperation, he swore at me and shouted, "Your job is to *tell* those bastards what they want."

I can't describe the impact of his words. McBreen was the senior elected official for the machinists in the ten western states. The members of the Spokane local had elected me to carry out their nearly unanimous decision, one that had been reached through many hours of open discussion. Now the general vice-president was ignoring the interests and decisions of the Spokane membership. Indeed, his whole posture was diametrically opposed to the democratic principles that are the foundation of this country and, in turn, of our union. Those were powerful ideological contradictions. The general vice-president was giving orders from on top. Because my orders were the result of a long series of democratic procedures carefully designed to develop a broad consensus among the workers, I ignored his suggestions and stayed with the membership. As a result of our firm unity, we won a settlement worth twenty-six cents, nearly twice the amount the general vice-president had berated me for not accepting.

The euphoria of winning a big settlement was tempered by the fact that it had earned me the enmity of the leadership of the machinists' union. I didn't know what the Grand Lodge would do about it, but expected that they would use their substantial resources to get a business agent in office who would follow their gentle ways with the companies. Before long, McBreen revealed his strategy when he sent in a Grand Lodge auditor to go over our financial records, the first audit of our local within the memory of old-timers. It didn't bother me, but it was an omen of more things to come. Later events proved my suspicions right.

The usual procedure for a Grand Lodge representative was to stay at a hotel and visit Local 86 for a few days at a time. That changed when a young Grand Lodge representative showed up in town looking for a house to rent or buy so he could move his family to Spokane. Ostensibly, his job was to organize the nonunion mechanics working in the shops of car dealers. One evening after he had been in Spokane for some time and after a few beers, he admitted that his basic job was to see to it that someone was elected to replace me who would take advice from the Grand Lodge. That left me in the position of being a great success with the members of the local who were paying my salary, because I didn't sell them out. At the same time, I was a thorn in the side of the Grand Lodge, one they wanted to remove.

Those events reminded me that the basic democracy cherished by the working machinists in the conduct of Local 86 business was lost in the apparatus of the Grand Lodge of the international. There seemed to be a substantial difference between the objectives of the local lodge and those of the Grand Lodge. The machinists and mechanics wanted better working conditions and pay that matched their skills. The Grand Lodge appeared to want all machinists and mechanics in the union, but it also wanted the union membership to get along with the companies in a congenial way. Since my place was with the men, I could see tough times ahead, with both the companies and the Grand Lodge aligned against me. Moreover, those circumstances came as a rude shock to my dreams of being part of a rank-and-file-controlled union that would represent the best traditions of workers, that would support broad social concerns, that would have the confidence of its members, and that would serve as a powerful voice for its own interests.

What caused the wide differences between McBreen and me? Or rather, how did McBreen come to support the Associated Industries position and ignore the democratic, nearly unanimous decisions of the working machinists? My assessment is as follows: McBreen recognized the power realities of the conflict, and Associated Industries was a much more powerful group than his own machinists; the working machinists' unity was fragile and inconsistent; therefore, because he did not trust democracy in the workplace, McBreen chose the powerful Associated Industries for an ally.

Part of a longer answer is that McBreen had been a working machinist at one of the bargaining companies in the Associated Industries group. Also, he was a former business agent of the same machinists' union; he had been chosen by the same procedures that elected me. At that time, it is reasonable to assume that he respected the democratic decisions of his fellow workers. However, when he informed me that my job was to tell machinists what they wanted, he had changed. McBreen had been working as an appointed Grand Lodge representative for several years. He first had been appointed to his position as general vice-president for the ten western states; therefore, when he faced the election process, he ran as an incumbent with the support of the Grand Lodge. That was true for all the general vice-presidents who held office in 1948.[5]

Because of those circumstances, McBreen had been removed from direct contact with working machinists for some time. His antidemocratic philosophy was similar to that of all the Grand Lodge representatives of the machinists' union and the international officers of the United Steelworkers of America. Because that twist of interests characterized all international union representatives, I decided that it must be a general impersonal force, unseen, like gravity, that pulled union representatives towards the company's position.

From 1956 until 1972 I worked under the jurisdiction of the International Federation of Professional and Technical Engineers. It is a very democratic but widely dispersed small union. During those sixteen years I knew three people who went to work as business representatives, who came on the job as strong supporters of the members' rights and needs, and who were elected by a democratic vote of their fellow workers. Despite their record of work for the union, the same process of erosion took place. All three of those people gradually leaned more toward an accommodation with the powerful employers or administrators. That forces me to conclude that there is something systemic about the process and that it comes from the capitalists' control over the workplace and its product. That power accommodates all other political, economic, and social institutions to the capitalist system. If they fail to follow this path, they lose their potential for growth. That is part of an overall struggle between the needs of the company and the needs of the workers. That is what the class struggle is all about.

Looking back at that problem, the evidence of the union representatives' drift to the right was visible in all my contacts with trade-union leaders since the 1940s. The pressure of the companies is a dominating influence. In nearly all cases, employers have the right to hire workers and, with some restrictions, to fire them. That amounts to the right to give or reject a family's meal ticket. It is a dominating position. The companies are few, powerful, and on many issues united. Workers are numerous and powerless unless united. Because of those conditions, union representatives are under constant pressure to support the companies. The only union leaders that I know who have resisted company authority and who have tried to strengthen the unity of workers were those who believed in the necessity of the people to collectively organize, to contribute, and to direct the workplace.

Despite my negative contacts with the Grand Lodge, my relations with the men in the shops was positive. There was a strong glow of pride in the success of our negotiations. The men had done it by themselves; all I had done was to support them.

*

As the summer of 1947 wore on, many machinists began to express an undercurrent of resentment toward the heavy-duty mechanics, who made up about half of the membership of the union. The machinists were the original founders of the local, but because their craft had stopped growing and that of the mechanics was increasing, the two groups became about equal in number. Most of the resentment on the machinists' part seemed to center on how to handle the finances of the union. Like many others, Local 86 came out of the Second World War with a sizable nest egg. The machinists liked the security of having that money in a savings account, but the mechanics wanted to use the fund to keep another business agent on the job. The latter were also generous in their contributions to other unions. The grievance was current, but the problem's origin lay deep in the history of the machinists and the mechanics.

The machinists' union was born in the railroad industry in the South during the nineteenth century.[6] Throughout its history, it was customary for a young man to serve an apprenticeship of four or five years in order to learn the trade. Those traditions were still cherished by the membership of Local 86. When a machinist served an apprenticeship and was graduated to journeyman, it was the equivalent of receiving a professional license. Talking about apprenticeship days was like alumni going over old college days. Men without an apprenticeship background were somewhat declassed.

It was different with the mechanics. Their trade was new and growing. Many of them had picked up the trade in a random fashion as they worked here and there. Apprenticeship programs were being inaugurated, but many shops and garages had none. There was also a difference in the work process between the two segments of the trade. A mechanic could get a stalled or broken-down car or truck fixed with his own tools and the parts that were available. That gave him a strong feeling of independence. On the other hand, if a machinist wanted to create a new part or a new machine from raw iron, he needed to use the multithousand-dollar machine tools that were usually owned by the boss. That left the machinist dependent on a company big enough to finance a machine shop.

The heavy-duty mechanics were strong union people, and as their numbers grew, they insisted on having a business agent to represent them. During the war, with lots of people working in the shops, the union treasury grew and it was easy to pay for an additional business agent for the mechanics. But by the time I was elected business agent for the machinists, the revenue was not sufficient to pay for two agents and a financial secretary. Therefore, every month or so the financial secretary would request permission to cash reserve bonds in order to pay the bills. That didn't bother the independent, tough-minded mechanics, but it irked the machinists, who didn't like to see the treasury reserve melting away.

Those different perspectives made it difficult to obtain the unity necessary to solve important problems, such as organizing the nonunion, auto-row shops or getting the financial recognition that both crafts deserved. The pressure from the machinists to cut back to one business agent was so strong that the mechanics' business agent resigned during the second year I was on the job. That left me as the sole person responsible for both segments of the union; it also left me with a heritage of bitterness in the union.

There were three big shops employing from twelve to twenty machinists, and I usually made arrangements to be at those shops during the noon hour so we could discuss problems confronted by the union. It also gave the men a chance to talk about their grievances. Trying to settle those problems during my own noon hour on an empty stomach was unsettling for me.

An especially difficult grievance came up over the firing of a welder at General Machinery, a shop that had a lot of problems because the foreman was not a machinist. He had been a millwright and knew a lot about machinery, but that is different from being a machinist who crafts intricate, precise machine parts out of rough blocks of iron. The welder at General Machinery called to tell me that the foreman had told him to add on two layers (or passes) of mild steel on a shaft with a certain size welding rod. The welder did as he was told and gave the built-up shaft to the foreman, who in turn gave it to a machinist to turn down to the correct size. The machinist put it on his lathe and started turning off the welded-on metal; by the time he got down to clean, new metal, it was too small. Several hours of the welder's and the machinist's time had been wasted. Those costs could not be passed on to the customer, and the foreman did not want to accept the blame, so he fired the welder. But it was the foreman's ignorance of the welding process that caused the trouble, and he should have admitted it and taken the blame.

When I met with the company partners, they were polite and considerate but backed their foreman in order to maintain authority in the shop. The machine-shop contract had a clause that expressly stated that the company had the sole right to decide on the competence of the employees. That unusual concession to the company came about because of several different factors. In order to get recognition, the machinists were very careful not to interfere with management's prerogatives. Besides, in the older shops almost all the men and the foremen were apprentice trained, and competence among those close-knit master craftsmen was not much of an issue. But all that didn't help the man who had lost his job at General Machinery. It was my miserable task to tell him that under the old clause in the contract there was nothing I could do to help him. Grievances of that kind made for bad days for a business agent. It is a very sad scene when a man has lost his job, the means to support his family, and his personal pride.

Some of the young machinists in the new postwar shops were derisive about a union contract that gave management the sole authority to determine competence. Their heightened awareness illustrated the changes that were taking place in the industry as the old traditions became inadequate in the face of the current conditions.

*

My involvement in organizing the H and U Clutch Shop illustrates the problems of fitting a standard contract to a small business of three or four workers. That case was unusual because the owners and the workers had agreed to try to go union. When I first went to the shop, the owners showed me around the operation and introduced me to the small crew. The business was set up to rebuild worn-out clutches in a way that used some of the old castings and yet turned out a product that was equal to the original one. In some cases, when high-quality clutch linings were used, the rebuilt unit might even be superior to the original. Signing a union-shop contract focused on the problem of fitting a standard machine-shop agreement to a production-type operation, or designing a new agreement for only three or four workers.

Making special provisions in a standard agreement for one shop opens a Pandora's box of future problems, because many other owners believe their businesses to be unique. In addition to the time involved in fashioning a particular contract, especially if there are dozens of different ones in effect in the same town, a union contract loses its basic standards. In the case of H and U Clutch we finally agreed with the workers and the owners to use the standard machine-shop classification of helper, specialist, and journeyman. Most of the workers who were doing production tasks would be paid the specialist rate, while the higher journeyman's pay would be available for the experienced employees who would operate, repair, and adjust the machines. Even then, dealing with a small shop is time consuming and no matter what answers you come up with, there are many potential grievances. However, I was happy to bring one more shop into the union fold, regardless of the work involved for only three or four new members.

The organizing procedures used at Alexander's Towing, Wrecking, and Machine Shop illustrated how an employer's right to hire and fire can intimidate employees; it also shows how the Wagner Act and the National Labor Relations Board (NLRB) provided a shield for workers by establishing some limitations on that right. Alexander, the owner, had a small machine shop that rebuilt motors and provided facilities for installing those engines in a vehicle.

One night a machinist called me to ask if I would come out to his home and help the workers in the shop join the union. A few nights later I met with the three or four men who were the entire crew of Alexander's shop. They wanted the protection of the NLRB so the boss could not fire them for wanting to go union. Under the provisions of the Wagner Act and the policies of the NLRB at that time, an employer was not permitted to fire his men during an authorized organizing drive. The men told me that they wanted to sign cards that night calling for an NLRB election. Then they asked me to present those cards to the NLRB before notifying the boss, a procedure that would give them the protection of the NLRB before the boss knew they wanted to join the union. I followed their suggestions and filed the cards and left the rest to the NLRB. The board notified the employer that his employees wanted an NLRB-supervised election.

Alexander was upset and hostile when he received the notice from the NLRB. But it was too late to use his unchallenged prerogative of hiring and firing at will, because the men were now under the protective wing of the NLRB. The board held the election and the men voted unanimously to go union. Only then did I contact Alexander about signing the standard machine-shop agreement. He gave me a lot of guff about the procedure we had used, because he considered it underhanded. I had little to say except that the men wanted some NLRB protection in case he was mad enough to fire them. After Alexander got tired of chewing me out for not dealing directly with him, he signed the standard union contract with no questions asked.

The signal point to that incident was not so much Alexander's anger, but how it illuminates the way the bosses' unrestrained right to hire and fire can intimidate a work force unless it is organized and has some community and legal support. In many cases the protection of the NLRB was of little help when an intransigent company wanted to fight the board. Since that period, the NLRB has been so weakened by Congress and the courts that it is of little help in organizing.

Yet another incident illustrates how a union can bring a modicum of industrial democracy to the shop floor and still maintain efficiency. That event occurred at the Columbia Electric Company, a local industry manufacturing fluorescent light fixtures and employing about fifty people. The employees included four or five tool-and-die makers, a few punch-press operators, and a crew of men and women assembling the fixtures. The machinists' union represented the tool-and-die makers and the punch-press operators. The International Brotherhood of Electrical Workers (IBEW) represented the people doing the comparatively unskilled production work.

The company did not negotiate with the other Spokane machine shops that were represented by Associated Industries. But after the other unions negotiated a contract with Associated Industries, Columbia Electric would sign for substantially the same provisions. We represented the higher-paid, somewhat-elite group in the plant, and our contract generally stipulated only three wage scales: journeyman machinist, specialist, and helper. There weren't many specialists or helpers employed in our shops, and the pay for those jobs had a tendency to be comparatively good, a fact reflected in the low turnover in personnel. We considered our contracts to be superior to the IBEW agreement.

The main group in the IBEW were the journeymen electricians. The Columbia Electric contract for production workers was an industrial agreement far removed from the union's mainline. Because the union agreement with Columbia Electric had no bearing on the basic agreements for their journeymen electricians, the union usually signed with Columbia Electric for a low industrial wage, much like that in effect in West Coast factories. The minimum wage under the IBEW contract was considerably below our agreement, yet we were able to maintain our higher wage scale with little pressure from the company.

However, that arrangement changed when Columbia Electric moved into a big, new, one-story plant during the first part of the Korean War. The company was awarded a big contract to make hundreds of thousands of brass artillery-shell components, a very complex piece requiring machine work of a very precise nature. The company planned on hiring three hundred women to do the assembly-line work, its first of that kind. Because the job was conceded to be machine work, it came under our jurisdiction. But the company found our wage scale for specialists too high and argued that it didn't fit the proposed assembly line. Company officials suggested that a standard IBEW contract be substituted for our craft-oriented agreement. Because that would involve allowing a lower wage scale than our contract required, we resisted the proposal.

The company's plan had two unusual features: a very low hiring-in wage rate and an automatic escalation. Every four months for a period of sixteen months, the wage rate would increase a certain amount. After sixteen months the employee would be receiving a relatively high wage—the highest rate we knew of for that kind of work. The company defended the low hiring wage rate through two lines of reasoning: the contract was already in effect with competing employers on the West Coast, and because the assembly line was just starting, it would take six to twelve months to get the kinks worked out. The low hiring-in wage rate was necessary, they argued, to get the line organized and working. If the contract lasted long enough and the employees stayed the full sixteen months, they would have the best wage scale for industrial workers, male or female, in the Inland Empire.[7]

However, my union resisted the very low hiring-in rate, one that was lower than any of our existing contracts. We refused to sign a contract with Columbia Electric that was cheaper than any of our contracts with Associated Industries. In addition, we were suspicious of the escalation features of the proposal. Under the agreement, the escalation was automatic as long as the employee stayed the required amount of time. There were no qualifications other than working the four months; then the escalation clause would go into effect automatically. If the workers didn't stay on the job, they would labor for four months at a very low rate; if they were laid off, others would be hired to work four months at the same low rate.

That feature of the contract made it susceptible to capricious hiring and firing on the part of the company. It had the potential to result in a large employee turnover, meaning that very few people would get the benefits of the higher wage rates. A solid impasse resulted. We felt we were on firm ground in resisting a contract with a lower hiring-in rate than those in effect in the metal-trades industry elsewhere in the Inland

Empire. For its part, the company felt it had the right to sign an agreement comparable with those already in effect on the West Coast.

In order to prevent the company from firing employees before they could get the benefit of the higher wages, I finally offered to sign a contract with the lower hiring-in wage if the company would agree not to fire any of the women on the assembly line unless a committee elected by the women approved the firing. That was quite a revolutionary idea, because it required the company to give up the right to fire the assembly-line people. The proposal required that approval of the firing would rest in the hands of the women's shop committee, which they elected themselves. After many days of discussion, the company finally agreed to those terms. We accepted its wage scales with the automatic escalation features, and it accepted our proposal that the firing would be under the control of the women's democratically elected shop committee.

Those unusual provisions in the contract came naturally to me because of my previous work experience. It was very commonplace for many people to be hired and fired for little reason. I had witnessed personally that common reference about companies needing three crews—one coming to work, one on the job, and one leaving. That practice was one of the old hiring-hall rackets of hard times. With that in mind, I was determined not to sign a contract that would allow such practices. The most dependable cure for that problem was to give the responsibility to the workers themselves.

The women responded collectively and in substance unanimously; their challenge and responsibility appeared to bring about a renaissance of spirit and talent. For that was a high-speed assembly line, and with three hundred people doing the arduous, repetitive work, one would expect a rash of grievances. To the surprise of many of us, they simply did not develop. Because the right of dismissal was collectively in the hands of the women, they were looked to for advice in handling personnel problems. That consultation fostered a sense of humanistic, creative responsibility that appeared to solve problems. Even though Columbia Electric had the largest concentration of people under our contract, there were few grievances. It was a pleasure to visit the plant. I attribute the smoothly running operation to the highly unusual fact that—in the major issue of whether a person is to work or be fired—the women, through their elected committee, had final authority. That responsibility created a subtle shift in the balance of power on the line. The women were asked rather than ordered around. Their collective judgment and talent were in command. Their authority took the place of the boss's authority—and it worked.

The company didn't try to evade the contract. The women felt their power; their concern that no one should be fired capriciously and their resistance to oppressive work schedules gave a sense of security to each person. Those conditions made each day better for all the workers, and the experiment supports the concept that workers' collective judgment and talent are essential in industry. To gain that talent, industry has to give up its prerogatives of autocratic power.

Because the women were hired under the jurisdiction of an existing union-shop agreement, they did not have a voice as to whether they wanted to belong to a union. However, they seemed to appreciate the working conditions, the job security in their own collective hands, and the egalitarian social relations of a union. They joined, attended meetings regularly, and took part in union business, and some of them were elected as delegates to the Central Labor Council. While I was business agent, the men accepted them as fellow workers and relationships were good. However, I must recognize that there was a shortage of labor during that period, so male workers did not feel a threat to their jobs.

Although it is somewhat rare, I have experienced the beautiful sharing of comradeship with fellow workers many times. The first time it happened in a waterfront union machine shop in San Francisco. There I shared a broad regard and respect for the other machinists who were united together. We negotiated for wages and working conditions; no one progressed at the expense of others; we won or lost together. A union is a product of those feelings, and a democratic union helps to preserve them. The Spokane women probably felt that in their shared work and union experience.

There are large, intangible, powerful forces at work in a shop because of the company's inherent right to hire and fire. When the company conceded some of that power to the workers, a bit of the aura of influence passed to workers. With that authority in their hands, the women could tame the line somewhat; their day-to-day struggle to keep the dehumanizing features of the work from being dominant was bolstered.

Workers have the same desire to perform as musicians who want to produce beautiful music. For those needs to be satisfied, a humane environment and a work pace at human rhythms are required. At Columbia Electric those conditions existed because the boss no longer had the right to fire anyone on the line. Because that right was in the hands of the women, problems of personnel and productivity had to be negotiated with the people working on the line. As a result of those negotiations, productivity was directly related to the women's experience in the work process. They had a sense for improvements that would make the work easier, more efficient, and in keeping with human rhythms of work and rest. Productivity in that sense was under human control. The company was pleased with the production figures that came out of that arrangement, even though it had lost the autocratic right to say who worked and who went home without a job.

nine

Union Activity During the Cold War

At the meetings of the Washington Machinists' Council there was an opportunity to confer with officers and business agents from the other big locals, especially those in the Seattle area. In that work I had no direct knowledge about their relations with the Grand Lodge, nor did I learn of any dramatic confrontation between workers' democracy and Grand Lodge authority similar to my own experience. However, there didn't appear to be any Grand Lodge activity that would indicate that my confrontation was unusual.

In the fall of 1948 I attended the Grand Lodge convention in Grand Rapids, Michigan, a massive gathering of several hundred elected delegates from all over the United States and Canada. The international president, Harvey Brown, chaired the meeting; behind him sat the nine-man Grand Lodge Executive Council, composed of the general vice-presidents and the Grand Lodge secretary and treasurer.

During the two-week convention I observed the Grand Lodge apparatus develop and carry out a nationwide program to circumvent the working membership's democratic and collective decisions. At the same time the Grand Lodge strengthened the power of the international president and its council. That was most forcefully demonstrated in its opposition to a proposal to give the working machinists in a given geographical area the right to elect their own general vice-president, similar to the way citizens elect representatives to Congress in Washington, D.C.

Members of the machinists' union did not have the right to elect a general vice-president to serve their area. For instance, the state of Washington is served by a general vice-president who also oversees approximately ten western states. Machinists working in the state have an opportunity to observe business agents in the different locals. Some agents and locals just follow the leader; others set exemplary patterns, protecting the standard of living and working conditions of their members. As time passes, it becomes obvious which business agents are doing their job and which ones are simply there for a free ride.

Left to themselves, the machinists in the ten western states would probably elect a proven business agent to be the general vice-president from their area, but that is not the way it works. Those machinists do not have the right to elect their general vice-president. That right is spread out over the fifty states. That diffusion of voting authority robs the machinist of the right to judge a candidate accurately, because members all over the United States have to vote on all nine general vice-presidents. There is no way for machinists in the Northwest, for instance, to be able to judge the work of a business agent in New York City. If a machinist votes only on the vice-president in his area, his ballot is voided. To know anything in detail about all nine general vice-presidential candiates is impossible for a working machinist. The only way he can learn anything about those candidates—even their names—is through the Grand Lodge press, and that medium is controlled by the incumbent general vice-presidents and the international president. Thus, incumbency becomes very important.

That issue was brought out at the Grand Rapids convention when a delegate from New York asked the international president how many of the nine general vice-presidents sitting behind him were elected to office the first time they held that position. International President

Harvey Brown laughed at the question and replied that all the general vice-presidents were elected. Many delegates laughed, but the questioner held his ground. He restated his question, reminding the international president that the issue referred to whether they were appointed or elected to office the *first* time. After some long pauses, the international president conceded that not a single general vice-president presently holding office had received his original office through an election.

As it turned out, all were first appointed by the international president, who manipulated the situation in this manner: shortly after a four-year election, an older general vice-president would retire; that gave the international president the opportunity to appoint a "reliable" Grand Lodge representative general vice-president from that area. By the time an election came along two or three years later, therefore, the new general vice-president would be running as an incumbent. His photo and his activities would be featured in the machinists' press, which was distributed throughout the states.

Effective democracy in the election of the general vice-presidents was aborted by requiring all working machinists in the forty-eight states to vote for all the general vice-presidents. From that experience of seeing how the international president and the general vice-presidents ran a self-perpetuating bureaucracy, it was plain to me that the general vice-president's haughty disdain for democracy in Spokane was not an aberration. Rather it was part of a nationwide policy to abort the working machinists' right to choose a general vice-president from their own ranks.

Not only was that form of union officialdom a self-perpetuating bureaucracy, it also made rules to maintain power at the local level. In the area of Grand Lodge authority, there was a constant skewing of power away from the local level. I observed this at the Grand Lodge convention, where the authority for initiating constitutional changes was limited to local lodges. Despite this the Grand Lodge Executive Council introduced a number of constitutional changes. At an appropriate time, I got the floor and asked the international president to show me where the executive council was given that authority. He and the general vice-presidents sitting behind him thumbed through the constitution for several minutes. Finally, the president replied: "Son, when we get a tough job in the shop we just go ahead and do it. That is called the shop method. When we in the executive council have a job to do, we do it. That is called shop authority." Because there were no other protests, the executive council's proposals were accepted.

Four years later, in 1952, some local unions introduced resolutions giving the Grand Lodge Executive Council the authority that it had ursurped four years before. I considered that change an admission that the previous action had been unconstitutional. It was through those little piecemeal changes that more and more authority was skewed toward the Grand Lodge.

One of the reasons delegates did not relish a floor fight against the international president was that the only way out of the rigors and the pervasive day-to-day grievances of the membership was to be appointed to the position of Grand Lodge representative. Those are prestigious jobs with good salaries and travel and expense accounts. The positions also are isolated from the election process of the membership. The authority to give or withhold those jobs gives the general vice-presidents and the international president a lot of subtle influence and allows the Grand Lodge to accrue to itself power that at one time belonged to the working members.

*

Dutch syndicalist Anton Pannekoek provided an analysis of the different ways that employers resisted trade unions that was especially pertinent to my work as business agent. In his view, employers resisted the formation of unions of any kind as long as they could, but if the unions were strong enough to force acceptance, the employers shifted their tactics by making concessions in areas that did not endanger their control over the workplace, their profits, or their priorities. Those concessions, he suggested, often created confusion and disunity among the workers.[1]

A classic example of that situation is the way an employer may agree to a union-shop contract. Under such a contract the employer agrees that all employees shall join the union and pay union dues. Union activists usually like such clauses because workers who are not union minded are required to join and pay dues. That concession from the employer, by itself, does not change the speed of the line or shape the control of the work process. But it does grant financial security to the union, one that is dependent on the employer's enforcement of the union-shop clause. Through that dependence on the employer for the union's financial security, power subtly swings away from the workers to the company. Dependence on the employer also intensifies the estrangement between the working members of the union and its full-time salaried officials, whose financial security is dependent on the continuance of the revenue that flows from the union-shop contract.

Given the lack of satisfaction with most atomized and repetitive factory jobs, workers are driven to push for more humane conditions, more human rhythms on the job, and more input in the design of the work process. Grievances such as those challenge the employers' historical autocratic and unilateral authority over the design and operation of the work. Because of that tendency, employers resist any concessions in those areas, even though resolving grievances is very important to the rank and file. However, grievances do not affect the international officers directly. For those people, a good financial statement is more important because that is where their salary comes from. Although the maintenance of union-shop agreements—with their accompanying steady flow of cash—is essential and inherently good for international officers, they do not necessarily produce better conditions for the workers. In fact, the flow of money to the international may skew the leadership's interests toward continuing the operation of the union-shop agreement rather than supporting the workers' struggles for better conditions.

This analysis illustrates the basic systemic forces that can cause a general vice-president to show up in Spokane to back the companies forcefully rather than support the members paying his salary. It also shows why international union officers use undemocratic procedures that discourage support for shop-floor grievances. This analysis also emphasizes that many union problems flow from the employer's basic power to control the workplace while granting concessions that are great for the international union officers but of little value to the employees, who must face the debilitating and inhuman rhythms of the workplace.

*

My work as business agent took place during the cold-war era from 1947 through 1952, a period when the social unity of the Second World War was lost. In its place, the postwar era experienced the Taft-Hartley Act, the loyalty purges, the Smith Act trials, and all the recriminations of the Truman-McCarthy period.[2] There was no way that I could be comfortable with any of those cold-war purges. I was certain that the only un-American activities I had ever witnessed were carried out by the government's un-American activities committees and their supporters. The purpose of the Truman-McCarthy purges, in my view, was to wipe out dissent against postwar capitalism's push for domestic- and foreign-policy ideological hegemony. Those were sad years.

As a result of signing non-Communist affidavits, some of my trade-union friends were jailed on real or contrived perjury charges.[3] I had the right to sign the affidavits, because during my tenure as business agent my associations involved no actual or implied connection with any organization other than the machinists' union. The only possible exception would be my ideological support for people who had the courage and perception to resist cold-war hysteria.

During that time, my favorite statesman was Glenn Taylor, the United States senator from Idaho. He understood the predatory influence of cold-war ideology and spoke out forcefully for more enlightened views. In northern Idaho I saw people standing for two hours at a time while he critiqued cold-war foreign policies. His interest in combating the cold-war programs led him to accept the 1948 vice-presidential nomination as running mate to Henry Wallace, the Progressive party's candidate for president. That important but unpopular decision cost Taylor his Senate seat.[4] Ironically, he was again defeated in the primary election in 1956 by Frank Church, who served a long career in the Senate and had the tables turned on him in 1980 when he was defeated by a Republican right-winger.

One of the saddest events of those years was to see the democratic, rank-and-file-controlled miners' organization—the Mine, Mill and Smeltermen's Union (CIO)—destroyed by the collusion of the undemocratic steelworkers' union, the mine owners, and the United States government.[5] I knew some of the activists and officers in Mine-Mill, and they were loyal Americans and stalwart defenders of trade-union democracy and fighters for workers' rights. For that, their union was destroyed.

I missed not being able to take an active part in the struggle to save those independent, rank-and-file-controlled unions. My time during that period was almost exclusively devoted to carrying out my job as business agent for the machinists' union. There was no way I could feel any rapport with either the policies of the day or the people who carried them out.

Although no one Red-baited me to my face during that time, I learned early on, from the perspective of the Grand Lodge and the employers, that anyone who stood up for rank-and-file democracy in the union was suspect. I plead guilty to that. In retrospect, it would have been better to serve as a rank-and-file member of the union rather than a business agent during those years. As a working machinist, the membership would respect personal views expressed openly at union

meetings. The disapproval of the Grand Lodge and the companies would not be as significant for an individual member. But for a business agent, every dissent from the establishment's views made it more difficult to maintain unity in the union. Those features of the cold-war hysteria contributed to the problems I faced as a business agent.

During the six times that I ran for office as business agent of Local 86, no one ever accepted a nomination to run against me, but in 1952 a sleeper write-in campaign upset me very much. The situation stemmed from the old division between the machinists and the mechanics. During the nominating process, a mechanic at the largest truck shop in town was put forth for business agent but refused to accept the honor. That left me unopposed. Because there were few other contended offices, there was little interest and a small turnout for the election.

On the appointed day the mechanics in the big shops turned out and wrote in the name of the person who had refused the nomination in the open election. I thought that a cheap trick—to refuse an open nomination and then run in a secret write-in campaign. Fair or not, it put me in a very compromising position. I did not want to leave under those circumstances, but the most ignominious part of it was my accepting the assistance of the international president, who ordered a new election. In the open election there was no contest and I was elected by a considerable margin. However, the loss of confidence of my friends among the heavy-duty mechanics hurt me deeply. They defended themselves by saying they only wanted me to pay more attention to them.

My job was to represent both the machinists and the mechanics, but I had so much more rapport with the militant, progressive mechanics that most of my time had been spent working on the machinists' grievances. The mechanics' unity, élan, and independent spirit contributed to a shop-level solidarity that protected them from abusive company action. Thus, the mechanics put fewer demands on me. Given that rapport, I took their support for granted. Obviously that had been a mistake.

The incident highlighted the difficulties of trying to maintain a strong, united union that involved two crafts in the postwar era. We had avoided that sort of disunity in the steelworkers' union at the aluminum rolling mill, where one local represented two thousand production workers and several hundred members of five different crafts. With all that variety of work, there seemed to be a special effort to get along. The very fact that we worked for the same employer provided a unifying background. The basic philosophy of an industrial union is to encourage workers to stand together against one company. In addition, wartime unity helped avoid internal bitterness. For me, the 1952 election was a warning that my hopes and dreams of building an especially strong, progressive, and united union were not working.

The difficulty of achieving unity was underscored one morning in the early summer of 1952 when I stopped to visit the picket line at the struck Union Iron Works shop and found the men in a happy mood and pleased with themselves. They had just come from a meeting with the company owner and liked the settlement he offered. Their exuberant pride in meeting with the company showed an appalling lack of sensitivity to standard union procedures. In effect, they were negotiating a personal contract that jeopardized the bargaining power of the rest of the union. Their satisfaction pained me, because they seemingly had repudiated me and all that I stood for. I had a rebellion on my hands. The men at the biggest shop in Spokane wanted to settle for the company's offer; they needed only a few votes from Washington Machinery and a few small shops to have a majority.

Before those events, it had been my position always to speak out against an owner's efforts to undermine the collective decisions of union workers. However, in that case I accommodated or engaged in toadyism to the bosses. In doing so, my integrity as a business agent for the union was compromised. I should have called a special meeting of all machinists and thrashed out the problem until we had reached a consensus. Instead, in a meeting with the company and its lawyers, it was agreed to present to the membership a settlement that was a slight improvement over the company's original offer. I did not offer a recommendation against it, because that was probably the best we could do after the cordial meeting between the Union Iron Works crew and the owner. My report to the membership did not mention that meeting; in fact, the negotiations placed me in a bad situation because of my decision to back away from our previous position without giving the real reason for it. That was close to a sellout for me. I had caved in to the most conservative sector of the union without an open discussion and vote by the members involved.

My inexperience had contributed to that fiasco. For years it had been customary for the business agent to conduct the negotiations and process the grievances. I continued that practice, but should have requested the assistance of a negotiating committee. The working members would have faced the Union Iron Works members squarely. Collectively, we would have presented a more impersonal position than I could offer acting alone.

At the time, I was ashamed of trying to settle the problem alone without facing up to the issue in an open meeting. It didn't occur to me at the time that the job was robbing me of my élan, my soul, and my energy. Looking back, there were disappointments, a lack of support, and a barrage of grievances that had eroded my strength and will to fight. I had backed away from a positive, open floor fight on the issue and had to face up to the fact that the prospect of confrontation was wearing on me.

One night at a union meeting later in the summer I began to look at the clock to see how close it was to adjournment. As member after member spoke, it was obvious to me that I didn't want disputes to arise that would require solutions. That was a far cry from my sense of confidence when my work as business representative began six seasons earlier. It was time for me to go back to work using tools and to regain my composure, my strength, and my will to carry on a good fight.

In the workplace you share the labor and companionship of your peers. Communication is multidimensional as people become involved in the common problems of the job. Individuals are judged through a long process of sharing, talking, and working together. The social and production problems of the workplace can be mastered by talented people, and often they become rank-and-file leaders and are elected to business-agent jobs for the union. That is when a quantum change takes place. The predictability of your comrades and the work process is gone. In its place you face day-to-day contradictions between industry's push for profits and the workers' desire for humane conditions on the job. A business agent becomes the focal point for those contradictions. It is impossible for one person to solve all of those complex problems, and if he doesn't resolve them to the workers' satisfaction, their only option is to elect a new, eager face and try again.

In my various places of work, those changes led to pressures on the business agent that usually contributed to one of the following: (1) the business agent would be defeated for reelection; (2) the agent would retire and take a job in private industry, such as industrial relations; (3) he would be elevated to a nonelective office with the international union; (4) he would become part of a corrupt organization that favored industry to the detriment of the workers he is supposed to represent; (5) he would take refuge in alcohol; (6) he would quit the job in weariness and disappointment. At one point it was my opinion that model fellow workers had become phony because of some hidden weakness. But as different versions of that phenomenon took place, I began to look for more fundamental reasons to account for that pattern of change in people.

One of the reasons for the business agent's problems rests in the reality that the power of the companies is concentrated, while the power of the membership is dispersed and divided most of the time. Only after a particularly glaring act of injustice on the part of the company will there be sufficient unity among the union membership to make a joint effort, such as a work stoppage, to resist management's power. The companies have economic, political, social, and mass-media power. As time goes by the business agent usually is pulled by the stronger gravity of the company's influence or is worn out trying to resist it.

Because of those circumstances, the idea of retreating to a job where I had served a long, full apprenticeship, even if it meant moving away from the comradeship of fellow workers in the machinists' union, looked attractive. It was time to enjoy a more restful, eight-to-five job while I pondered the lessons of the last ten years and savored the fellowship and sharing with so many beautiful people.

Finding another job would not be easy. I had held two good jobs in Spokane, one as a layout machinist at the aluminum rolling mill. But my activity in the steelworkers' union had cost me that position. My skills also qualified me to work at my old job in the small highway shop, but after I quit to go to work for the union, someone was hired to take my place. It would not be fair to ask for that job back.

About that time my friend Joe Bernardy asked me to consider going to work for him as a transitman on a highway-survey crew. Russ Parsons, the district engineer, confirmed the offer, which would mean working for Bernardy at Wallace, Idaho (map 1). But I was saddened to leave machinist's work, the comradeship of union members and friends, and the opportunity to continue in the union as a rank-and-file member. In some ways it was a bitter pill to swallow. It meant returning to the highway game, where there was no union and where everyone

was on a hierarchical ladder of classifications, pay, and authority. Those relationships did not foster comradeship or rapport among workers. My decision meant returning to the politics of state jobs and to the problem of corrupt contractors.

In addition, working with machinery, either repairing old machines or building new ones, appealed to me. In the machinist's craft there was the satisfaction of seeing my work become reality. Now it was back to an industry where my effort was often an abstracted part of the whole, where a boss or contractor might repudiate or nullify my work, and where there was no mechanism for protest. That was the basis of my disappointment and personal hurt in returning to highway work. If the conditions of the 1920s had still prevailed—when we did the work ourselves—or if there was the comradeship of Hugh Cochran's location crew, I would have felt better. But the same features of highway work that prompted me to leave ten years earlier still existed. Yet, in order to work at a paying job, I was back at it again.

As we headed for Idaho, the ashes of another burnt-out dream saddened my days. But as time passed my view broadened, as did my appreciation for the knowledge and experience gleaned from the ten years of work in trade unions. At least I was not going back to the woodyard at the Winton Mill. My lot actually was much better than that of many other workers who had tried to organize in support of humane job conditions. That relatively gentle confrontation with the ethics of big business and big unions increased my respect for others who have struggled for the trade-union movement. After that experience it was easier for me to understand why the capitalists had destroyed the Wobblies and other militant rank-and-file unions. Their democratic approach threatened the capitalists' autocratic control of the workplace, its profits, and priorities.

From that point on, I would be more chary of criticizing democratic unions that had not succeeded. It seemed apparent that Joe McBreen—who told me that my job as business agent was to tell workers what they wanted—probably once had dreams of being part of a big worker-controlled machinists' union. His feelings for workers likely had been eroded away by years of facing company opposition and associating with reactionary international officers. His once-warm association with machinists had been replaced by a refusal to listen to workers and a willingness to get along with the companies. I had not fallen into that trap; even being out of the trade was better than that. So, I was off to Wallace, Idaho, and a transit on my shoulder.

ten

Highway Engineering in Idaho and Montana, 1952–1956

Wallace, Idaho, the county seat of the rich Coeur d'Alene mining region, was a unique town. Within a radius of fifteen or twenty miles there were many world-famous silver, lead, and zinc mines. The Bunker Hill and Sullivan mines reported in 1952 that they had five hundred miles of underground tunnels and shafts. Another one, the Morning Mine, had eight miles of track to transport miners in to a hoist that lowered them four thousand feet into the bowels of the earth, where rich lead ore was mined. The Sunshine Mine yielded millions of dollars' worth of rich silver ore every year.

Only six miles from Wallace in the mining town of Burke, the canyon was so narrow that the tracks for the ore trains went through the first floor of the only hotel in town and the crews had to stop to ask local car owners to move their parked vehicles so the train could get through. That gives some idea of what the terrain was like in the canyons that lead to Wallace.

Because of its industrial base, Wallace had a special character all its own. Mining towns, like seaports, are somewhat cosmopolitan because miners move about from one mining region to another. Because of its open atmosphere, Wallace was an interesting place to work.

I worked for the telephone company in 1926 in the neighboring mining town of Kellogg, and in 1928 and 1929 the Idaho Highway Department hired me to drive trucks that were involved in repairing and oiling the roads just below Wallace. Just before the war I had been the office man (and Joe Bernardy the transitman and field chief) in Wallace for the resident engineer. Wallace, therefore, was rather like home.

This time Bernardy, who had inherited the position of resident engineer, hired me as his crew chief and fieldman. It was good to be on a mainline job pushing U.S. 10 (now I–90) through the steep, narrow canyons to Lookout Pass (map 1). It was a responsible and challenging job, and a busy place. I had little time to cry over the disappointment of the business-agent job that went sour.

My assignment was to lay out the big cuts, fills, and details of a new four-lane section of the highway west of Wallace, called Rocky Point. One solid-rock cut on that job towered 247 feet above the roadway. One of my major jobs was to set the stakes for the contractor on that impressive rock cut. After the big cut was drilled, blasted, and hauled away, the contractor built up the roadway with crushed-rock surfacing in preparation for paving with asphaltic concrete (oil pavement). As the finishing touches were being applied to the surfaced roadway, we ran into trouble.

The difficulty arose because the grader operator was not making the transition from a crowned roadway, characteristic of straight sections of a road, to the flat section that is used on the tilted-up, or "supered," section required on curves. By carrying a crowned shape through the curve, the contractor was leaving the outside of the curve deficient in tilt, or "super." That deficiency could cause drivers to lose control of their cars. Joe Bernardy pointed this out to the contractor, but the flawed subgrade was not corrected. An impasse developed: Bernardy was determined not to approve a grade that did not meet Idaho's standard specification, and he was also determined not to make illegal bribes to the contractor.

The impasse lasted a couple of weeks. Eventually the contractor brought in another superintendent who worked with the blade man until the super on the curve met the standard specifications. However, by that time the high-country summer had dissipated and the oiling contractor did not have time to complete the planned high-type pavement. A low-type temporary application of asphalt was made in the hope that it would last through the rainy season.

A short time after the temporary oiling job was finished, Sam Johnson, the state location engineer who was in charge of all highway-location work in Idaho, offered me a job as the top field location engineer in southern Idaho. The position involved the supervision of a highball location crew doing the mainline location work on U.S. 30 in a troublesome but important route across southern Idaho. It was a flattering job offer. I would be locating a major transcontinental highway alignment through that terrain and using my own judgment. Truly it was a dream! It tasted even better in that it came so soon after my disappointment in the union job.

There was only one drawback: it would take me all over the southern part of Idaho and it meant living away from home. There had been times in the past when the traveling would have been welcomed, but at that moment I simply did not want to live in a lonely motel room, waiting for the weekend to make the long drive home. Besides, I was uncertain about my ability to make the proper decisions on a major highway in relatively flat or gentle terrain. All of my experience in building roads had been in the mountain country.

Eventually, I turned it down and told Johnson that, although the offer was flattering, staying in Wallace as Bernardy's transitman was preferable. A few days later Johnson offered me work on a location project in Shoshone, Idaho (map 5), one that would bring me home almost every night. That was still a big move, but since he had gone out of his way to negotiate the job with the district engineer, I accepted it. The new position meant a promotion to resident engineer. That kind of offer was not easy to resist, so we moved to Shoshone.

Actually, working as resident engineer in Shoshone was sort of anticlimactic, because it involved the same work that I had done for years as a transitman. Of course, there was more independence in that it did not involve working under a resident engineer (although occasionally the district engineer would contact me). Johnson, the location engineer, also spent quite a bit of time with me explaining his concepts for choosing the precise location of the highway. That was very informative and it was flattering the way he detailed his views and the nature of my job. Through all of that, I felt that he showed confidence in me.

As time passed, it seemed to me that we were a long way from what I considered my home range. Shoshone just didn't feel right; the country and the people seemed different. Moreover, it was at least five hundred miles from all of our friends in Spokane and northern Idaho. I asked Johnson to find a job for me back up north when he could. He remarked: "What is the matter? Do you miss the trees? Don't you like sagebrush?"

About four months later Johnson told me that the Highway Department wanted to transfer me back to Wallace as resident engineer. That was the most responsible residency in the state of Idaho; but because of my concern about taking Joe Bernardy's job, I got in touch with him. Joe said they were transferring him because of the delay on the Rocky Point job, which caused me to consider refusing the appointment to make it more difficult for the department to transfer Joe. But he said it wouldn't save his job and that he would rather have a friend take his place than to turn the office over to a stranger. Joe then went on to say that heavy fall rains had washed out the temporary oil job at Rocky Point. That left the subgrade exposed to the weather and, as it deteriorated, the road became very rough to drive over. There were many complaints from the public, and the Highway Department decided to replace Joe as resident engineer. A transfer from Wallace would have been welcome for many engineers, but Bernardy's case was unique. He had grown up in Wallace and it was the only place he had ever worked. He was justifiably proud of having reached his position as resident engineer in his hometown. Being transferred, to Bernardy, was the same as being fired.

I felt some responsibility for Joe's transfer because of my work on the same job and the fact that I had pointed out the problems in the subgrade and had supported Joe in his request that it be brought up to specifications. My sense of guilt also included a feeling of negligence in allowing the construction schedule to fall behind, because my advice did slow the progress of the work. And I do not recall reminding Bernardy of the impending fall rains that would make it impossible to complete the paving job. Only a high-type paving job can protect the roadbed through a high-country winter.

But the incident also points out the dilemma faced by all quality-control personnel on major highway projects. If you get a reputation for being tough on a contractor, you wind up out in the boondocks or in a basement office reviewing someone else's work. If you try to get along with the contractor and don't insist on the work outlined in the standard specifications, the job will probably go smoothly, but the finished road will lack the fine details required in the original plans.

In removing Joe from his post as resident engineer, the Idaho Highway Department ignored the day-to-day problems of getting quality work from a contractor. In fact, by blaming Joe Bernardy for the foul-up, the state made it more difficult for other state engineers and inspectors to stand up to contractors. Although the decision to transfer Bernardy gave the appearance of solving the problem, it actually covered up the realities surrounding the contractor's de facto control of the work. An accumulation of incidents like that eventually led older resident engineers to give up on quality control and bribe the contractors by cutting corners on quality while at the same time paying the full price for inferior work.

As the resident engineer in Wallace, I was responsible for the location, construction, and maintenance of over forty miles of U.S. 10. The eastern terminus of that section of highway was the Idaho-Montana state line at Lookout Pass, an elevation of 4,700 feet. The fall rains that come to Seattle in late September or October usually dump an inch or so of wet, sloppy snow on the hill at Lookout Pass; therefore, snow removal was a major problem six or seven months of each year. At lower elevations, overnight and morning ice on the winding highway was another dangerous problem. The thirty miles from Pine Creek to Lookout Pass was in the narrow, rough valley of the South Fork of the Coeur d'Alene River. Because it was expensive and time consuming to build a highway through that rough terrain, there was nearly always a major location or construction job under way. For those reasons the Wallace residency was one of the most challenging jobs in the Idaho Highway Department. The assignment was an honor.

*

Soon after my arrival in Wallace, an unusual problem with unsuitable material illustrated the efficiency of the department's administrative and inspection procedures when senior personnel are directly involved in the work. The situation was in sharp contrast to the inefficiency that occurs when senior personnel are deeply involved in reports and employees several steps removed from the resident engineer do the actual on-the-job inspection.

On a big construction project at Pine Creek we encountered large amounts of unsuitable material. The valley floor was covered with several different layers of mine tailings. Some were coarse enough to provide a good highway foundation; others were as fine as white kitchen flour—in fact, so fine that they would float on water. That fine material was unsuitable for a roadway foundation. Preconstruction sampling had shown large amounts of that material, so provisions were made in the contract to pay for removing several thousand cubic yards of the unsuitable material. However, the excavation for several miles of riprap trenches revealed more cubic yards of the material than had been expected. Before the additional work could be authorized, an improved work order was needed that would include a more realistic estimate.

Because the estimate would only be another guess, I called the district engineer, and he advised me to contact the man who represented the U.S. Bureau of Public Roads in northern Idaho. That shortcutting of the lines of authority was unusual, but it was direct and efficient. On the telephone the bureau representative, a man named Oakley, chided me for my concern: "What are you worrying about?" I told him of my worry about cost overruns and of the need to avoid a lot of static for such a big work order without having prior approval. He told me that the department had confidence in my abilities to produce a high-quality roadway, that I should get rid of the unsuitable material, and that he would sign the work order and the department would pay for it. Amazed by his directness and confidence in me, I left the telephone booth in exhilaration at the indirect compliment paid me by the district engineer in having me talk to Oakley directly. Oakley's reply was a beautiful pat on the back.

If a situation like that had arisen on a similar job during the late 1960s or early 1970s when I worked for the construction division of the Washington State Highway Department, the bureaucracy would have been cumbersome, expensive, and inefficient. The latter bureaucracy had developed as a response to the problem of avoiding collusion and corruption between the resident engineers and contractors. Consequently, the authority of the resident engineer was severely limited. Reports and multiple layers of administrators to review, approve, or disapprove the reports had become a fetish.

The procedure would have been something like this: The resident engineer would not have been put on the job to see the extensive and unsuitable mine tailings. He would have had to depend on personnel several steps of authority below him. He would have notified the district construction engineer, who probably would have called the geologist or the district materials engineer. They probably would have made a trip to the project to look at it first hand. The standard response then would have been to call for more sampling by ordering a portable power drill to do more drilling and sampling. Then a survey crew

would have been called to locate the drill holes so that an office man could prepare a map of the sampled area. In the meantime, the geologist would have prepared a report to accompany the map. By that time the wheel of the administrative world would have begun to spin. A letter with recommendations, data, and maps would go to headquarters in Olympia. In due time Olympia would take the matter up with the U.S. Bureau of Public Roads engineer. (By that time, the bureaucracy would be at the same stage as I was on my second phone call—the one to Oakley). In time, bureau representatives and state engineers would make a decision and probably authorize the removal of the unsuitable material. By that time the contractor might have prepared a claim for delay on the work, asking for rental pay for expensive machinery that had been standing idle waiting for a decision.

The worst part of that tendency for administrative layers, lines of authority, and reports is not the expense and inefficiency. It is that the highest-paid and theoretically the most-qualified engineers spend most of their time away from the reality of work. That absence leaves less-qualified people to make important decisions or to transmit information. The paper reports and the handling of them become such a fetish that they take on a reality of their own. Because of such a cumbersome allocation of authority, some problems of the real job may not even see the light of day in that world of paper.

Another interesting feature of the Pine Creek job was that much of the roadbed was built from river gravel dug out of big borrow pits on the valley floor. It was hauled out on the grade with new state-of-the-art Caterpillar scrapers, massive machines that weighed more than sixty tons when loaded. Because of their weight, I realized that those machines had the potential to compact the grade as it was being built. Their weight per bearing area was much more than the approved compactor and more than any vehicle that could be licensed to use the finished highway. Therefore, I asked the contractor to see to it that each driver use a different track from the one before him so that the entire roadway would be compacted by those giant machines. He was also instructed to tell the drivers to spread each load in a long, thin layer as listed in the standard specifications and to break track on each trip so that the full width of the roadway would be compacted. That wouldn't hold up the progress of the job to any appreciable extent, so he readily approved. I stayed on the job long enough to see that those stipulations were carried out.

At that time, the density inspection and the quality-control measurements for a roadbed were under the control of the district materials engineer. His crew found that the roadbed tested out 104 percent of the maximum density that the laboratory had been able to obtain under controlled conditions. They were amazed at such densities and complimented me for the high-quality job. That work was accomplished without even starting up the roller that was required in the specifications.

Another problem developed with the riprap (heavy rock protection). On most jobs where riprap is required in order to protect a roadbed from erosion from a nearby stream, it is added outside the regular roadway template. But on that project the riprap was so extensive that it was also designed as part of the supporting roadbed. In spite of this, no provisions were made for compacting the riprap. The regular practice was to build the supporting roadbed embankment and then dump the riprap over the side so that it would roll down the embankment and form a protective blanket of heavy rock. Because the addition of a layer of heavy rock was too narrow to support any compaction equipment, only the top portions of the riprap could be compacted. From the previous tests made by the materials division, we knew that the big Caterpillar scrapers had a potential for compaction beyond that of the laboratory or the roller approved by the standard specifications.

On that same section I had obtained free rolling of the roadbed by judiciously directing the big scrapers as they hauled along the roadway. But there was no way to get rolling for the riprap except at the hourly rate for the inadequate roller approved in the contract. There was a lot of money in the contract, however, to pay by the hour to rent one of the big scrapers. I got a rental figure which was very reasonable. Besides the effective compaction job of the rubber-tired scrapers, they also traveled faster than the approved crawler-pulled roller. The contractor selected a skilled veteran operator and asked him to do the hazardous work of driving a loaded scraper along the edge of the narrow slice of riprap to compact it beyond the loading that it would get from future use of the highway.

In order to pay for that quality rolling, I had an inspector keep track of the time in the usual way. The hourly rental rate was considerably more than the contract allowed for the approved roller, but since it didn't cost the state anything to get the regular roadbed compacted, there was plenty of money left to pay for the loaded scraper to roll the outside layer of riprap.

That process of conversion—shifting money from one item in a contract to another—was common practice in Idaho at that time. Through the use of conversion and the close control of the hauling equipment, we were able to produce a dense, stable roadbed beyond the ideal specifications of the laboratory. Under late 1980s regulations in the state of Washington, conversion would be illegal, and under the reporting system then in vogue—where the resident engineer is busy supervising the reporting forms and low-rated personnel are doing the inspection—it is unlikely that those beyond-the-model densities would be obtained for the roadbed.

*

The district engineer in Coeur d'Alene didn't like going to public meetings to hear complaints about the Highway Department, so he asked me to attend a meeting of the Kellogg Chamber of Commerce as his representative. I was happy to go, because it was an honor for a resident engineer to be delegated to attend such meetings on official highway business. My background in political protest and my six years' experience as business agent for the machinists' union provided a good basis for communication with businessmen. I felt that the members of the Kellogg chamber would present authentic criticisms of the Highway Department in their area.

The Kellogg chamber members, as it turned out, all spoke in a similar vein. The town was located in a narrow canyon in the mountains surrounded by steep hills, and during the fall, winter, and early spring, the sun would cause thawing conditions during the daytime. Each night the roadway would freeze into a treacherous, icy surface. Sand put on the evening before would be blown away by the air blasts from the cars, therefore, in order to provide safe traveling for the miners going to work in the early-morning hours, the roads had to be sanded before the heavy morning traffic hit the highway. The state highway crews, ignoring the heavy early-morning traffic, usually did not get out on the road with sand until 9 A.M. Although that was convenient for them, it really was an inexcusable way to serve the public.

I agreed completely with the Kellogg Chamber of Commerce. The present sanding schedule was wrong, and I promised to change it immediately. That seemed to surprise the chamber people, but they were happy about the promise to get the roads sanded early.

At a meeting with the highway day-shift crews to talk over the problem, they were concerned that state highway wages were set by the dominant southern part of the state, which was largely agricultural. Living expenses and wages were much higher in a community dominated by the hazards and high costs of the mining industry. Idaho wage scales were not flexible enough to adjust to local conditions; there was, for instance, no provision for premium pay for unusually long early-morning work schedules, a standard practice in many industries. Because of my work driving a truck for the state from 1928 to 1930, the issue was not new to me. All I offered the crew was the soundness of the proposal and a willingness to go to bat and to do the best for them within the state's regulations.

The situation was exacerbated by the fact that Shoshone County was quite insular by comparison to the rest of Idaho. The county was a collection of mining communities whose economic health revolved around the price of silver, lead, and zinc and the rich veins of ore in the deep mines that dotted the rugged, narrow canyons. The highway maintenance men were under the nominal authority of a long succession of civil engineers who had neither the training nor the experience necessary for a close relationship with maintenance men. That lack of rapport had allowed many of the maintenance workers' problems to accumulate in such a way that the quality of the crews and their interest in the work had deteriorated. The feeling of isolation from the district office of the Highway Department and a pay scale well below that of the miners were the basis of most of their grievances.

I advised updating their equipment and made all the pay accommodations that were possible within a scale set by the farming-community standards of southern Idaho. There wasn't much room to maneuver, but the men appreciated what was possible. Adjustments of days off, vacation schedules, and other schemes were worked out, and most of the men accepted the early-morning schedule in a way that was acceptable to them and excellent for the traveling public.

The chamber of commerce and the district engineer were pleased with the new sanding schedule. A representative from the chamber told the district engineer that its members were surprised to see his representative listen to them rather than make excuses. The district engineer was especially glad to have such rapport with the mining towns, where problems were the regular fare. Previous resident engineers were trained professionally for engineering problems, but listening to the problems of small businesses and the maintenance workers was a nuisance to them and did not receive high priority. My years of experience as a truck driver and business agent for union workers and my study and work in the arena of radical politics had prepared me for those kinds of problems; solving them was a pleasure.

*

Regardless of the successes at Wallace, political events not connected with my work caused me to lose my job as a highway engineer. During the height of the Truman-McCarthy Red scare, a former Communist-party official in the Pacific Northwest presented a list of people she had seen at party meetings. My name and Catherine's were included. As soon as the news appeared in the newspaper, I drove to Coeur d'Alene and talked to the district engineer about it. I said that Boise was sure to fire me, because it was embarrassing to the state administration to have all this publicity about a state employee in the papers and on the radio. The district engineer was not moved: "Norm, don't worry about it. You're too valuable to me. I need you up there in Wallace. You just go back and go to work. I won't let them fire you for this old depression stuff."

The next day a reporter from the local newspaper asked me if the reports of my attendance at Communist-party meetings were true. I told him yes and volunteered to meet with him in his office and tell him all about it. At that meeting I admitted to being a member of the Communist party as described in previous chapters. My explanation included a discussion of the days before the Second World War when the social fabric of the United States was being torn by misery and unemployment in the midst of overproduction. All over the country people were trying to solve the problems of farm families living in poverty because they had produced more than they could sell; coal miners' families were cold and hungry because they had produced so much coal that could not be sold. They had no jobs and no money to buy coal for themselves or to buy bread from the farmers' bumper crop of wheat. That, I told him, was the pattern all over the land.

Many of us were trying to find a cooperative formula to put that puzzle together. If the capitalists gave us cold houses and bare cupboards in the midst of plenty, then many of us thought it was time to share, to get together, and to elect representatives to cure those problems. That was done in the finest tradition of United States democracy. I also told the reporter of my decision to stop my affiliation with the party in 1946 because times had changed in the country. During the McCarthy era I felt a need to work out my own answers, and as an employee of the union, to avoid any other associations. The Taft-Hartley Act also gave me no other option but to disassociate from the party. My interest and commitment to political and industrial democracy did not wane, but it was necessary to work on my own.

None of that interested the newspaperman, or at least none of it showed in the paper. Headlines screamed about a Communist being a state employee and a resident engineer at Wallace. At the height of the cold war and in the wake of the Korean War, I was ostracized as a disloyal citizen, one to be shunned by society. My work to protect the interests of the state of Idaho and to preserve democratic traditions were as nothing. Another postwar wave of hysteria against dissent was sweeping the country. It was a reminder of the way the IWW was treated during the First World War. There weren't the right-wing vigilantes of those early years, but radio and television commentaries were directed against a broad spectrum of loyal dissent in a pervasive way. Some old friends shunned us, but it was rewarding to find warm, sympathetic understanding from unexpected sources.

In a few days a wire came from the state personnel director in Boise. In substance it read: "You are dismissed effective upon receipt of this communication. You have embarrassed the governor so much that your continued employment is not acceptable." That was tough to take, but there were no regrets about my association and work with all those people of good will in the late 1930s and early 1940s. I am still proud of my activities and those people during those years and would not trade their fellowship for a resident engineer's job. During my membership in the party we had supported FDR and his programs; we had worked to extend the Bill of Rights to workers and to establish democratic controls over the giant monopolies; we had supported all the basic democratic ideology of the U.S. Constitution. It was the corporate monopolies, their spokesmen, and the governor who had subverted the Constitution and denied us the right of peaceful petition, free speech, and the right to work.

There was little to do but pack up and move on to where someone needed an experienced road builder, someone who would accept me for my skills, someone who was not worried about my political philosophy. Although the governor of Idaho could fire me, he could not take away the knowledge and experience gained through more than fifteen years of work in highway engineering and road building. He couldn't deny me the reality of the labor and the association with other workers which had fostered a feeling of confidence in doing the job that needed to be done on any road-building project.

A lot of good people came to our support in those difficult times, and it gave me a good feeling as we set out looking for a job. It pleased me, too, that I had been the resident engineer for a short time and could now look forward to getting rid of the tensions connected with that position and return to using the tools of the trade.

A published article about the state of Colorado, in which the director of highways said the state believed in developing its engineers through experience rather than depending on college degrees, attracted me. We borrowed an old house trailer, loaded up a few essentials, and headed for Colorado.

En route we went through Missoula, Montana (map 6), and drove by a building with signs identifying it as the district office of the Montana Highway Commission. The district engineer responded to my query about a job as a transitman: "Yes, we have a job for you. It is a big job in a little town some distance from the railroad." As he talked, I realized he was making a solid offer of a job and that he was trying to talk me into taking it regardless of the remote back-country location. He asked no questions about my experience, background, or my reason for looking for a job. Although elated at that turn of events, it was necessary to let him know about my firing in Idaho. After my recital, he replied, "Think nothing of it. During the old days I used to carry a Red card myself." So there I was with a job on a big construction project in the back country of Montana. It was a good feeling to have a job of work, as Woody Guthrie would say, and to be accepted by another old-timer in the highway game. We drove on to the job site at Lincoln.

*

Lincoln was adventure—adventure, that is, in the rugged mountains of Montana's Continental Divide. It was a village of 150 people nestled against the western slope of the Rocky Mountains and without a year-round road or access to the west. It was only fifty-five miles from Helena, the state capital, but that was a two-hour drive because one had to cross the Continental Divide on a county road where twenty miles an hour was good time. Great Falls was ninety miles to the northeast, and that trip also took two hours because it crossed the Continental Divide on a paved state highway through gentle Rogers Pass. Missoula was ninety miles to the southwest, but a rugged twelve-mile section of Blackfoot Canyon blocked all traffic on that route from fall to spring. The road was usable in the summer months by hardy souls who braved the rough, narrow, and steep hills of the canyon. Our job was to do the surveying and layout work through Blackfoot Canyon so that a contractor could build a modern year-round highway. When we went to Lincoln in that summer of 1954, it was so isolated that people didn't even have up-to-date license plates. They licensed only the cars and trucks they drove outside.

My new boss, Kenny Lawrence, was cast in the mold of C. R. Short, the tough disciplinarian I had worked for at Oregon's Santiam Pass in 1932. Lawrence expected a full day's work, but reliable, quality performance was the top priority.

My first assignment was to run the transit as we staked out the centerline of the new highway. There was no limit to the artistry or refinement of skill in setting up a transit in rough, mountainous terrain. We had to overcome obstacles, such as getting the transit set up directly over the survey control point. And there was the problem of keeping the base of the instrument level so that the vertical axis could be easily plumbed. It was also necessary to have the tripod and head in a stable, tension-free position. After all that was done, the apparatus should end up with the tripod legs positioned so I could stand comfortably and look through the telescope without a lot of stooping or awkward reaching. Last but not least, I wanted to have all of the tripod legs positioned so that the chainman could pull up his hundred-foot tape without finding a tripod leg in the way. Chainmen get critical when they find that the transitman has blocked their passage; therefore, it was helpful to avoid that embarrassment. In order to facilitate such maneuvers, all tripods have legs that telescope, either to shorten or lengthen each one.

While pulling out the tripod at Lincoln, I learned that we did not have a transit tripod in the truck. We had a nontelescoping level tripod with stiff legs but with no way to shorten or lengthen them in order to get a precise fix on a position. To compensate for the loss of adjustable legs and still make good time, I decided to let the tripod stand as easy as possible and then to push the legs around in the ground instead of adjusting them in or out. To make up for those deficiencies, I handled the transit gently and kept compensating the level screws as the work progressed.

My strategy got us through the first setup in fair time without the whole crew standing around commiserating or ranking me too much. As the chaining crew took off, putting in the survey stakes every twenty-five feet and carefully measuring every hundred-foot station, I gave line to the head chainman with voice signals. My job was to keep the survey stakes on the calculated line. As they got farther away, beyond the reach of my voice, I shifted to arm signals that showed the head chainman the direction and, hopefully, the distance he had to move the range pole to get it on line. My signals included a little quick move of the right hand for a small move to the right and a big, slow move of the arm if he needed to move a longer distance. The chainman read my hand signals and set the range pole on line as if he, too, were looking through the telescope. That precise communication meant that I was over my first hurdle. It was a good feeling to find a head chainman who moved as precisely as if we had worked together for years; his expertise hastened my acceptance by the other workers.

After proving myself to a new crew and a new boss, the highlight of my surveying experience in Montana was the job of finding control points on approximately fourteen miles of an old survey that had been run fourteen years earlier. That assignment was especially notable because there was no evidence of the old line to be seen above ground. With the help of the original notes, we had to dig as much as six inches into the ground to find remnants or signs of the old line. Besides the digging for old clues, we faced the bitter cold and deep snow of a Montana winter in the high country not far from the Continental Divide.

The first day on the job introduced us to both the difficulty of finding the old points and the inhospitable winter weather. We had two control points in the little town of Ovando, about one hour's drive from Lincoln. According to the original notes, all we had to do was to extend that line about a quarter of a mile up a slight grade and we would find an iron pin buried in the old road. We chained the quarter-mile in a frigid wind that was nearly more than we could take—and found nothing. That was a discouraging day. We would not be able to find the rest of the line unless we started our next course on the same spot as the original survey. All we had to show for the day's work was the experience of facing cold weather.

The success or failure of recovering fourteen miles of completed roadway plans hinged on locating the old line in the field, so I racked my brain for a solution. If we had made a mistake in chaining up the long grade, then we would be digging in the wrong place. In order to settle that question, we chained up the road again the next day as carefully and precisely as possible. All that was to no avail, because we came out in the same place we had dug before.

I tried another tactic—to put myself in the position of the crew that did the original survey. Years before, as the head chainman in northern Idaho, we did not chain as precisely as we were doing now. Instead of checking the chain with a hand level, we would eyeball it or guess whether it was level. That gave me the idea of chaining up the old road again without properly compensating for the slope of the hill. I walked up the long hill and tried to visualize how it might have been done twenty years earlier—with a boss wanting to know why we didn't do a mile or two each day. Rather than break chain every thirty or forty feet, my scheme was to ask the rear chainman to hold as high as he could and I would pull out the whole hundred feet and call it good. The men chained up the hill with that procedure, which brought us to a point about four or five feet shorter. We dug there and presto! we found the old control point. That was a very rewarding experience for the whole crew, and it gave us a start on the fourteen miles of lost line.

Over the years, cattle, people, and the elements, or soil bacteria, had combined to destroy the survey stakes, so we had to develop a procedure to find clues that might indicate where they had been. Our key tools turned out to be a Pulaski (a tool something like a carpenter's adz on one side and an ax blade on the other used for firefighting) and a whisk broom. With the blade we chiseled off thin slices of dirt, and with the whisk broom we cleaned off the chiseled surface.

Before long every member of the crew was trying to be the first to find a clue as to where the stakes had been set. Sometimes a remnant of the bottom of a stake would show up, but usually we had to chisel away two or three layers of topsoil to get below the surface bacteria before we found anything. As the digging got deeper, everyone played detective or archaeologist, hoping to find any sort of clue. One of the crew spotted a distinct hole in the frozen ground the size of a survey stake. That was a beautiful sight and all we needed. We put in a new stake, placed a tack in the middle of it, set up the transit, and turned an angle onto the forward bearing and took off again, measuring along for the next control point. Finding the next intersection was the real proof that the frozen hole was the location of the old control point. At one key control point two or three inches below the surface, we found a column of sawdust in the shape of a survey stake. That was good enough; a new stake fit into the hole; we tacked it and went on with our work.

Our best piece of archaeological work took place near the end of the job. At one point we were unable to find any sign of a hub or any evidence that one had been there. As we planed off deeper slices of earth, we uncovered a large flat rock with still no signs of the old survey. However, on closer examination, we noticed a hole in the center of the buried rock, and there were pie-shaped or radial cracks running from the center to the outside. We deduced that it was possible that the survey crew had driven a frost pin into the rock as they worked at making a hole for the stake. We took a chance on that idea and drove in a new hub in the hole in the rock, turned the angle and anxiously headed for the next control point, which would be the proof that our theory was correct. Sure enough, we found the next point and proved that our deduction about the cracked rock was correct.

On most of the jobs that I worked on, especially those in the high country of Montana, Idaho, Washington, and Oregon, there came a time when the fieldwork stopped because of extreme cold or deep snow. Thus, as the snow began to pile up and the temperature was consistently below zero, I asked the boss what he wanted me to do about working through the worsening weather. He wanted us to drive down to the canyon every morning and see how bad the weather was. If we could stand it, he wanted us to work, but he added, "If it is too cold for the men to work, I don't want you to build a fire and sit around it all day or to stay in the truck. I want you to drive back to the office and I'll find something for the men to do."

We carried out those guidelines all winter long. Day after day the temperature was in the range of twenty below zero, but every day we got in the truck and headed down the canyon. Besides the deep blanket of snow, the high-country weather meant that the ground was frozen iron hard. Penetrating the hard ground for hubs and witness stakes was a most challenging job. Even with heavy sledgehammers and tool-steel frost pins, it took a lot of precise hammering to inch through the frozen earth. The crew accepted the challenge and took turns sledging on the frost pins. At each control point we left four witness stakes driven so deep into the frozen ground that they could not be dislodged, even if the tops were broken off. I was especially proud of the way the crew

12. Norm Best with transit, Lincoln, Montana. Courtesy of the author.

responded to the challenges of that bitter winter by leaving a durable record of work.

As for cold-weather clothing, it was every man for himself. I got my first pair of insulated boots through a local grocery-store owner who drove a stage to Helena to pick up mail and supplies. For fifty cents he would do shopping for the Lincoln people. My feet were never cold after the boots arrived. Our landlord gave me a surplus army parka, which put me in good shape for the sub-zero temperatures that we confronted through January, February, and March. I remember that it was forty below zero on the twenty-fifth of March that year. The flu kept me home that week and the crew stayed in the office, so thankfully we all missed that frigid weather.

One day the snowdrifts were so deep across Kleindschmidt's Flats that we didn't get to the job until nearly noon. Because of the storm, the driver pulled in to a little grocery store with a lunch counter, where we had a bowl of soup. I didn't want to get stuck in the snow late in the day, so we waited there for the state snowplow and followed it back across the flats to the mouth of Blackfoot Canyon, where we turned off and headed for Lincoln. That day we didn't do any surveying because it took the whole day to get to the job and back to Lincoln. On another occasion the snowdrifts in the canyon were so deep that we couldn't get through. But with those few exceptions, we faced the bitter cold and deep snow for about two months and worked at surveying and locating the control points.

Anytime we were passing a cattle ranch in those remote areas, the people usually came out and visited for a minute or so. Once, down on Kleindschmidt's Flats, a woman asked us where we stayed at night. When we told her that we drove back and forth from Lincoln, she was shocked. Though she had never seen any of us before, she volunteered the hospitality of her home to the whole crew. "If a northeaster comes up anytime you are working around here, you men come and spend the night with us," she said. That was a good indication of the respect that local people had for a Montana high-country winter.

My fellow workers at Lincoln were a mixed crew, comprised mainly of local people, inexperienced at surveying, but seasoned at working and facing Montana's bitter winters. Every man responded well to the challenge of finding clues for the lost line and toughing it out through the winter. I am proud to have worked with those men, each of whom contributed to our success. Experiences like that renewed my confidence in the ability of people to meet challenge and opportunity and to work on solutions with their own talents.

*

The working year for 1954–55 at Lincoln was interesting, my relations with the boss and the crew were good, and my health was excellent. All of those things turned sour during the season of 1955–56 at Philipsburg, Montana.

We couldn't stay in Lincoln for another year because our older son, Michael, was ready for high school. Lincoln was too small to support a school, and it was too far away to bus students across the mountains to towns with high schools. The usual practice for Lincoln students was to board in Helena or Augusta on the east side of the mountains. We didn't want Mike to do that, so I told my boss that we needed to be in a community large enough to have a high school. The district engineer was very cooperative and arranged for a transfer to Philipsburg, a town of more than a thousand people and a high school. He said I would be my own boss. Although it did not make me a full-fledged engineer, it did mean a promotion to acting resident engineer. The only thing that turned out according to plan was that Mike did get a year of high school and was able to live at home.

At that time the state of Montana didn't pay moving expenses, so we pulled a trailer loaded with our possessions behind the family car. With only two days off for the move, most of the actual moving took place on weekends and after work. When I finally started the survey for the proposed new construction, one thing after another went wrong. The fine young man who had been head chainman on that first day at Lincoln had moved to Philipsburg but decided to return to Lincoln. The next-most-experienced man on the crew wanted to live with some friends in an isolated area, where he was often snowbound and unable to get to work. The other chainman's only qualifications, at least that I could determine, was that his mother ran a restaurant that the district engineer patronized. That form of patronage would have been all right, but he didn't appear to have any interest in learning the techniques or the art of surveying. In order to compensate for the lack of personnel, I pushed myself hard, hoping to make a half-decent showing.

When we got far enough along to set slope stakes for the contractor, I discovered that the right-of-way shown on the plans was not wide enough to allow the new road to be built without encroaching on some of the ranchers' irrigation ditches and watering facilities. That stopped the job, because no contract could be let until the state made arrangements with the ranchers for the right-of-way and for rebuilding the irrigation ditches and water facilities. Those developments left me sitting in Philipsburg without a project, and my crew was melting away. There was another resident engineer there, so the district boss told me to help him until they got my job straightened out. Because of all the accumulated frustrations, I came down with the flu.

After a week or so I returned to work with the understanding that my assignment would be in the office for a while. But instead of giving me a chance to recuperate at the drafting table, the boss sent me out on a small construction job. I still wasn't feeling well but didn't know what the trouble was. After a visit to the doctor, he sent me home with orders to stay in bed for thirty days because he was concerned with my general health. Eventually I got back to work but was unable to handle anything out in the field; as a result, the rest of the winter was spent in the office trying to recuperate.

While working for the resident engineer in Wallace, I had learned the best procedures for building a map and calculating the latitudes and departures of the survey line. That was a challenging task and it gave me pleasure to do it. The only unusual feature of that winter's activity was my work in observing the star Polaris and in my hour-angle calculations to determine a true bearing for the field crew. That was difficult because my prescription medicine left me quite woozy. That was the only time that I took a bearing from a star. Making that observation on Polaris was the one redeeming feature of the year's work in Philipsburg.

When spring came, the boss assigned me to one of the elementary jobs on the survey crew while he and one of the pets did the work that I was classified for. Actually, he did me a favor. My immediate concern was that carrying the rod for the young man running the level might be too much walking for me. But the terrain was gentle and the combination of sun, fresh air, and the easy walking was good therapy and helped me out of a winter of debilitating poor health and office routine. Still, the walking was an effort, but the novice running the level had a hard time focusing the high-powered telescope on the level. That gave me a restful pause waiting for him to read the rod. By noon of the first day it became apparent that I would be able to hack the outdoors and to regain some strength. That was a great moment for me. The worst of the long, rough winter was over; spring had come and I was fit enough for the lowest job they could assign me. That was the highlight of my Philipsburg work.

As the summer progressed my convalescence was the only part of the work that was good. We had two small construction jobs. The supervision of the work was flawed and made me ashamed. And the crew was too irresponsible for me to accept as long-term fellow workers. Those jobs reminded me of the City Garage in Coeur d'Alene years earlier in that I learned how *not* to build roads rather than how to turn out quality work.

An unfortunate example of that took place on a back-country road a few miles south and west of Philipsburg. The plans called for hauling solid rock from a big cut up a steep hill to build a stable roadway embankment. The contractor didn't like the long, slow haul up the hill, even though he had signed his name and furnished a bond to the state as a pledge that he would construct the road according to the plans. In one flagrant violation, the resident engineer allowed the contractor to use inferior black garden dirt to take the place of the stable rock. That violation gave the public an unstable and muddy road that will continue to plague the driving public and maintenance crews as long as it exists. It might even be washed out some dark, stormy night.

That situation was not a case of graft or corruption. The only thing the resident engineer got from the contractor was acceptance as a good guy, a reasonable engineer, or a smile instead of a bitter glance. In order to protect the public, an engineer or inspector must have what it takes to stand up to the contractor, even if it means being labeled as unreasonable or tough by the construction fraternity.

On another construction project, the resident engineer put in a new and larger culvert to carry irrigation water to an adjoining field. He and the design team ignored the significance of the height of the old culvert and lowered the water-flow line of the new one a couple of feet. They didn't understand—or didn't care—that the lowered culvert meant that the farmer would not be able to get the water high enough to irrigate several acres of nearby land. By lowering the flow line of the new culvert, they were, in effect, stealing the use of fifteen or twenty acres of farmland. They could have designed the new highway grade to accommodate a larger pipe and could still have kept the water high enough for the farmer's use. Even after the farmer complained they didn't seem to understand the enormity of their mistake; instead, they indulged in ridicule.

The flawed design and construction of that culvert taught me a good lesson. Years later it was my responsibility to design culverts, siphons, and irrigation ditches on the Interstate Highway System west of Ellensburg, Washington. On every design it was necessary to consult with the local farmers and to ask them to show me how their irrigation system worked. Then I drafted plans that would fit the highway's needs and that would also efficiently irrigate the farmers' fields. That is the essence of a good design. Seeing it ignored at Philipsburg was a powerful lesson for me.

Late in the summer after we had finished the two small construction jobs, we were sent to the village of Helmsville, about fifty or sixty miles from Philipsburg, to stake six miles of new road (map 6). We were supposed to stay near the job site in a couple of motels, but the rest of the crew decided that they would rather commute from Philipsburg and use the per diem money to pay for car expenses.

That turned out to be a nightmare for me. The crew was a close-knit gang of hot-rod car buffs and the two youngest men were the wildest drivers I have ever had the misfortune to ride with. The man who drove most of the time had a worn-out Lincoln that shimmied on the old road. He drove ninety miles an hour on a narrow road that had been designed for safe driving at thirty-five miles an hour. Because we were on state business, it was my opinion that the resident engineer was responsible for the safety of the crew. But when I protested about the excessive speed, he didn't feel there was anything wrong with the reckless driving.

On the way home one night the situation got to be too much for me. When my protest didn't do any good, it seemed to me that the only way to get them to stop was to offer to buy a drink at the next tavern. When we pulled into the joint, I got out of the car and told them to go on, that I had had enough of that kind of driving. I went into the bar and called my wife and asked her to come and get me. The next day, the boss gave me a stumbling apology for the excessive speed. That cooled it for a few days, but as the summer wore on it was apparent that I was stuck on those little back-country jobs.

Because I was a new man with little seniority, there seemed little chance for improvement. Moreover, Montana also presented special problems for people with families. Because the state is so large and sparsely settled, construction jobs are usually distributed as widely as possible throughout the state. That means jobs may be miles apart from one year to the next, which means a lot of moving around. With two daughters and a son in school, that was not a good situation for us. I began to send résumés to West Coast states looking for a location with a lot of heavy construction in one area. I got a solid offer of a permanent job in New Mexico and a conditional offer—dependent on my passing the highway engineer's exam—from California and Oregon.

The job I finally took didn't come from those résumés. It happened by chance or a fortuitous incident one day in the survey truck. A young man on the crew had a clipping from a Missoula newspaper, an ad from the Washington State Highway Department, offering jobs for highway engineers. The young man said, "Look at this. I'm going to get a job in the state of Washington." I said to him, "Give me that clipping. You aren't going anywhere, but I am." And I did. Even though it took me some time to complete the process of negotiating for a new job, I was able to take advantage of that news clipping.

eleven

The Big Job

Quitting the Montana job and starting all over again made me nervous. The bad year in Philipsburg had shaken my confidence, but Catherine and I decided to drive to Yakima, Washington, to talk to the district engineer about a job.

The personnel director of the Washington State Highway Department had offered me a job as a junior highway engineer. I assumed that his description meant what the word implied, but the district engineer in Yakima told me that it was merely the personnel director's language for transitman. However, the district head added that my qualifications were equal to those of an assistant highway engineer, which meant a field-party crew chief. That classification would have made me happy, but the district engineer said the department didn't hire at that position. That was a major disappointment and caused me to consider returning to Montana. But the district engineer seemed sympathetic to my plight and advised me to stop in Ellensburg and talk to M. D. McMahan, the resident engineer, if I changed my mind. I followed his advice and went to see McMahan and everything turned around 180 degrees.

Sometimes there is instantaneous rapport between two people with similar backgrounds, professions, or crafts. It was that way between Mac and me when we met for the first time. Here was a man I wanted to work for and he was pleased at the prospect of having me as his assistant and crew chief, regardless of the payroll designation. He assured me that there would be no one between us and that he would get my payroll title raised to that of his assistant. In the meantime, he appointed me as his assistant and chief of the survey crew.

With that settled, Mac told me about the impressive, challenging work we would be doing on the mainline Interstate Highway System. As Mac explained it, when he had the choice, he had asked to be assigned to the location and design phase of highway engineering. As a result of that decision, he had avoided the problem of getting along with the contractors on the construction phase. That was all right with me. There was lots of heavy highway work within easy driving distance from Ellensburg, and that was what I was looking for (map 7). Another advantage to being in Ellensburg was the state college, where the family could go to school on a small budget.

Still, it was not easy to quit an existing job and take the children out of school and to move five hundred miles to a new position, a new town, and new schools. If my work had been on a big, steady job in Montana for a top engineer like Kenny Lawrence, C. R. Short, Hugh Cochrane, or Chet Adams, I would never have left Montana. I am fortunate in a way that things at Philipsburg turned out poorly. That helped me get to Washington and a better future for all of us.

*

The job at Ellensburg was better than I had even hoped for. The school system was fine; Central Washington State College was only a block from our home; and there were miles of roads to be located, designed, and built—eighty miles of them through Snoqualmie Pass and eastward to the Columbia River. It was a privilege to be part of that big construction program and to associate with the many fine construction workers and engineers who built that highway system.

My first day on the job was October 1, 1956, and my initial task was to work on a contour map projecting the detailed location of the Interstate Highway in the Upper Yakima River Canyon west of Ellensburg (map 8). That is a difficult section of the Interstate 90 system. The sides of Yakima Canyon were so steep that the highway had to be carved out of the hillsides, and there was little room by the river because the mainline of the Burlington Northern Railroad claimed the north bank and the Chicago, Milwaukee, St. Paul and Pacific Railroad had laid track on the other side of the river. The Washington State Highway Department was trying to lay out a four-lane highway in the space remaining on the high, steep slopes above the river and the two railroads. My job was to find a place on the steep hillsides where it would be feasible to build a modern road.

My only introduction to the job had been a morning's ride over the route with Mac. He had driven along the existing narrow canyon road, pointing out places where he thought the Interstate could be built. When we got back to the office, he handed me a heavy book on the geometric standards of the Interstate Highway System and laid down the big roll of contour maps with the admonition that I could lay any line on those maps that I had guts enough to defend. With those words he went into his office to work on the details of another big job.

The brevity of those fast-moving events amazed me, because here I was doing the work of a senior location engineer my first day on the job. It was just me against the steep, rough Yakima River Canyon with the curving contour lines of the Aero Service map as my guide. Somewhere among those contours I had to find the best place to carve out four twelve-foot lanes for a seventy-mile-per-hour highway.

My previous location and construction work with experienced locators like Hugh Cochran, C. V. Adams, C. R. Short, C. V. Chamberlain, and Sam Johnson was immensely helpful. With those resources and a lot of apprehension, it was good to wade into the task. Although there was little time to savor the prestigious assignment, I was happy with those developments. After the ignominy of being fired at Wallace and the flawed back-country work at Philipsburg, the Yakima assignment gave me a feeling of buoyancy.

McMahan had a professional office engineer and a competent crew working on detailed plans on some big jobs farther up the mountain towards Snoqualmie Pass. The office engineer was a prewar Regular Army veteran who had done mapping in many faraway places. I soon learned that he was a dedicated union man, an extra bonus for me.

During the winter and part of the spring I worked on the contour maps. By the summer of 1957 my work of mapping Interstate 90 from Teanaway Junction near the small town of Cle Elum to the open country west of Ellensburg was completed. As a consequence, Mac put me in charge of the survey crew to locate and stake the line that I had developed on the maps.

Staking the centerline of the proposed Interstate Highway was a far cry from running a line in the back country of Montana. On the Washington job almost all of the line was close to—or on—existing U.S. 10 from Seattle to Spokane. Working safely around all of that traffic was a constant and hazardous problem. Because the safety of the crew was my first responsibility, I used all my resources to develop and maintain proper working procedures. The heavy traffic on the existing road, and the rough terrain, made for slow progress, but we kept plugging away at putting in secure stakes every fifty feet along the centerline for the new highway. After almost a year's work we had placed the centerline stakes to a point about eight miles west of Ellensburg. We were quite proud of our effort, because we had traversed the steep slopes of the Upper Yakima River Canyon and the rough country at the mouth of Swauk Creek and Hayward Hill. The only easy going lay between us and Ellensburg.

While we were savoring that accomplishment, we got orders to go over to the Thorp Prairie region, the route of one of the old pioneer wagon roads, and put some horizontal and vertical controls on reconnaissance photographs. Those orders meant that the selection of the Yakima River route was being questioned after years of work and thousands of dollars had been invested. Everything was highball on that job, because construction on I–90 via the river route was being held up until a quickie, shotgun estimate could be completed on the Thorp Prairie proposal. We liked the excitement, the importance, and the attention being paid to our rush job.

A few weeks after we finished the fieldwork, word came from Olympia that the Thorp Prairie route had been chosen for the mainline Interstate Highway system. That decision meant a whole new ball game. With three or four years' work abandoned, the administration of the Washington State Highway Department needed new maps in a hurry, and it was our job to produce them. McMahan was responsible for locating the highway on the new route, and as his assistant, I was in charge of all the fieldwork. Our job was to produce precise contour maps of all the rough terrain for Thorp Prairie; a lot of people were waiting for them.

We would not have the benefit of the fine photogrammetric maps or the control points that had been set along the river route. In order to complete a contour map covering that rough country, it was necessary to measure out a preliminary line very accurately. That is the baseline for a contour map. Once that is determined, levels are run over the line to show the elevation of the ground along the route. The contour map is drawn in the field by measuring the distance to the right or left of the map baseline on every five-foot change in elevation. In other words, the location of every five-foot change in ground elevation is shown on the map. That is done for a distance of several hundred feet on both sides of the baseline. To do that on the ground for twelve to fifteen miles on rough terrain is quite a lengthy project, but it is necessary if circumstances do not permit making a map by aerial photogrammetric procedures.

When the contour map is completed, the location engineer—in this case McMahan—has to develop the L, or location, line. That line is the culmination of years of work. It represents the collectively approved location of the center of the highway that is soon to be built. The L line is staked in the field with substantial, secure stakes so that a new process of running line, running levels, and cross-sectioning the side slopes is started all over again. Before plans, specifications, and estimates can be made up for purposes of bidding, all the details of the terrain have to be shown on the blueprints so that the contractor will have detailed drawings of all the work that has to be done to convert the hillsides to a modern highway.

We were now starting our third or fourth line from Cle Elum towards Ellensburg, but that was the one that would count. This time we started a mile or so west of Cle Elum and worked towards Ellensburg. On most of that route there were two L lines because the eastbound and westbound lanes were to be independent of each other. They would be in the same vicinity, but each one would have its own independent, separate alignment and geometry designed to fit into the existing terrain with as little destruction of the landscape as possible. It took years of work through rotating seasons to complete all the staking, mapping, and measuring. I was responsible for its progress and accuracy. If the contractor found during construction that the terrain was not exactly as shown on the maps with their profiles and cross sections, he would be able to file a claim for extra expenses. For that reason, the fieldwork had to be like Caesar's wife: above reproach. Yet, because so much time had been wasted on designing and staking the Yakima River route, there was a lot of pressure from headquarters to get our work done.

We had a top-notch crew of experienced young men who worked summers and winters on the project for two or three years. I gave them the benefit of my experience with top engineers in Idaho, Oregon, and Montana, and we gradually developed routines, skills, and confidence as we worked through all kinds of weather and terrain. Through that process, the young men learned to master the craft and to assimilate the skills passed on to them. It was an awkward feeling when I realized that they didn't need me anymore. Now they were doing the work, applying their own skills and ingenuity, and, in some cases, developing ideas and techniques of their own. They became masters of the engineering equipment and the terrain. As they went about their task, their abilities were catching up with or surpassing mine.

Because there was lots of work in the office where Mac toiled at the projection table by himself, I talked it over with the crew and then offered to help in the office. He was glad to have my assistance. I told the crew—Harold Porter, Don Morfield, Cecille Gillette, and Norm Martin—that the fieldwork was up to them, and joined Mac at the projection table as he developed the line that represents today's highway.

That was another good experience, because I had an opportunity to watch Mac as he tried line after line through the curving contours. His patience was amazing. When he had a line that looked good to me, many times he would abandon it and try for something better. His patience and sensitive skill has paid off for millions of drivers who use the highway between Ellensburg and Seattle. He chose a route that presents an ever-changing view as the road crests several hills and glides through the country with relatively little disturbance to the natural beauty of the landscape. Mac had few peers at that art. He called it "going with the country." Years later, when the route was built according to Mac's alignment, it won national honors for a safe, seventy-mile-an-hour highway that blended with and accented the natural beauty of the gently rolling hills. The highway did not slash through the country in what Mac called straight-edge location.

*

After Mac took me on that quick ride through the steep, narrow canyon of the Yakima River, I had a very pleasant experience getting acquainted with our office engineer, a veteran of the peace army of the early 1920s. There he had learned mapping techniques, from the most primitive to modern stereo-photography, the latter capable of producing a contour map from aerial photographs. He was a fine person to work with; the

years in the army had not eroded his sensitive concern for people. And, for a bonus, he was a union man, as was his assistant. So that put me back on a union job only four years after leaving the machinists' organization in Spokane in 1952. I was happy to join the crew and became a member of the International Federation of Professional and Technical Engineers, Local 17, AFL-CIO.

Local 17 was a statewide union of technical engineers. The larger geographic jurisdiction was necessary because there were so few of us in any given area. In order to give the widely dispersed membership a voice, local chapters were located where there were a dozen or more members in an area and an AFL-CIO Central Labor Council.

Although Ellensburg met those conditions, members who wanted to attend had to drive forty miles down the Yakima Canyon road to the meetings. In order to avoid that, I petitioned the regional executive board of Local 17 to authorize an Ellensburg chapter. The petition was granted, we organized a chapter, and from then on we had union meetings in Ellensburg. In small organizations like ours, the election process for officers and delegates is usually a question of finding someone who will accept the work. Having a chapter in Ellensburg also entitled us to a member on the regional executive board. That person had the privilege of driving after work to and from Seattle four times a year in order to attend an all-day meeting of the regional executive board, the governing body for our statewide local.

Through my interest in the union and through the default of others, I became the regional executive board member for the Ellensburg chapter. There were delegates from all the major cities of the state of Washington at those meetings. I began to learn about how work was accomplished in a large, mostly public employees' union.

Local 17 lacked the broad social concerns of the San Francisco machinists' union. It also lacked the wide spectrum of interests that are an integral part of most groups of industrial workers, such as we had at the Trentwood rolling mill. In Local 86 of the machinists' union in Spokane, the heavy-duty, long-haul freight mechanics never failed to send money and support to most any union asking for help. But the narrowness of the highway engineers tended toward a parochial view of the world, focused only on their own day-to-day problems. That narrowness disturbed me, and I was unable to broaden their perspective very much. Yet the technical engineers were a union, and that meant a lot to me.

Much of the narrowness of the technical engineers had to do with their work relationships with other crafts and among themselves. The old-line craft unions dominate highway and bridge construction jobs and have their own building and construction trade councils. Because they are the best organized, the best paid, and the most adequately represented, they have become an aristocracy within the labor movement. The best known of the old craft unions are the carpenters, the cement finishers, and the operating engineers. The latter are the men who operate heavy equipment, such as power shovels, cranes, large tractors, and self-loading scrapers. Within each of those crafts, there is a lot of sharing.

But the technical engineers, in addition to being a small group of specialists, also have an internal hierarchy of job classifications. On the usual field crew, each person has a separate classification for the work, pay, and its perceived importance. Those job categories include flagperson, stake driver, rear chainman, head chainman, transitperson, and crew chief. The implementation of those hierarchical job classifications presents many personnel problems.

Fitting all those job categories to people is bad enough, but then comes the Civil Service Commission with a pencil and paper and a true-false test to measure a worker's qualifications for advancement in job and pay. The Civil Service test score takes precedence over the resident engineer's evaluation of the progress of the work being done by the field crew. As a result of those dual evaluations, it sometimes takes two people to accomplish the work assigned to one; it takes one who is qualified by Civil Service to get the higher pay, and another who can do the work but did not meet the Civil Service test requirement.

Unsolvable grievances like those made the union business agents old before their time. In the sixteen years I was in Local 17, three business agents wore themselves out on the job. The first one, who organized and built Local 17, lasted for quite a while until he just petered out on the job. The regional executive board didn't want to fire him, so it lowered the retirement age and let him go. The next business agent had a lot of talent and lasted about five years. But when the pressure in the union built up, he quit and went to work as the labor-relations boss for the county. Another agent began to resent the members' militant stand on their grievances. Before long he resigned and sought gentler and more satisfying work.

With simpler problems, however, the union made a lot of progress. For instance, for one six-month period our crew in Ellensburg was assigned to a job at Pomeroy, Washington, two hundred miles away. The district engineer from Yakima told us that we had to get to Pomeroy by 8 A.M. every Monday morning and were not to leave there until 5 P.M. on Friday. That forced us to leave Ellensburg at 4 A.M. on Monday and drive to Pomeroy on our own time. The drive home on Friday also was on our own time. The district head outranked McMahan, our resident engineer, so we drove the two hundred miles to and from Pomeroy on our own time for six months.

Because the union examined standard procedures for other agencies and travel plans for administrators, we were able to prove that most administrators did their traveling during working hours whenever possible. Our union, therefore, stopped the practice and from then on we traveled on Highway Department time. That was a big victory, but it was the usual process for unions representing employees of public agencies.

Besides saving on travel time, one of the biggest accomplishments of the union was the implementation of seniority in determining transfers of people to distant locations. In my previous highway experience, I was unable to resist an order to move, sometimes several hundred miles, to a new job site. Just before my retirement, the Washington State Highway Department wanted to transfer a lot of people to a new job more than two hundred miles from Ellensburg. That would have meant a permanent transfer for my family, or living away from home and driving back and forth every weekend on my own time. Local 17 negotiated for those transfers to be made according to seniority. The district office wanted to move a person of my classification, but since there were younger men with less seniority, my boss simply asked: "You don't want to go to Clarkston, do you, Norm?" I answered no, and that was all there was to it. That right to refuse was great!

Another big accomplishment of the union was winning a good retirement plan. The lobbyist for the Washington state employees, supported by the state legislature, won that battle in the 1970s when the lawmakers approved a fine retirement program for themselves. For each year in the legislature, they set aside 3 percent of their salary for a pension with a maximum of twenty years' accumulation. That would allow legislators to retire at 60 percent of their salary. The lobbyist for the Washington Federation of State Employees supported the legislature's generous plan. The next year he organized a drive for a 2-percent-per-year pension plan for all state employees. The legislature was in no position to resist. That was a classic example of successful lobbying by the state employees' unions, as they asked for comparable pay and conditions already established for others.

In most of the day-to-day grievances each union has a good degree of autonomy. However, that autonomy is sacrificed when unions work through city, county, state, and national labor councils affiliated with the AFL-CIO. All of those labor councils are chartered by the president of the national AFL-CIO councils and are under his personal supervision.

In the archives of the University of Massachusetts at Amherst I read the minutes of the Massachusetts State Labor Council meetings and its correspondence with the AFL-CIO president, George Meany. That demonstrated how absolutely the president controls the state labor councils. In that instance, the Massachusetts State Labor Council passed a resolution instructing its delegates not to sign the ballots they cast in elections for state council officers. Meany ruled that the Massachusetts council should rescind that action because signing the ballots was required. Further, Meany's letter stated that if the Massachusetts council didn't comply, he would put it under receivership, appoint new officers, and have the vote rescinded.

That sordid picture of subverted democracy demonstrated again the way national labor organizations keep labor councils removed from the influence of rank-and-file workers who might want to implement industrial democracy. In other words, the same subversion of democracy that I experienced in both the steelworkers' union and with the head office of the International Association of Machinists is endemic in the national AFL-CIO.

I don't want to leave this discussion without reminding readers that on the local level all unions are enthusiastic followers of Jeffersonian democracy. It is only the pressure of big business—trying to protect its authority from workers—that encourages international and national unions to subvert democratic procedures in order to keep the troops under control.

*

One of my biggest assignments in highway engineering was completed in 1963. For seven years my days had been spent in the field surveying and mapping in a search for the best possible route for the new Interstate Highway through the eastern approaches to the Cascade Mountains. Now that fieldwork was over. There was a sense of euphoria over that accomplishment and also a sense of nostalgia in leaving the world of surveying.

In the mountains, surveying owes its challenge to the myriad problems that arise when you are trying to fit highways with long tangents or gentle curves into ever-changing hills, ravines, sharp ridges, and rolling slopes. We measure with a one-hundred-foot steel tape that has to be pulled up straight, taut, and level regardless of the deviations of the terrain. The transit also presents problems. That versatile instrument measures angles in degrees, minutes, and in some cases seconds, but it cannot see around or over hills or through brush or trees. All of the highway maps have horizontal angles and distances, so it is a continuing challenge to fit the straight horizontal geometry into the ever-changing terrain of the mountains and foothills. Each setup of the transit, each pull of the hundred-foot tape requires an accommodation to the curving and sloping hills. There are always brush and trees to cut down or triangulate around.

Besides all that, there are the changing seasons through summer, fall, winter, and spring. In rainy country like the Cascades, you can't stop working just because of the rain or you would never get anything done. In winter seasons it is necessary to spend time in the cold and the snow. In the heat of summer, work is done early and late, not through the worst of the heat. All those kaleidoscoping, ever-changing problems are what make a field man gradually fall in love with his work. In Idaho, in Oregon, and in Montana I served a long apprenticeship at the art of surveying. Here in Washington, a pull of the tape for whatever we could reach, a setup of the transit where the transitman could see only a few feet, or perhaps half a mile, that is what a day's work is all about. The days stretch into weeks, into months, and even years as you develop an affection for the job, the mountains, and the slow turning of the seasons. That was my working world for the first seven or eight years in Ellensburg.

*

In the summer of 1963 we finished all the field and office work required to locate the horizontal and vertical alignment for Interstate 90 on the fifty-mile stretch through Kittitas County. Instead of some nebulous idea, we now had maps showing the precise position of the proposed new highway. For seven years I had worked with McMahan on that major project, and it gave me a good feeling to realize that we had accomplished the first basic task. My only regret in moving on to the next phase—which consisted of the preparation of the plans, specifications, and contractor estimates—was that I would not be working with Mac.

Joe Aimone, a young engineer in charge of all the remaining design details, was my new boss. My assignment was to design the culverts on major segments of the highway. That required calculating the amount of water that would run off the hills traversed by the highway and designing a culvert that would pass that water under the Interstate in a dependable way to avoid flooding or washouts from the storms that sweep down from the mountains.

That was a whole new world for me. It was also the beginning of a new era of highway standards for the state of Washington. In an attempt to improve and standardize the design of culverts, the Highway Department had established elaborate criteria for designing drainage structures thirty-six inches in diameter or larger. Because of that, I was introduced to the science of hydrology: the study and determination of the amount of water that may intercept the highway from the drainage areas of the adjacent mountains, hills, valleys, and ravines. On major streams, government agencies have statistics on observed runoff from major floods and these can be used to project future floods. But for the smaller draws and ravines, there are usually no records.

Hydrology is not an exact science. It derives formulas from rainfall and snowmelt where weather records and runoff figures are available, and it applies them to similar adjacent areas. The state of Washington had approved runoff formulas, studies, and maps for the drainage areas from Cle Elum to Ellensburg. My first job was to make up small-scale maps of the major areas that drained across the highway and calculate the volume of water that might bear down on the roadway in the worst possibile conditions of rainfall and snowmelt for the next fifty years. It was fascinating work, but since the statistics were incomplete, wherever possible I tried to find people who might have personal experience or knowledge about high water in particular areas. From those observations and information about the dimensions of old culverts, I made calculations of the actual volume of floodwater runoff. That gave me a figure to use in verifying the official equations of the Washington State Highway Department.

The first big culverts, where the Interstate crossed the Chicago, Mil-

13. Norm Best at work on the hydraulic equations for Interstate 90, Ellensburg, Washington. Courtesy of the author.

waukee, St. Paul and Pacific Railroad, made the job very interesting. I came up with one estimate for high water from the Highway Department equations and another—three times as large—from an interview with the railroad roadmaster, who had observed the high-water mark at the railroad culvert some years before. That presented a dilemma, because I had two answers with a 300 percent difference between them.

The roadmaster's observations, I thought, were impeccable, so my formulas for calculating the volume of water that would pass through the culvert were very precise and reliable. My estimates were based on an observed runoff volume, one that in my view would be more reliable than the figure extrapolated from the approved runoff formulas furnished by the Highway Department. I prepared a large sheet with maps, calculations, and drawings to support both answers and a recommendation that the observed estimate be used. To my delight, the bridge department approved my recommended design for the big culvert.

I faced a similar experience at the mouth of Rocky Canyon, near Taneum Creek, where a local rancher had observed the flooding of the county-road culvert near his house. Using his observed flooding elevations, my calculations showed that seven times as much water had come down that canyon as was indicated in the approved hydrology formulas. I followed the same procedures as those used at the culvert by the railroad bridge and presented both sets of figures and a design for a big box culvert to handle the larger capacity. Again the bridge department approved the one based on my calculations, which took into consideration the rancher's observations.

For the remaining small culverts on that sixteen-mile stretch of highway, there were no observed runoff data, so I had to depend on hydrology equations that had been extrapolated from other data. Although it made me uneasy to trust the safety of the public to that sparse information, I did my best and those culverts have been handling the storms and spring runoffs with no problems.

Another part of the hydraulic work was to design the siphons, culverts, and ditches required to transport the local irrigation water safely and efficiently under the new highway. My confidence in the ranchers' knowledge about their own irrigation systems led me to consult them about how they wanted to irrigate after the new highway was built. With that background information, I was able to design new structures and ditches that met the ranch owners' needs. Combining my knowledge of the ranchers' practices and hydraulic theory enabled me to avoid the usual complaints from property owners about the way the new highway often interfered with their irrigation systems. The successful operation of those systems, coupled with the proven adequacy of the culverts, was and is a source of much personal satisfaction.

When I finished the hydraulic-design assignment, I realized that the location and design work on I–90 through Kittitas County was complete. Now it was time to bring all that effort to fruition through the actual construction process. To that end I now turned to laying out the culverts and bridges that we had dreamed about for ten years.

As we moved to the construction phase, I began working for Bob Patrick, a young resident engineer cast in the mold of Hugh Casey and a man who had mastered his own work and gave his men support and an opportunity to do theirs. He was in charge of several big construction jobs. Patrick assigned me to bridges where there had been problems in either the elevations or the layout. I had spent years resolving errors in the laying out of bridges and culverts, and while working for Patrick, it was possible to develop procedures that would help eliminate errors by exposing them before they were incorporated into the construction of a bridge. It is easy for a levelman to read the wrong mark on the rod, for the recorder to write down the wrong figure, for someone to make an error in addition or subtraction, or for a carelessly written number to look like another.

The contractors first task on bridges is to dig footings. Before the contractor shows up, the field crews run levels at the site and establish bench marks of proven elevation. Once that is done, they set stakes at the bridge site to show the contractor how deep to dig. Those first stakes do not have to be set to fine tolerances, but they have to be reliable and accurate within a required range. The contractor's crews then come in with their big machines and dig out the trenches or holes for the footings. When they have the excavation roughed out, the contractor sends for the engineering crew to set precise hubs showing the correct depth and dimension of the footings. Errors in the rough layout, or in the second, more precise one, don't happen very often. But when they do, they are very troublesome, so it is imperative to avoid those errors.

My system was simple and a little cumbersome. I established procedures for all calculations and readings to be written down so they could

14. Franklin Falls bridge, one mile west of Snoqualmie Pass, Washington, a seven-hundred-foot bridge spanning two avalanche courses and carrying westbound lanes of Interstate 90. Courtesy of Clyde and Doris West.

be checked by a second person. All level readings were checked by a different member of the crew and all of that information was systematized through a big operational chart. It sounds rather complicated, but once I had the charts and forms photocopied and on hand for each job, the plan worked out nicely. Contractors and project engineers began to notice the improved reliability of our work, and they began to ask for our crews on responsible and troublesome projects.

The peak of my construction layout work came when Patrick assigned me to the Franklin Falls bridge on the west side of Snoqualmie Pass (map 7). Today, it is a big steel bridge that spans two avalanche courses through very rough terrain. He gave me the choice of any of our field men for the crew and urged me to be careful and to see that no one got hurt. He showed me the plans for the bridge, and they were impressive. There were two steel spans, each 350 feet long. We talked over the personnel for a few minutes, Patrick handed me the fat roll of blueprints, and it was off to a job that was worthy of capping thirty years of highway work. After I left Patrick's office, he never monitored or even mentioned the project. That was his style. He didn't need to remind me that it was imperative that we locate the piers and abutments precisely so that the long, massive steel girders would fit.

In a few days Patrick's assistant, Bill Briggs, and the bridge inspector, John Wines, took me out to the site. The view from the east abutment was impressive, because we were not far from the summit of Snoqualmie Pass. Ahead and a little to the left lay the deep valley of the South Fork of the Snoqualmie River. Directly to the west were the deep ravines of the two avalanche courses, and a little to the right stood a big rock massif towering hundreds of feet into the sky.

In all of my working years—in the Cascade Mountains in Oregon, the Rocky Mountains in Montana, and the foothills of Idaho—this was the most impressive job site I had ever worked on. The country fell away so fast to the left and rose so high on the right that the heights gave one an eerie feeling.

It was easy to choose personnel for the job, because Patrick had about fifty good men working for him. I chose a young graduate engineer to do the transit work and a young man who had worked for me on the Menastash Ridge job to be the head chainman. Two others, one from Walla Walla and one from Odessa, filled out the crew. Our first job was to calibrate our one hundred- and three-hundred-foot steel tapes. To do that, we obtained a special hundred-foot tape from the district office in Yakima that had been calibrated by the U.S. Bureau of Standards. The tape had a note with it from the bureau telling us how many pounds of pull was required to produce an accurate measurement at certain temperatures. With that for our standard, we set some points on level ground near Cle Elum and used those points to calibrate our own tapes. After a day or two at that work, we were ready to head for Franklin Falls and tackle the job of traversing the avalanche courses and measuring out the actual location for the two abutments and the center pier for the bridge.

Each time we arrived at the bridge site it was nice to savor for a moment the awesome view of the landscape. The face of the rock massif looked like Rocky Mountain goat country. One day the crew pointed out an adult goat grazing along a narrow ledge of that immense rock. When we turned the transit on the goat, we could see the muscles ripple under its white fur as it moved along the high, narrow ledge. That was a beautiful introduction to our job; we were all impressed with the way the agile goat made its way along the ledge, finding summer grass here and there. Somehow that view of our high-country companion seemed like a good omen for the project.

The main purpose of our work on the bridge was to set control points on both sides of each abutment and pier so that it would be easy for construction crews to show the contractor where the footings should be placed. When all the concrete was built up, the piers would be in the proper spot to receive the long steel girders that were being fabricated in some faraway steelyard. It was imperative that all the reference points correspond to the length of the steel girders when they were set on the piers. On level or gentle ground that is a simple, though important task, but on that job we had to drag our long steel tapes out over the precipitous avalanche courses and find places where the transit could be set up to measure the steep angles and the slope distances. With that data we would be able to calculate the horizontal distance we had traversed for each setup and thus would continue along until we had found the location for the center pier. I kept the notes in a bound transit book, and the transitman doubled his angles in order to eliminate casual errors as the chainman carefully read the tapes and called out the distances.

We worked on that job before the magic of the little shirt-pocket calculators; therefore, all of the slope distances had to be reduced to horizontal measurements by longhand arithmetic and trigonometry. Everybody took turns looking up the trig functions and doing the involved arithmetic as we looked for corroborating answers. It would have been easy to make those reductions in the office, but because it was so slow and tedious to get in and out of the steep terrain, it was more efficient to do the longhand calculations right there on the job.

Patrick was concerned about the safety of the crew—especially where we had to traverse the remaining ice bridges—so I bought three hundred feet of three-quarter-inch rope. The east abutment was on high, gently sloping ground, and we secured one end of the rope to a tree and pulled it over the steep slopes and sharp ridges to use as an aid in traveling back and forth. The young crewmen got over the rough ground a bit like the goats above us, but it was all I could do to make one trip a day along the centerline of the bridge site and then crawl back up the steep slopes at quitting time. There was no easy way out of the deep courses cut by the avalanche. Ahead were the long talus slopes toward Denny Creek. Below was the South Fork of the Snoqualmie River, which was too deep and fast to wade; thus, it was down in the morning and up in the afternoon. Each of those trips tried my physical resources, but doing reliable work that conformed to the planned dimensions was my central concern.

It took a myriad of readings and calculations to accumulate the seven hundred feet of horizontal distance over the up-and-down world of the bridge site. Because reliability was the name of the game, I never pushed anyone. After we had carefully located the centerline of the two abutments and the center pier, I turned the job over to the crew and had them repeat the measurements using different intermediate points. The transitman and the crew responded beautifully and came up with the same locations for the bridge foundations, so we had done all we could to verify our data. It would take two more years of work to dig the foundations and to build the high pier and abutments before the fitting of the steel would prove out our calculations for sure.

It was customary to bring in a special crew with electronic gear to measure the seven hundred feet to verify the accuracy of our work. That verification was tried at Franklin Falls, but the electronic machine required a clear line of sight through the length of the bridge. On that project, unobstructed vision was impossible because of the trees, brush, and the roughness of the terrain, so they were unable to do the check. That was disappointing. It would have been better if the department had sent in another crew with conventional transit and chain to check us out, a procedure that is done on major bridge jobs. Only the verification of a second crew would have settled questions about accuracy. But at Franklin Falls, the proof of our complex pudding was left until the contractor got the piers out of the ground far enough for the electronic machines to take a reading across the site. The real satisfaction from our work would come only when the contractor set the massive steel beams in place and they fit.

When the contractors began working on the job, my work brought me by Franklin Falls occasionally, but my day-to-day assignment was at another bridge about a half-mile away. That bridge, over the South Fork of the Snoqualmie River, was not as spectacular as the one at Franklin Falls, but the trigonometry and arithmetic of curves and angles were more intricate. I was crew chief on all the layout and stayed there for two construction seasons. That enabled me to be with the contractor, providing information whenever it was needed. It was good work. The site lacked the spectacular views of the Franklin Falls area, but it was gentler for me.

15. A reinforced-concrete bridge over the South Fork of the Upper Snoqualmie River, one-half mile west of Snoqualmie Pass on Interstate 90. Courtesy of Clyde and Doris West.

On the latter job I passed the magic age of threescore and five and still didn't feel the years. My goal still was to produce reliable layouts in an expeditious manner. I was especially pleased that the state of Washington had not tried to promote me to an administrative job. The real accolade of success came when Patrick or one of his young engineers assigned me to trouble spots. The two important bridge jobs were evidence of that. When my bosses looked to me to do the tough, responsible tasks, it gave me a good feeling. That was better than being promoted to administrative tasks or being pensioned off to some cushy site. Nothing is better for a person than to have an opportunity to do meaningful work. If anything, the feeling of being needed tastes even better when you are a little older.

*

One of the highlights for me was the exhilarating experience of taking part in the last day of work before the Cle Elum-Ellensburg-Vantage section of I–90 was opened to the public in the fall of 1968. Because I had been involved in most phases of the project since the reconnaisance and location work began in 1956, that was an especially notable day.

Even though we worked a fifteen-hour day, the extra hours all felt good.

That section of the highway was the long-awaited missing link, enabling traffic to avoid the long, narrow grade that climbed up from the

Columbia River at Vantage. The old two-lane road, used regularly by heavily loaded trucks that seemed barely to crawl up the hill, was the bane of tourists and local drivers. People became frustrated when they got caught behind one of the trucks, because it might mean miles of slowly moving traffic until an open stretch would allow a precarious, hurried opportunity to pass. Even then one might encounter another slow truck on one of those seemingly interminable curves. Because of that infamous grade, local people and the Highway Department were looking forward to opening up the new four-lane route that traversed Rye Grass Canyon with widely separated lanes. There were two eastbound lanes on the south side of the canyon and two westbound lanes some distance away to the north. With those separate two-lane highways, drivers would be able to pull out safely and pass the slow trucks without being concerned about a car coming at them from the opposite direction.

For me, the impending completion of the new highway was even more meaningful. Twelve years earlier it was only a dream, but we had worked hard to make that dream come true. I had been part of the project from the beginning, when we pored over contour maps and aerial photographs or walked through potential routes doing evaluation studies. After years of surveying, mapping, designing, and construction, the last twenty-eight-mile segment was approaching completion. And now, by chance, I had to work a fifteen-hour day on the last details that had to be completed before the highway was opened to the public. The opening ceremony was a big event for the Washington State Highway Department, and the agency was making a big public-relations splash with it. Because a popular cross-state football game between the University of Washington at Seattle and Washington State University was scheduled at Pullman, the department announced that the new highway would be open to handle the heavy traffic on the Friday before the game.

For reasons that slip my memory, I was out on the job with a small crew of construction workers installing Highway Department monument cases in big eighteen-inch holes. Everyone on the crew knew that our job had to be completed before the opening-day traffic came pouring through the next morning. At our regular quitting time, several miles of those big holes lacked monument cases, so there was nothing to do but stay with the job until it was finished. Only a few people remained: the concrete mixer's truck driver, a couple of the contractor's men, and I. None of the contractor's bosses were on the job. We couldn't leave to eat because we had green concrete in the truck, so at approximately seven or eight o'clock in the evening I drove to a nearby tavern and bought fried-chicken dinners and a six-pack of beer for the crew. The food and drink were most welcome and buoyed everyone's spirits. It was about midnight when we finished, but everybody was feeling great because we had completed the work.

For me that was an unusally good day, and the fifteen hours seemed to speed by. All of the men had responded beautifully to the challenge of finishing the task before we quit. Through that long night of working a double shift, I never heard a word of complaint. Because all the bosses had gone home for dinner and relaxation, the men were free to do a high-quality job of fitting the cases and the green concrete into the holes. When we left the job, we realized that we had done our part in getting the road ready for the opening-day ceremonies.

twelve

A Look Ahead with the Benefit of Hindsight

With the four lanes of I-90 open to traffic from Cle Elum to Vantage, the only work going on was the two bridges on the west side of Snoqualmie Pass. Winter comes early there. Bridge and road jobs are usually shut down in October or November. When the snow drove us off the Snoqualmie River bridge, my thoughts turned to getting out of Ellensburg. There was only one gap in my experience with highway construction and that was to work on a big-city freeway project. I thought it would be nice to return to Seattle, fifty miles to the west of the pass. From riding a bicycle and motorcycle for Western Union in the twenties to working on the layout on a big freeway job seemed to me to be a lot of progress. So, when the bridge work shut down, I volunteered for the freeway job east of Seattle on I-90. That is where I retired from highway work, having filled out my mountain experience in heavy construction with a big-city freeway project.

When my memory turns back to the big jobs and the heavy equipment that has taken the place of the horse outfits and all the hard work on the paving jobs, I have a strong feeling of sadness. But it is the pervasive and systemic corruption of the quality-control process by the big contractors that saddens me the most. But those problems of corruption in highway construction date back to my experiences in the early 1920s on a little road job at Fighting Creek in northern Idaho.

The Kootenai County project at Fighting Creek illustrates how road building with publicly employed construction workers can unite the need for a quality and economical highway with the construction workers' need to use their creative skills. Between 1928 and 1930 the Idaho Highway Department created a similar unity between the highway administration and the construction workers when they oiled the Fourth of July Canyon section of U.S. 10 between Coeur d'Alene and Kellogg. On those projects the entire construction program was under the direct control of the Highway Department administration.

That unity of administration was severed on the Santa job in 1931 when the construction work was awarded to a contractor. In that case the Jay Company submitted the lowest bid, accompanied by an acceptable financial bond that guaranteed completion of the work. But that created a duality of interest and authority. The state of Idaho needed a quality, year-around road in the Santa area, while the contractor had a compelling interest to get the road built as quickly as possible and make a profit. To the extent that the state hired its own engineers and inspectors to supervise the layout and the quality control of the work done by the contractor, it recognized that duality of interests.

Under the contract system, highway engineers lost direct control of the construction workers because the actual orders and the right to hire and fire the crew went to the contractor. The reality of the contractor's control of the work force in the interest of production for profit at the expense of quality created a conflict with the state engineers, whose duties and interests were to produce a high-quality road.

When I look back at years of work trying to build quality pavements under the contract system, it is obvious that quality was compromised on one job after another. That indiscriminate compromising of public-works projects illustrates the power of the contractor and the way society and our educational system have isolated professional engineers from the experience and knowledge that flows from the work process. That has allowed the contractor and his workers to become the sole custodians of the knowledge gained from the process and reality of work. Under the contract system, that knowledge is used to increase profits for the contractor rather than to build durable roads for the public.

During my stay in Ellensburg, I was at the center of many big highway-construction projects. Those jobs were built by contractors who were using state-of-the-art construction equipment. Being around those modern machines gave me an opportunity to compare them with the machines and technology used during my early years in the highway game. Perhaps the most sensational of the modern machines was the slip-form finishing machine, usually referred to as a slip-form paver.

Portland cement, usually called concrete pavement, has always been the most durable of roadbeds. It has additional values in visibility for night driving and good traction in the rain. But the finishing process is very difficult and fraught with hazards as the soft, green mix goes through a metamorphosis and becomes stone-hard concrete. During that process, the uncured mix has to be confined by heavy wooden or steel side forms. Installing those forms in the proper alignment and elevation is a time-consuming job. After the concrete has set up and gained some initial strength, the forms have to be removed, cleaned, and reset in front of the paving machine as the project slowly proceeds down the grade.

Sometime after the Second World War someone had the audacity to design and build a paver that would work without any of the cumbersome, time-consuming, and expensive side forms. That is why it was so revolutionary and why I was so excited about its potential. It was in the late 1950s when I first heard of the slip-form paver. It sounded like the perfect answer for quality-control inspectors, who dream of building concrete pavement without the contractor's continual pressure for mix that is compromised by too much water.

The slip-form paver is a big, powerful machine that can walk right through good-quality concrete that is not overwatered. In fact, the slip-form paver requires a mix that doesn't have too much water because it works without fixed side forms to confine the concrete while it cures. In other words, the mix cannot be overwatered or it will crumble away. In order to use the big, fast labor-saving paver, the contractor must let the state engineers design and produce a good, stiff mix.

When I got a chance to see the new paver in action, it was all that I had hoped for. Instead of a small machine riding on steel forms set to confine the green concrete mix until it cured, the slip-form paver was supported by large steel Caterpillar- and tank-style tracks. Those tracks had the solid support of the finished subgrade. The state materials division had produced high-quality aggregates, and the water-cement ratio was carefully controlled at a big central batching and mixing plant. The dump trucks were unloading a top-quality concrete mix, and the heavy, well-supported machine was working its way through the stuff.

When I went back to where the finishing was in progress, my elation turned to bitter disappointment. In the final finishing process, the machine being used behind the slip-form paver was spraying large amounts of water on the mix. Although most of the mix was still of high quality, the top wearing surface was being recklessly compromised by excessive amounts of water.

There were no state inspectors in the area where the all-important final finishing was in progress. The state personnel were busy up ahead of the paver taking samples of the green concrete mix. Those samples are cured and then sent to the state's testing laboratory to prove the quality of the mix. But those samples did not include the mix with the excessive water that was being added during the finishing process.

My thoughts turned to my first big four-lane paving job in 1938. The contractor on that job was J. H. Collins, whose work was 180 degrees different from the slip-form paving job. With Collins there were no machines to strike off, consolidate, or finish the concrete. All those steps were done by hand—the hands of proud journeymen finishers. Because the contractor was so dependent on the finishers, he deferred to their judgment. Under those conditions, the finishing crew wanted a mix that was sufficiently workable and cohesive to allow them to use their skill to produce a quality job. Because of their need as craftsmen to do good work, their objectives were similar to those of the Idaho Highway Department and the public. When the job was finished, all of us were proud of our work. We had produced a road that was so durable that it provided the public with years of comfortable and safe use.

Memory also takes me back to when a contractor purchased a small paving machine to consolidate and roughly finish the concrete. With that machine to do the rough work and an experienced crew to do the finishing, I expected another quality job. But only a few days into the project my fond hopes for good work were destroyed. The little machine was unable to make the speed that the contractor wanted, so he persuaded the resident engineer to allow enough water to make a wet, soupy mix so that his flimsy paving machine could make better time through the soft mix. Within two years that compromised pavement had to be patched over with asphalt.

With the advent of the finishing machine, the contractor lost his reliance on the cement finishers and those craftsmen lost control over the quality of the mix. Now the machine was in charge and the mix was designed to accelerate the contractor's ability to produce profits. That shift, away from the ethics of the craftsman and the needs of the public, took place forty years ago.

Today, the monstrously efficient machines that followed the little paving machine are still in charge. The slip-form paver requires a stiff, high-quality mix to begin, but then, in order to make good time, the contractor needs a lot of water so the machine operators spray on the water in the finishing process. That excess of water compromises the surface of the concrete, which has to resist the abrasive effects of modern traffic in addition to the hardened, steel-studded tires during the winter months.

Highway departments' literature and that of the Portland Cement Association continuously remind field inspectors of the necessity to avoid water beyond that allowed by the standard specifications. Yet the present operation of the slip-form pavers shows that the contractors' long history of violating standard specifications continues.

That problem is not due to flaws in the character of the inspectors, but, rather, flows from the structural relations of the contract system of construction for profit, the social and educational systems that support the contractor's monopoly of modern technology, and the right to hire and fire the men who operate the equipment. The power of the contractor is focused on expediting the progress of the work in order to maximize profits.

*

You don't have to be a concert violinist to understand or appreciate the beautiful sounds that come from the playing of the Beethoven violin concerto. However, it takes years of sustained work with a violin before a person can create those beautiful sounds from the quiet notes on the score. That is similar to the art of changing wet, green concrete mud into a durable, high-quality highway pavement. You must spend years working with the soft mud while it goes through its own magical process of returning to the stonelike qualities of the ingredients from which it was derived.

Our society and its educational institutions respect the learning process that the future violinist must go through. We know that you do not become a violinist by reading about the great performing artists. But our society does not respect the worker, his craft, or his experiences in the work process.

In the field of highway engineering, society expects a person with professional classroom expertise to supervise the processing of the soft concrete mud into the smooth, stonelike finish of modern concrete pavement. But present educational and personnel procedures consider experience in the actual work process beneath the dignity of a professional. Employees who come out of the work process are usually blocked off from promotion and held to menial positions in the hierarchy of responsibility and authority.

All of the problems with methods and procedures and all of the skill and knowledge that flow out of experience in the work process are left to the domain of the contractor who uses all that expertise to push down the road for more profits. That condition is illustrated by the slip-form paving job I described, where the personnel in charge were professional engineers with little or no experience with Portland-cement pavements. On that job, the contractor's men were adding water at will during the finishing process, thus compromising the essential hard and durable surface that is required if pavement is going to stand up to the punishing, abrasive forces of modern traffic.

After my retirement, I visited with an informal group of Highway Department inspectors who still face the contractors on a day-to-day basis. A young man who was still doing layout work told me that he was considering filing a citizen's civil suit against the state in an attempt to force the Highway Department to enforce its own contracts. It was useless, he said, to complain to the higher-echelon highway officials. One person in the group reported that another experienced on-the-job inspector wrote a letter to the Highway Department stating the reasons why he recommended that a certain contractor be barred from future contracts. His recommendation was ignored by the Highway Department.

Those continuing protests by on-the-job personnel illustrate that people do take pride in creating quality work. Furthermore, it demonstrates that my experiences are only a tiny part of similar compromises of quality, endurance, and safety on public construction projects. Long after my departure from highway work, I reviewed some of those old quality-control problems with a friend who is a very respected engineer on major construction projects. He reported that there were many state personnel who were sick of seeing contractors getting away with defective work.

The persistent ability of contractors to extract privileges from the public bureaucracy and from legislatures indicates that there is a lot of economic, social, and political power flowing from the contractors' monopoly of modern technology and the personnel who are trained in its use. If public agencies shared some of that authority, the theory, practice, design, and construction of public works would be more efficient. Then, perhaps, a force powerful enough to corrupt our society would be contained or eliminated altogether. At the same time, the workers' creative drives would be released and the public would benefit from higher-quality and more-durable public works.

The contract system is not efficient when all the relevant costs are accounted for, such as the expense of an elaborate organization of engineers, inspectors, and reports whose major function is to provide a secondary form of supervision over work that is already directly controlled by the contractor. That duality of supervision is both expensive and ineffective.

The array of nonproductive government engineers, inspectors, and accountants gives the government the reputation of being expensive and wasteful. That is true, but the basic cause of all the waste is the fact that the contract system cannot be trusted to turn out quality work. That wasteful duality of supervisory personnel is the price of the contract system and would be unnecessary if public agencies were doing their own work. Workers' and consumers' councils could provide a unity of purpose and priority that is not possible when the basic authority of a contractor is directed towards production, regardless of quality.

A glance at what has been built in the United States in the last two hundred years will show the potential of workers. We are now a mature capitalist system. The corporate profit motive is not producing jobs of any kind for millions of people, and it is producing meaningful jobs for only a tiny few. It is time to abandon the corporate push for profit as the driving engine of our society. A more dependable vehicle would be a democratic synthesis of people's needs with the workers' demonstrated ability to produce. That kind of people-oriented cooperation can provide jobs, goods, and services.

Two hundred years ago the people of this country broke the restrictive limitations of England's monopoly on political power. That released the democratic potential of citizens to create a growing, viable political movement. It is time once again to break the restrictive limitations of contractors who are limiting people's opportunity to work and grow. The democracy that has allowed this country to grow for two hundred years has proved itself in the political arena. The energy of our people must be released to allow democracy to grow in the domain of industry.

*

The legitimacy of capitalism's autocratic control of the workplace and the investments of its profits are being questioned today. The basis of those questions lies in the system's shrinking ability to provide jobs, housing, affordable health care, and a healthy environment. Using the fetish of profit to drive the engines of our society worked during the pioneer days, but government intervention was necessary to provide the war materials for both destructive wars and the reconstruction work that resulted from the Second World War. In the nuclear age, dependence on a war-related economy cannot be a viable option. Even with an unprecedented peacetime military buildup today, the U.S. economy is stagnant and presents fewer options for working people.

With the advantage of hindsight, I know of two examples of production organized for basic needs rather than corporate profits. I worked at both. During the depression, the Works Progress Administration built schools, roads, and water and sewer systems. It was an efficient construction program that depended on the experience and skill of the workers, both blue and white collar. During the Second World War massive industrial projects were created and organized to win the war against the Axis powers. Today, similar projects could be organized to win the war against unemployment and poverty. All that is stopping us from such a mobilization are the profit-making priorities of today's capitalists. It is time to abandon our dependency on the whims of corporate profit sheets. That is like making a partnership with the devil. For society's basic needs, we should use our resources to produce for people's needs.

A meld of WPA and war-production programs suited to human needs could bring a renaissance, both material and spiritual, to American society. That can take place when the social, economic, and political power of workers and consumers matches that of corporate America. Such a change took place in the political arena two hundred years ago; it is time to do the same in the world of industry.

*

Looking back at all those years in the workplace, a few strong impressions remain. Among those is a faith in working people, a belief that they are qualified to inherit the mantle of the defenders of democracy worn by Jefferson's freeholders. People respond well to being treated with the respect that flows from the New Testament's Golden Rule. Indeed, their positive response proves its efficacy seven days a week. Corruption, I found, was systemic rather than personal. Corruption flows from non-Jeffersonian concentrations of economic power that is used to multiply profits rather than for the production of goods for the use of people. In a more general way, the growth of the labor movement is a principled resistance to the monotony of a modern factory assembly line that uses concentrated economic power to multiply profits rather than to produce for people's needs. Generally, the capitalist system has had the economic, political, legal, military, and social power to protect itself from the applications of Jeffersonian democracy to industry.

Time has illustrated that the health of unions is influenced by national or worldwide cataclysmic events beyond the workers' present power to control. For example, there was nothing the craftspeople or the freeholders could do to stop the march of industrialization that destroyed their independent and democratic subsistence economy. The attempts of their descendants to apply Jeffersonian democratic and egalitarian concepts to a fast-moving assembly line were repulsed until the Great Depression of the 1930s gave birth to the people-oriented political renaissance that produced FDR's New Deal. From that movement came the legal and moral strength for workers to overcome capitalist resistance to industrial democracy; industrial unions were born. Thus, from the Great Depression, a union movement and a system of people-oriented law was given birth.

Another cataclysmic event, the Second World War, teamed up with the capitalists' fear that employees would control the workplace. It also brought about power relationships that devastated the growing industrial union movement and besmirched FDR's New Deal with the suggestion that those efforts to help people were part of a Communist plot to destroy our cherished free-enterprise system.

As a result of Hitler's attempt to destroy and take over the Soviet Union, the Russian army grew strong enough to resist, then to destroy the German war machine. The powerful Red Army dominated all of Eastern Europe after the Second World War. Such a powerful army under the control of a noncapitalist state gave rise to more fears of socialism. Those fears, when added to the industrialists' fear of unions and workers' control, gave a powerful impetus to the Truman-McCarthy witch hunt and loyalty oaths. United States workers had no control over that configuration of events powered by Hitler's push to war. Yet, the culmination of those events stopped both the labor movement and the New Deal programs that were enacted during the Great Depression.

*

Today, thirty years after the Truman-McCarthy era, a new fear of the Russians has spawned another great war program designed to defend us from the Soviets. That fear, similar to the those of the McCarthy era, has stifled dissent. It has changed the thrust of the government away from a concern for people to a concern for free enterprise, with a special emphasis on the profits of the multinational segment of industry and finance.

Fear of being called a Communist has silenced the democratic dialogue that is the hallmark of our country and guaranteed by our constitution. The radical antiwar movements of the 1930s were silenced by the first wave of real or perceived fears of the Soviets. The antiwar thrust of the American Communist party lost its credibility in the McCarthy era. Most of the trade-union movement now supports the military buildup while looking for crumbs in defense jobs. Yet, among the common people, opposition grows to a military program that allows our family farms and our cities to decay, all in the name of building more planet-shaking weapons in response to a perceived fear.

In an organized form, only the churches have both the Christian concern for people and the independence from the war machine to be the cutting edge of a new political renaissance, one strong enough to turn our country away from destruction back to the service for people that supported the founding of our country. My only complaint about the churches' antiwar work is that most of their workers have personalized the drift towards war as if it were caused by bad people. In my years in the workplace, I found good people corrupted by powers beyond their ability to understand or resist. My objective was to use my experience to expose those forces within the capitalist system that led to war.

So I had come full circle, back to my first interest: implementing the parables of the New Testament. I was coming home to work with the churches in the antiwar movement in the 1980s. Here and there a few voices are being raised to support the coalition for peace. A few twenty-five-year Central Intelligence Agency officers are writing books, telling us that the Soviets are not a military threat to either Europe or the United States. A few economists are telling us that we have the people and the resources to produce for use and prosperity without profit-making multinational corporations.

The Second World War presented that challenge to us. Without the benefit of foreign trade and a worldwide market, we the people, through our government, built many defense plants that supplemented free-enterprise production to produce those works of war. We won that production battle and the war. But now, in the nuclear age, we have the further job of using our resources to reclaim the peace. With our experience during the Great Depression and the early 1940s, we can learn to build production for our economy and neutralize our dependency on fear and military responses.

That is a worthy project, to build the people-oriented sector of our economy, one that can lead us away from war and towards peace. As a nation we have responded to challenges before. There is no greater challenge today than to dedicate our heritage of resources to its success. That is good work, for it is there that we find both personal and collective fulfillment.

Notes

INTRODUCTION

1. Norman Best to William G. Robbins, October 25, 1987. The term *Wobblies* is a popular reference to Industrial Workers of the World (IWW), the radical syndicalist-oriented industrial-union movement founded in 1905. For two works on the IWW, see Melvyn Dubofsky, *We Shall Be All: A History of the IWW* (Chicago, 1969), and Joseph R. Conlin, *Bread and Roses Too: Studies of the Wobblies* (Westport, Conn., 1969).
2. A sampling of recent studies in the new labor history includes Jeremy Brecher, *Strike!* (San Francisco, 1972); Stanley Aronowitz, *False Promises: The Shaping of American Working-Class Consciousness* (New York, 1973); Harry Braverman, *Labor and Monopoly Capital: The Degradation of Work in the Twentieth Century* (New York, 1974); Jeremy Brecher and Tim Costello, *Common Sense for Hard Times* (Boston, 1976); Herbert G. Gutman, *Work, Culture, and Society in Industrializing America: Essays in American Working-Class and Social History* (New York, 1976); David Montgomery, *Workers' Control in America: Studies in the History of Work, Technology, and*

Labor Struggles (New York, 1979); James R. Green, *The World of the Worker: Labor in Twentieth-Century America* (New York, 1980); David Brody, *Workers in Industrial America: Essays on the Twentieth-Century Struggle* (New York, 1980); Michael H. Frisch and Daniel Walkowitz, eds., *Working-Class America: Essays on Labor, Community, and American Society* (Urbana, Ill., 1983); and David Montgomery, *The Fall of the House of Labor: The Workplace, the State, and American Labor Activism, 1865–1925* (New York, 1987).

3. Braverman, *Labor and Monopoly Capital*, 90.
4. The best interpretations of Taylorism are in Braverman, *Labor and Monopoly Capital*, 85–123; Montgomery, *Workers' Control in America*, 113–19; Green, *The World of the Worker*, 70–71; Brody, *Workers in Industrial America*, 11–14; and David F. Noble, *America By Design: Science, Technology, and the Rise of Corporate Capitalism* (New York, 1977), 82, 264–78.
5. For a discussion of work as purposive activity, see Braverman, *Labor and Monopoly Capital*, 49.
6. See Green, *The World of the Worker*, 109; Braverman, *Labor and Monopoly Capital*, 192–96; and David M. Gordon, Richard Edwards, and Michael Reich, *Segmented Work, Divided Workers: The Historical Transformation of Labor in the United States* (New York, 1982), 173.
7. For accounts of the Nonpartisan League, see Robert L. Morlan, *Political Prairie Fire: The Nonpartisan League, 1915–1922* (1955; reprinted St. Paul, Minn., 1983); Elwyn B. Robinson, *History of North Dakota* (Lincoln, Nebr., 1966); and Larry Remele, "Power to the People: The Nonpartisan League," in Thomas W. Howard, ed., *The North Dakota Political Tradition*, (Ames, Iowa, 1981).

CHAPTER I

1. William Hinton is best known for his study of village life in China under the Chinese people's republic. His classic work, based on research conducted during the 1950s, is *Fanshen: A Documentary of Revolution in a Chinese Village* (New York, 1966).
2. Editor's note: the author acknowledges an intellectual debt to the work of Vernon Parrington for his argument in this section. See especially Parrington's *The Beginnings of Critical Realism in America: 1860–1920* (1930; reprinted New York, 1958), vol. 3, *Main Currents in American Thought*.
3. For the struggles of industrial unionism between 1880 and 1930, see Dubofsky, *We Shall Be All*, 5–16; Brecher, *Strike!*, 134–35; Brody, *Workers in Industrial America*, 3–47; Green, *The World of the Worker*, 58–101; Montgomery, *Workers' Control in America*, 91–112; Steve Fraser, "Dress Rehearsal for the New Deal: Shop-Floor Insurgents, Political Elites, and Industrial Democracy in the Amalgamated Clothing Workers," in Frisch

and Walkowitz, *Working-Class America*, 212–55; and Melvyn Dubofsky, *Industrialism and the American Worker, 1865–1920* (Arlington Heights, Ill., 1985).

4. The best sources on labor militancy during the New Deal years are Green, *The World of the Worker*, 133–73; Aronowitz, *False Promises*, 232–45; Brody, *Workers in Industrial America*, 120–72; Sidney Lens, *The Labor Wars: From the Molly Maguires to the Sitdowns* (Garden City, N.Y., 1973), 283–375; and Melvyn Dubofsky, ed., *American Labor Since the New Deal* (Chicago, 1971), 31–127.

5. In the midst of the production crisis of the Second World War, leading business executives already were laying the groundwork for a counter-attack against the gains made by labor. See Jack Stokes Ballard, *The Shock of Peace: Military and Economic Demobilization after World War II* (Washington, D.C., 1983), 15–59; Marty Jezer, *The Dark Ages: Life in the United States, 1945–1960* (Boston, 1982), 24–32.
6. For production problems associated with the war, see Richard Pollenberg, *War and Society: The United States, 1941–1945* (Philadelphia, 1972); Richard R. Lingeman, *Don't You Know There's a War Going On? The American Home Front, 1941–45* (New York, 1970); Paul A. C. Koistinen, *The Hammer and the Sword: Labor, the Military, and Industrial Mobilization* (New York, 1979); Gerald D. Nash, *The Great Depression and World War II: Organizing America, 1933–1945* (New York, 1979); and Allan M. Winkler, *Home Front U.S.A.: America During World War II* (Arlington Heights, Ill., 1986).
7. The demobilization period is treated in Ballard, *The Shock of Peace*, 15–59; Seymore Melman, *The Permanent War Economy: American Capitalism in Decline* (New York, 1974), 15–20, 262; and Allan M. Winkler, *Modern America: The United States from World War II to the Present* (New York, 1985), 60–62.
8. The evidence that employers sought to use a perceived Soviet threat abroad to discipline workers at home is discussed in Lawrence Lader, *Power on the Left: American Radical Movements Since 1946* (New York, 1979), 2–9; Brody, *Workers in Industrial America*, 181–82; and David Caute, *The Great Fear: The Anti-Communist Purge Under Truman and Eisenhower* (New York, 1978), 349–400.
9. For sources that show the implications of the Taft-Hartley Act for American workers, see Aronowitz, *False Promises*, 333; Lawrence Wittner, *Cold War America: From Hiroshima to Watergate* (1974; expanded edition New York, 1978), 47–48; Green, *The World of the Worker*, 174, 198–99; Lader, *Power on the Left*, 31–33; and Caute, *The Great Fear*, 354–59.
10. The reference here is to secondary boycotts, prohibited under the Taft-Hartley Act. See Green, *The World of the Worker*, 198.

11. For accounts of the loyalty hearings and the purges of union leaders suspected of leftist politics, see Lader, *Power on the Left*, 56–86; Caute, *The Great Fear*, 349–400; and Michael Belknap, *Cold War Political Justice: The Smith Act, the Communist Party, and American Civil Liberties* (Westport, Conn., 1977).
12. Jeremy Brecher, "Crisis Economy: Born-Again Labor Movement?" *Monthly Review* 35, no. 10 (March 1984): 1–17; David Montgomery, "Comment: Making History But Not Under Circumstances Chosen By Ourselves," *Monthly Review* 35, no. 10 (March 1984): 18–23; Norman Best, "Workers and State Power: A Reply to Jeremy Brecher," *Monthly Review* 36, no. 5 (September 1984): 45–48.
13. The struggle between labor and capital for control of the workplace in the twentieth century is treated in Aronowitz, *False Promises*, 333–34, 428–30, 434–38; Braverman, *Labor and Monopoly Capital*, 192–233, 424–47; Montgomery, *Workers' Control in America*, 113–34; and Roy Rosenzweig, *Eight Hours for What We Will: Workers & Leisure in an Industrial City, 1870–1920* (Cambridge, England, 1983).
14. On the Canadian bishops' statement, see *Commonweal* 110 (February 25, 1983), 104–5.

CHAPTER 2

1. The Farmers' Equity mentioned here probably was a rural insurgency organization similar to the various Farmers' Alliance factions. Such groups ranged from the American Society of Equity to the Nonpartisan League and the Farmers Union. See Larry Remele, " 'God Helps Those Who Help Themselves': The Farmers' Alliance and Dakota Statehood," *Montana: The Magazine of Western History* 37 (1987): 33; and James M. Youngdale, *Populism: A Psychohistorical Perspective* (Port Washington, N.Y., 1975), 16–17.
2. The standard history of James J. Hill and the Great Northern Railroad is Albro Martin, *James J. Hill and the Opening of the Northwest* (New York, 1976).

CHAPTER 3

1. For an account of the most recent literature on the Sacco-Vanzetti trial, see Katherine Roberts, "Books in Collision: The Continuing Case of Sacco and Vanzetti," *New York Times*, May 25, 1986. The article is a review of two books, the viewpoints of which clash on the issue of the guilt or innocence of Sacco and Vanzetti: Francis Russell, *Sacco and Vanzetti: The Case Resolved* (New York, 1986), and William Young and David E. Kaiser, *Postmortem: New Evidence in the Case of Sacco and Vanzetti* (Amherst, Mass., 1985).

2. Cataldo is a small settlement at the eastern end of the Coeur d'Alene mining district, a stretch of rich silver and lead mineral country that reaches along the South Fork of the Coeur d'Alene River and includes the historic mining towns of Kellogg, Wardner, Osburn, Wallace, and Mullan. See Richard E. Lingenfelter, *The Hardrock Miners: A History of the Mining Labor Movement in the American West, 1863–1893* (Berkeley, Calif., 1974), especially 198–218.

CHAPTER 4

1. Blue top is the term for heavy stakes driven into the roadway so that their tops indicate the design elevation of the new grade. Their lateral position indicates the width of the new grade.
2. Hogg Rock, high in the Cascade Range, derives its name from T. Egenton Hogg, an investor who made an abortive attempt to build a railroad through that section of the mountains. See J. Kenneth Munford's foreword in Wallis Nash, *Oregon: There and Back in 1877* (1878; reprinted Corvallis, Oreg., 1976), xi-xii.

CHAPTER 5

1. Falsework is the temporary supporting framework for a structure during construction. In this case, it was the structure that would support the heavy, wet concrete in place until it dried.

CHAPTER 6

1. For an account of grass-roots influence on New Deal policies and programs, see Barton J. Bernstein, "The New Deal: The Conservative Achievements of Liberal Reform," in Barton J. Bernstein, ed., *Towards a New Past: Dissenting Essays in American History* (New York, 1968), 271–75; Donald R. McCoy, *Angry Voices: Left-of-Center Politics in the New Deal Era* (Lawrence, Kans., 1958); and Bernard Sternsher, *Hitting Home: The Great Depression in Town and Country* (Chicago, 1970).
2. The Works Progress Administration is treated in William E. Leuchtenburg, *Franklin D. Roosevelt and the New Deal 1932–1940* (New York, 1963).
3. On the Civilian Conservation Corps, see John R. Salmond, *The Civilian Conservation Corps, 1933–1942: A New Deal Case Study* (Durham, N.C., 1967).
4. The author returned to Seattle in the fall of 1937 amid the alarming advances made by the forces of fascism and national socialism in Europe. The Roosevelt administration had refused to support the democratically elected Loyalist regime in Spain, while Germany and Italy were offering both overt and covert assistance to the forces of Francisco Franco. The German army had already occupied the Rhineland and was on the verge

of aggressions against Austria and Czechoslovakia. See Leuchtenburg, *Franklin D. Roosevelt and the New Deal*, 222–27; Robert Rosenstone, *Crusade on the Left: The Lincoln Battalion in the Spanish Civil War* (New York, 1969); and Manfred Jonas, *The United States and Germany: A Diplomatic History* (Ithaca, N.Y., 1985).

5. A comprehensive study of the Communist party in the United States during the Great Depression is Irving Howe and Lewis Coser, *The American Communist Party: A Critical History* (New York, 1957), 175–386; see also Frank A. Warren, *Liberals and Communism: The "Red Decade" Revisited* (Bloomington, Ind., 1966).
6. For incipient fascism in the United States in the late 1930s, see Alan Brinkley, *Voices of Protest: Huey Long, Father Coughlin & the Great Depression* (New York, 1982), 143–241; and McCoy, *Angry Voices*, 115–57.
7. Steffens's reference to facist tendencies in the United States during the 1930s is in Christopher Lasch, *The New Radicalism in America, 1889–1963* (New York, 1965), 251–85, especially 279–80. See also Lincoln Steffens, *Autobigraphy* (New York, 1931).
8. The United or Popular Front of the late 1930s is treated in Howe and Coser, *The American Communist Party*, 319–86; Leuchtenburg, *Franklin D. Roosevelt and the New Deal*, 282; and John P. Diggins, *The American Left in the Twentieth Century* (New York, 1973), 121–35.
9. For a recent account of the International Woodworkers of America, see Jerry Lembcke and William M. Tattam, *One Union in Wood: A Political History of the International Woodworkers of America* (New York, 1984).
10. Referred to as the Magna Charta for organized labor, the National Labor Relations Act (or Wagner Act) of 1935 threw the weight of the federal government behind the right of labor to organize and bargain collectively and required employers to accept unionization. See Leuchtenburg, *Franklin D. Roosevelt and the New Deal*, 150–52.
11. During the summer and fall of 1917, the lumber industry in the Pacific Northwest was operating at about 15 percent of capacity because of widespread strike activity led, in part, by the IWW. See Dubofsky, *We Shall Be All*, 412–14. For a case study of the effects of the strike in northern Idaho, see Keith C. Petersen, *Company Town: Potlatch, Idaho, and the Potlatch Lumber Company* (Pullman, Wash., 1987), 160–68.
12. The authoritative account of the 4L is Harold Hyman, *Soldiers and Spruce: Origins of the Loyal Legion of Loggers and Lumbermen* (Los Angeles, 1963).
13. In a sense, the AFL and CIO organizing drives revolutionized the work force in the lumber industry. The more militant unionists broke from the craft-dominated AFL and formed CIO affiliates under the International Woodworkers of America in 1937. See Lembcke and Tattam, *One Union in Wood*, 47–74.

14. The miners' struggles in northern Idaho are chronicled in Dubofsky, *We Shall Be All*, 28–42; and William S. Greever, *The Bonanza West: The Story of the Western Mining Rushes, 1848–1900*, (1963; reprinted Moscow, Idaho, 1986), 277–85.
15. Blacklists were circulated informally among employers. On them were the names of undesireable employees, especially those who were union organizers.
16. The International Union of Mine, Mill, and Smelter Workers was a lineal descendant of the militant Western Federation of Miners. See Green, *The World of the Worker*, 151, 163; Aronowitz, *False Promises*, 344–46, 349–50; and Howe and Coser, *The American Communist Party*, 457, 468.

CHAPTER 7

1. On the International Association of Machinists, especially Local 68 in San Francisco, see Mark Perlman, *The Machinists: A New Study in American Trade Unionism* (Cambridge, Mass., 1961), 85–88, 112–16. Perlman claims that Local 68 was more independent than most locals and that "it had always embraced a self-defined Populism." See also Perlman's *Democracy in the International Association of Machinists* (New York, 1962).
2. The freeze on wages during the Second World War went into effect in September 1942. See Vernon Jensen, *Lumber and Labor* (New York, 1945), 278. For a case study of the problems that developed under the wage freeze, see William G. Robbins, "Timber and War: An Oral History of Coos Bay, Oregon, 1940–1945," *Journal of the West* 25 (July 1986): 37–40.
3. For the reference to Tom Mooney, see Gerald D. Nash, *The American West in the Twentieth Century: A Short History of an Urban Oasis* (1973; reprinted Albuquerque, N.M. 1984), 69–70, 170; and Robert E. Burke, *Olson's New Deal for California* (Berkeley, Calif., 1953), 48–58.
4. On Culbert Olson's pardon of Mooney and the commutation of the sentence of Warren Billings, see Burke, *Olson's New Deal for California*, 58, 233. Mooney, an American Federation of Labor organizer, and Billings were arrested in 1916 and subsequently sentenced to death for a bomb explosion in San Francisco during a Preparedness Day parade. The highly circumstantial evidence eventually brought a reduced sentence of life imprisonment. Mooney, however, continued to serve as a symbol for the working-class fight for justice. See Robert K. Murray, *Red Scare: A Study of National Hysteria, 1919–1920* (New York, 1955), 114–15.
5. For the West Coast longshoring struggles of the 1930s, see Charles Larrowe, *Harry Bridges: The Rise and Fall of Radical Labor in the United States* (New York, 1972), 14–174, and Betty V. H. Schneider and Abraham Siegel, *Industrial Relations in the Pacific Coast Longshore Industry* (Berkeley, Calif., 1956), 12–15.

6. The accomplishments of the ILWU are detailed in Larrowe, *Harry Bridges*, and Charles A. Madison, *American Labor Leaders: Personalities and Forces in the Labor Movement* (New York, 1950), 404–33.
7. On the ILWU as a pattern-setting union, see Green, *The World of the Worker*, 213.

8. For the repeated prosecutions of Harry Bridges, see Caute, *The Great Fear*, 237–38; Lader, *Power on the Left*, 44; and Larrowe, *Harry Bridges*.
9. The Victory ships, also known as the Liberty class, were mass-produced merchant ships constructed with remarkable speed in the shipyards of Henry J. Kaiser. See Lingeman, *Don't You Know There's a War Going On?*, 130–31, and Carl Abbott, *Portland: Planning, Politics, and Growth in a Twentieth-Century City* (Lincoln, Nebr., 1983), 125–26.
10. Thomas Fitzgerald, "Why Motivation Won't Work," *Harvard Business Review* (July–August 1971): 43.
11. Michael H. Best and William E. Connolly, *The Politicized Economy* (Lexington, Mass., 1976), 153.
12. By then the Aluminum Workers of America (CIO) had been absorbed into the United Steelworkers of America (CIO). See Mark McColloch, "Consolidating Industrial Citizenship: The USWA at War and Peace, 1939–46," in Paul E. Clark, Peter Gottlieb, and Donald Kennedy, eds., *Forging a Union of Steel: Philip Murray, SWOC, & the United Steelworkers* (Ithaca, N.Y., 1987), 79.

CHAPTER 8

1. The reference is to the Popular Front. For Earl Browder's role in moving the party toward that position, see Howe and Coser, *The American Communist Party*, 319–86.
2. On the Molotov-Ribbentrop Pact of 1939 and its consequences for the Soviet Union, see Adam B. Ulan, *Expansion and Coexistence: The History of Soviet Foreign Policy, 1917–1967* (New York, 1968), 272–79, 287–88.
3. For the argument that the Molotov-Ribbentrop Pact gave the Soviet Union time, see Isaac Deutscher, *Stalin: A Political Biography*, 2d ed. (New York, 1966, 1st ed. 1949), 429–41.
4. On Anton Pannekoek, see Serge Bricianer, *Anton Pannekoek and the Workers' Councils*, trans. Malachy Carroll (St. Louis, Mo., 1978), and Pannekoek, *Workers' Councils* (Somerville, Mass., 1970).
5. The Grand Lodge election process is described in Perlman, *Democracy in the International Association of Machinists*, 32–42, 66–77.
6. See Perlman, *The Machinists*, 3.
7. The term *Inland Empire* is a geographical reference point centering on the great Columbia River drainage in eastern Washington, with Spokane at

its hub. See John Fahey, *The Inland Empire: The Unfolding Years, 1879–1929* (Seattle, 1986).

CHAPTER 9

1. See Pannekoek, *Workers' Councils*, 61–66.
2. An excellent assessment of this period is Wittner, *Cold War America*, 30–110; see also Caute, *The Great Fear*.
3. One of the provisions of the Taft-Hartley Act required union officers to file affidavits if their unions were to be eligible for the services of the National Labor Relations Board. See Howe and Coser, *The American Communist Party*, 465–66; and Caute, *The Great Fear*, 354–59.
4. On the defeat of Taylor, see Caute, *The Great Fear*, 37.
5. For the destruction of the mine, mill, and smeltermen's union, see Aronowitz, *False Promises*, 344–46, 349–50; Lader, *Power on the Left*, 65; and Caute, *The Great Fear*, 356–59.

maps

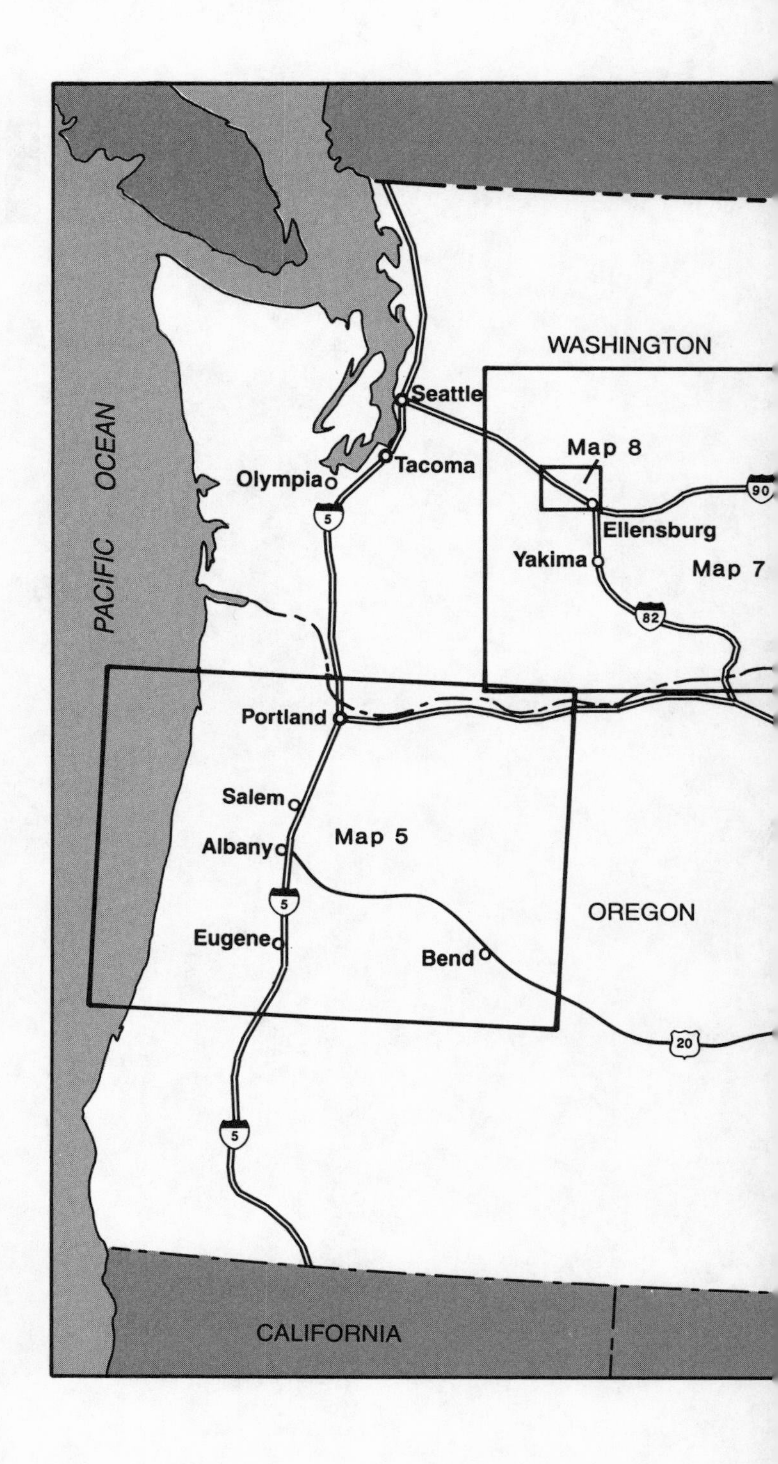
WASHINGTON
PACIFIC OCEAN
Seattle
Tacoma
Olympia
5
Map 8
90
Ellensburg
Yakima
Map 7
82
Portland
Salem
Map 5
Albany
5
OREGON
Eugene
Bend
20
5
CALIFORNIA

Index Map

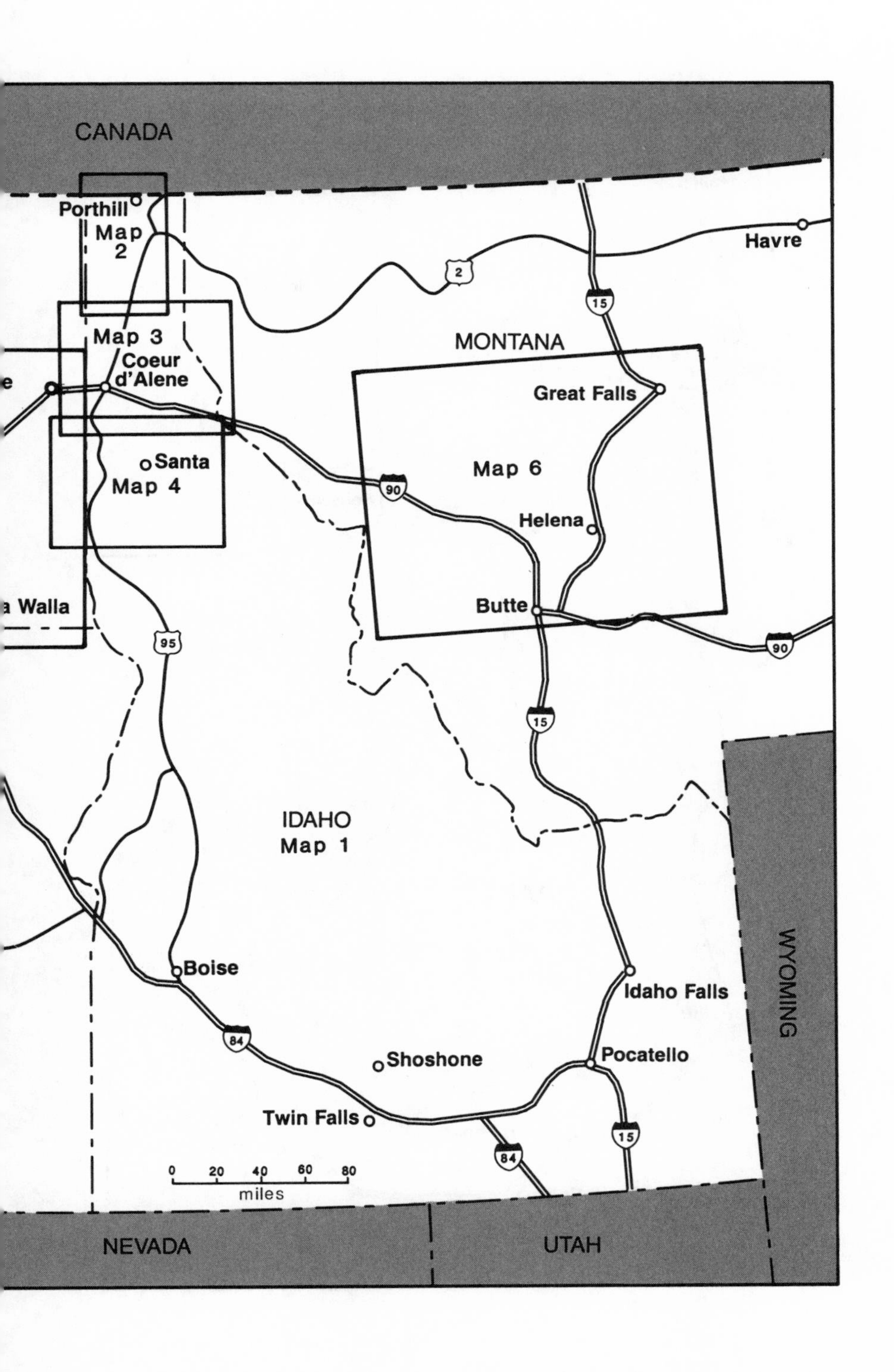
CANADA
Porthill
Map 2
Map 3
Coeur d'Alene
Santa
Map 4
a Walla
2
Havre
15
MONTANA
Great Falls
Map 6
90
Helena
Butte
90
95
15
IDAHO
Map 1
Boise
84
Shoshone
Twin Falls
Idaho Falls
Pocatello
15
84
WYOMING
0 20 40 60 80
miles
NEVADA
UTAH

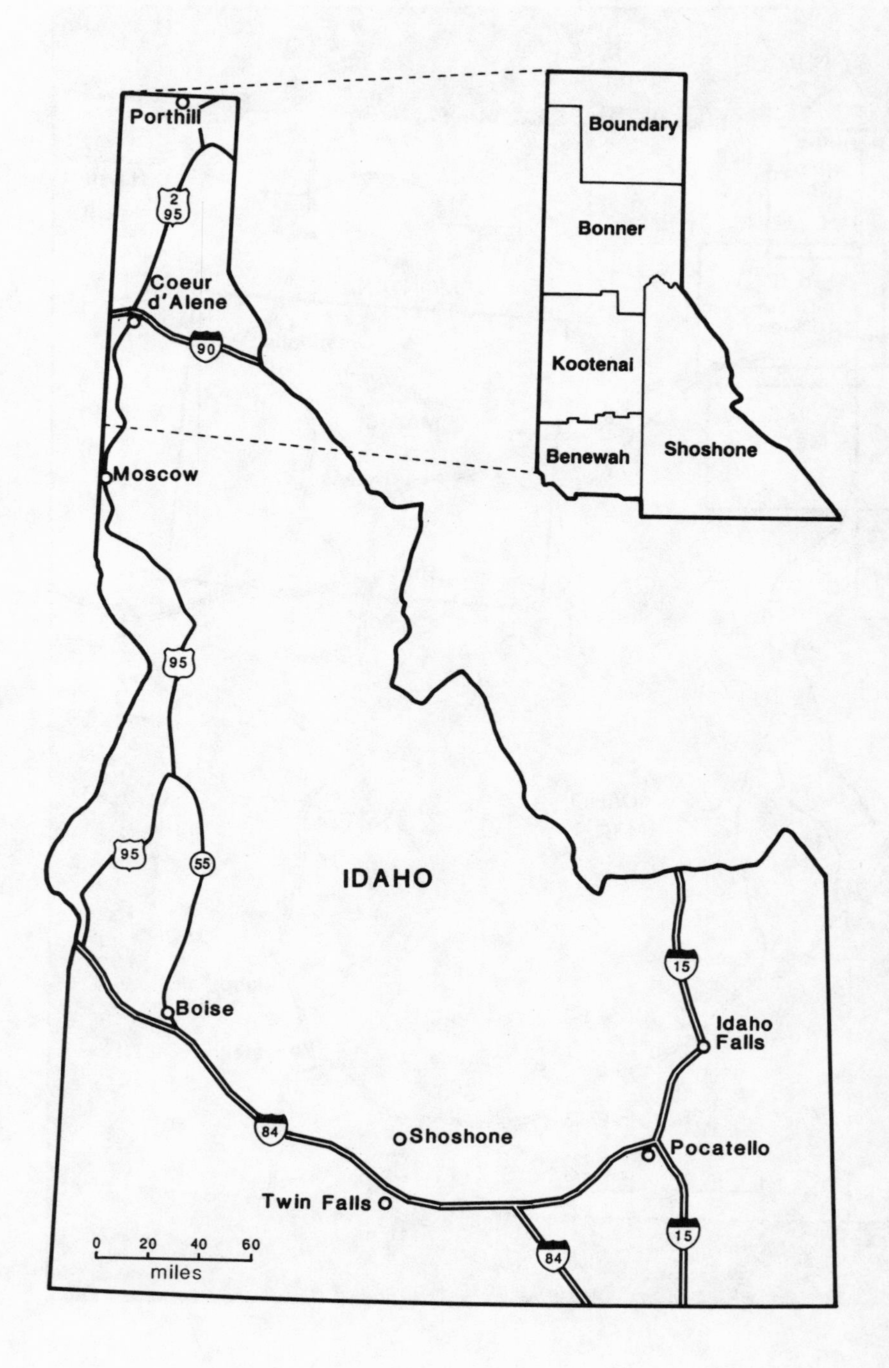
Porthill
2
95
Coeur
d'Alene
90
Moscow
95
95
55
IDAHO
Boise
84
Shoshone
Twin Falls
84
15
Idaho
Falls
Pocatello
15
0
20
40
60
miles
Boundary
Bonner
Kootenai
Benewah
Shoshone

Map 1

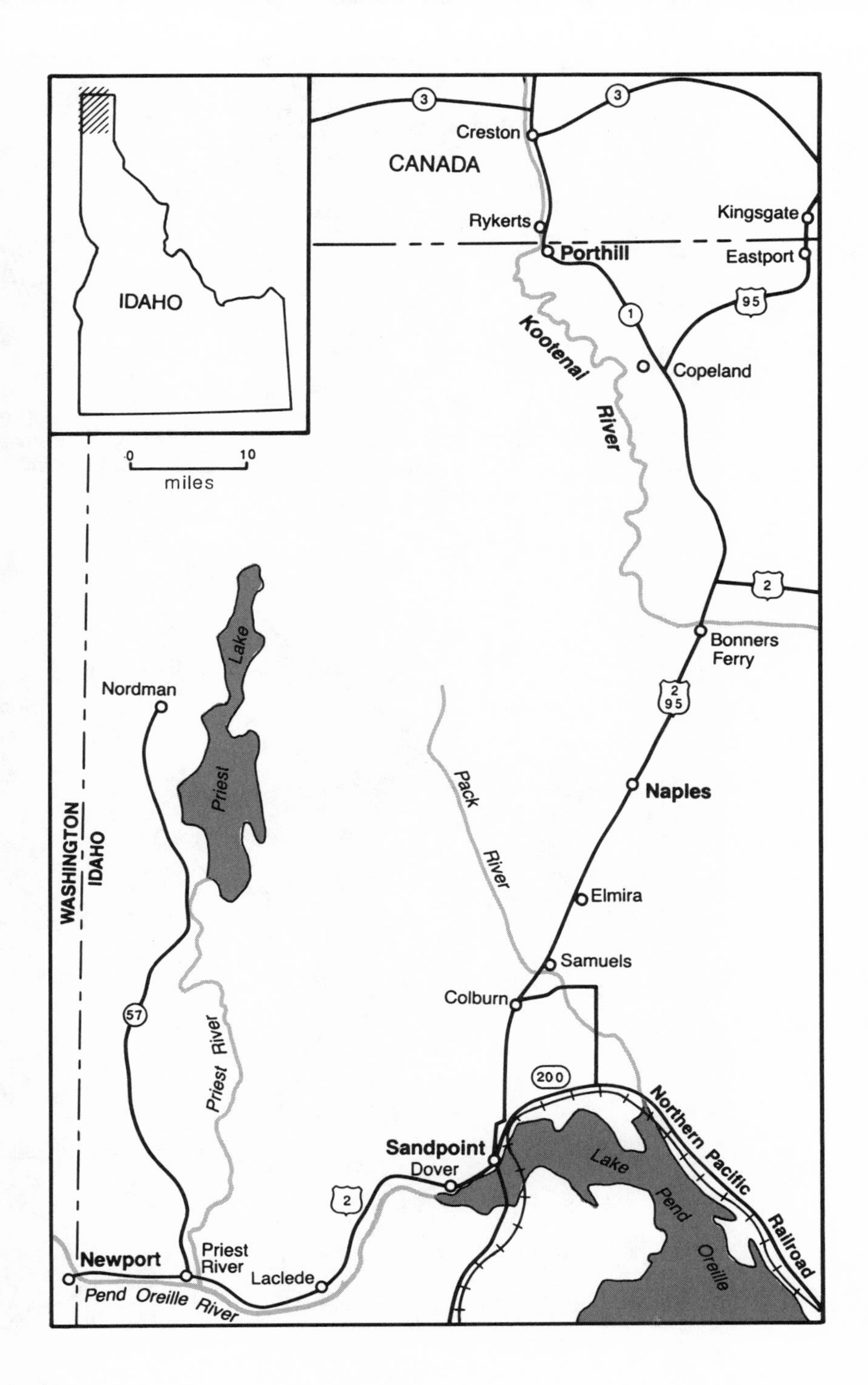

IDAHO
CANADA
Creston
Rykerts
Porthill
Kingsgate
Eastport
3
3
1
95
Kootenai
River
Copeland
0
10
miles
2
Bonners
Ferry
2
95
Priest
Lake
Nordman
WASHINGTON
IDAHO
Pack
River
Naples
Elmira
Samuels
Colburn
57
Priest River
200
Northern Pacific
Railroad
Sandpoint
Dover
Lake
Pend
Oreille
2
Newport
Priest
River
Laclede
Pend Oreille River

Map 2

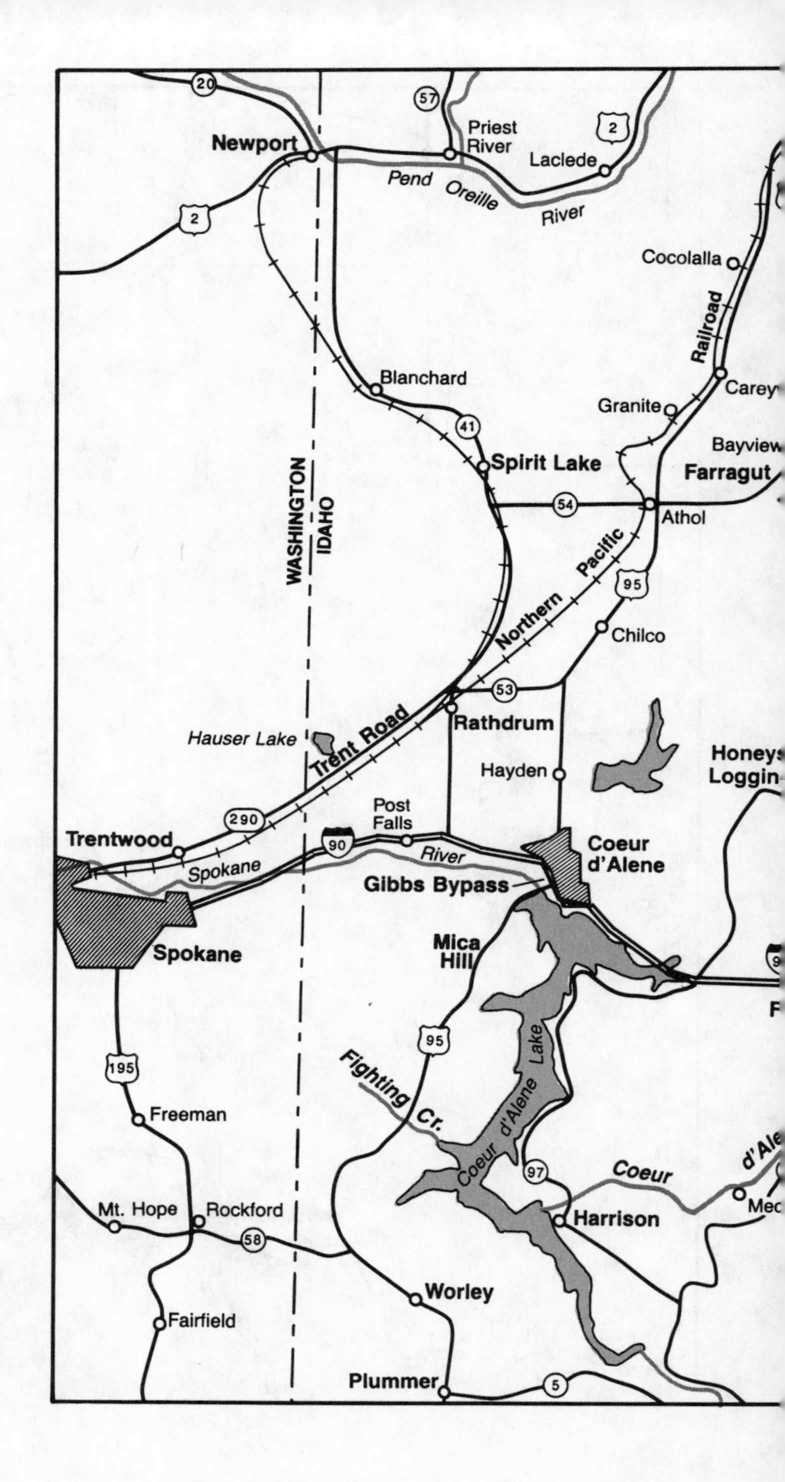
Newport
Priest River
Laclede
Pend Oreille River
Cocolalla
Railroad
Blanchard
Carey
Granite
Bayview
Spirit Lake
Farragut
Athol
WASHINGTON
IDAHO
Northern Pacific
Chilco
Rathdrum
Trent Road
Hauser Lake
Hayden
Honeys
Loggin
Post Falls
Trentwood
Spokane River
Coeur d'Alene
Gibbs Bypass
Spokane
Mica Hill
Fighting Cr.
Coeur d'Alene Lake
Freeman
Coeur d'Ale
Harrison
Mt. Hope
Rockford
Worley
Fairfield
Plummer
20
57
2
41
54
95
53
290
90
195
97
58
5

Map 3

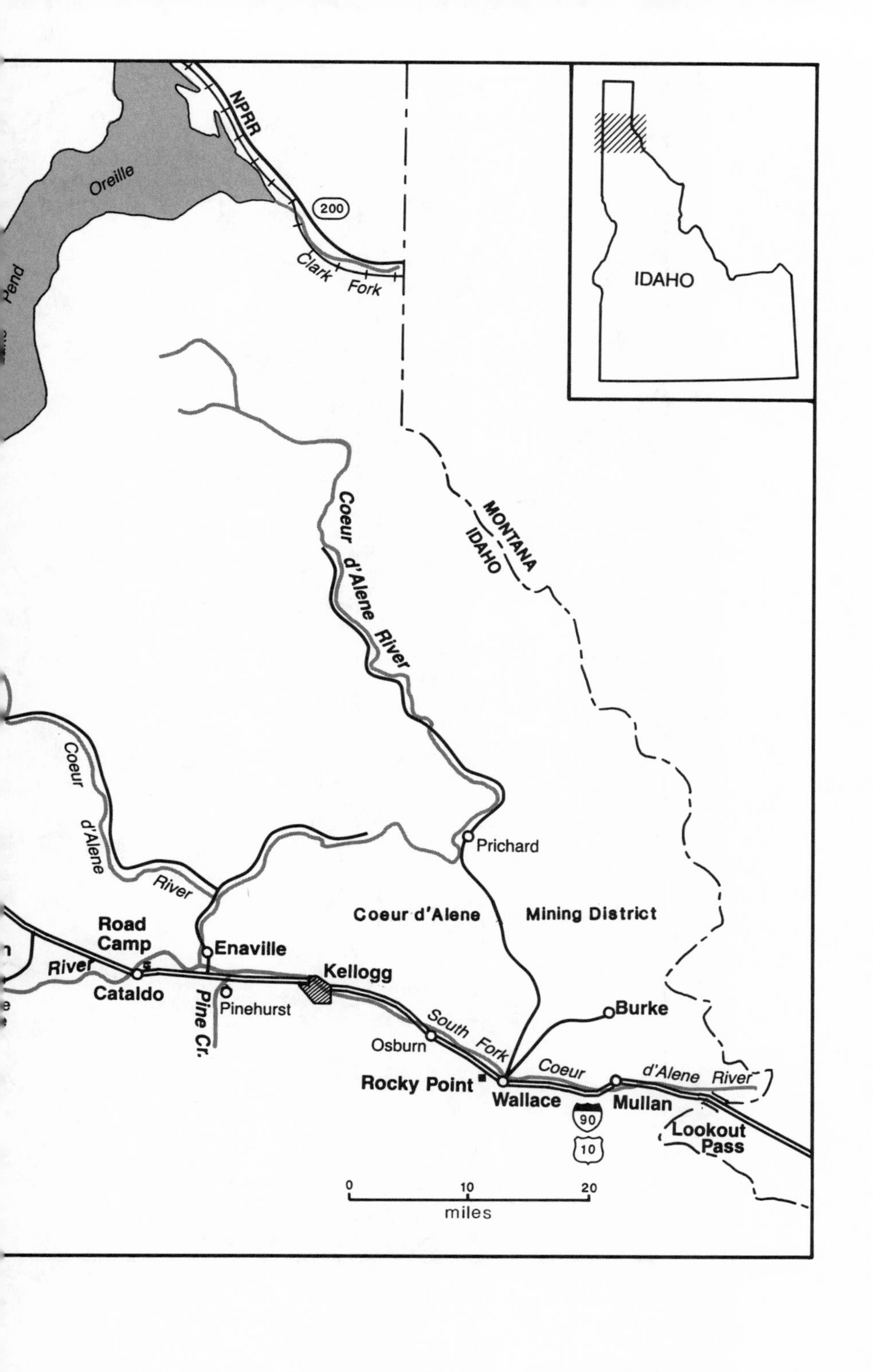

NPRR
Oreille
Pend
200
Clark Fork
IDAHO
MONTANA
IDAHO
Coeur d'Alene River
Coeur d'Alene River
Prichard
Coeur d'Alene Mining District
Road Camp
Enaville
River
Cataldo
Kellogg
Pine Cr.
Pinehurst
South Fork
Osburn
Burke
Rocky Point
Wallace
Coeur d'Alene River
Mullan
90
10
Lookout Pass
0 10 20
miles

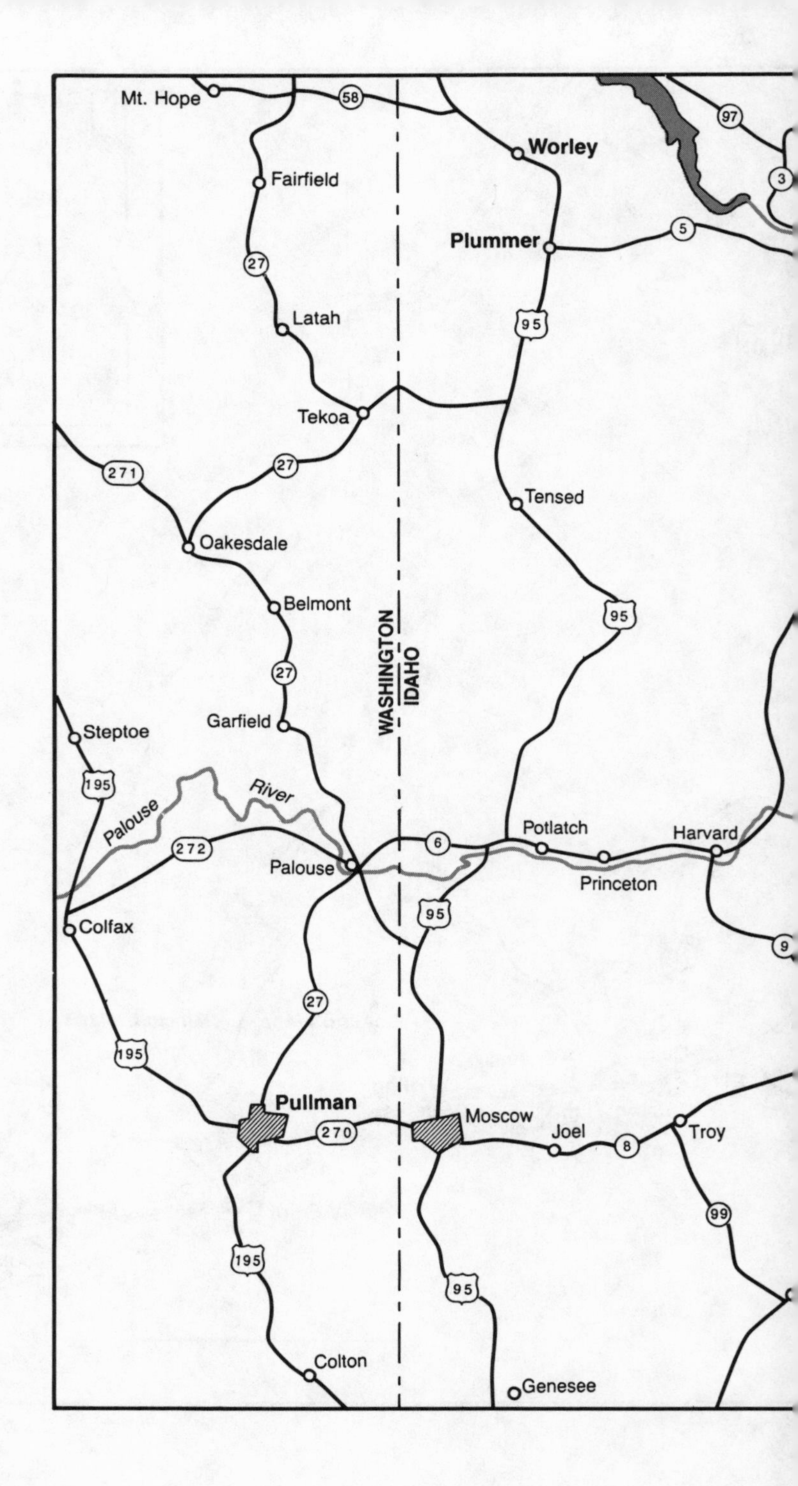
Mt. Hope
58
97
Worley
3
Fairfield
Plummer
5
27
95
Latah
Tekoa
27
271
Tensed
Oakesdale
Belmont
95
WASHINGTON
IDAHO
27
Garfield
Steptoe
195
River
Palouse
Potlatch
Harvard
6
272
Palouse
Princeton
95
Colfax
9
27
195
Pullman
270
Moscow
Joel
8
Troy
99
195
95
Colton
Genesee

Map 4

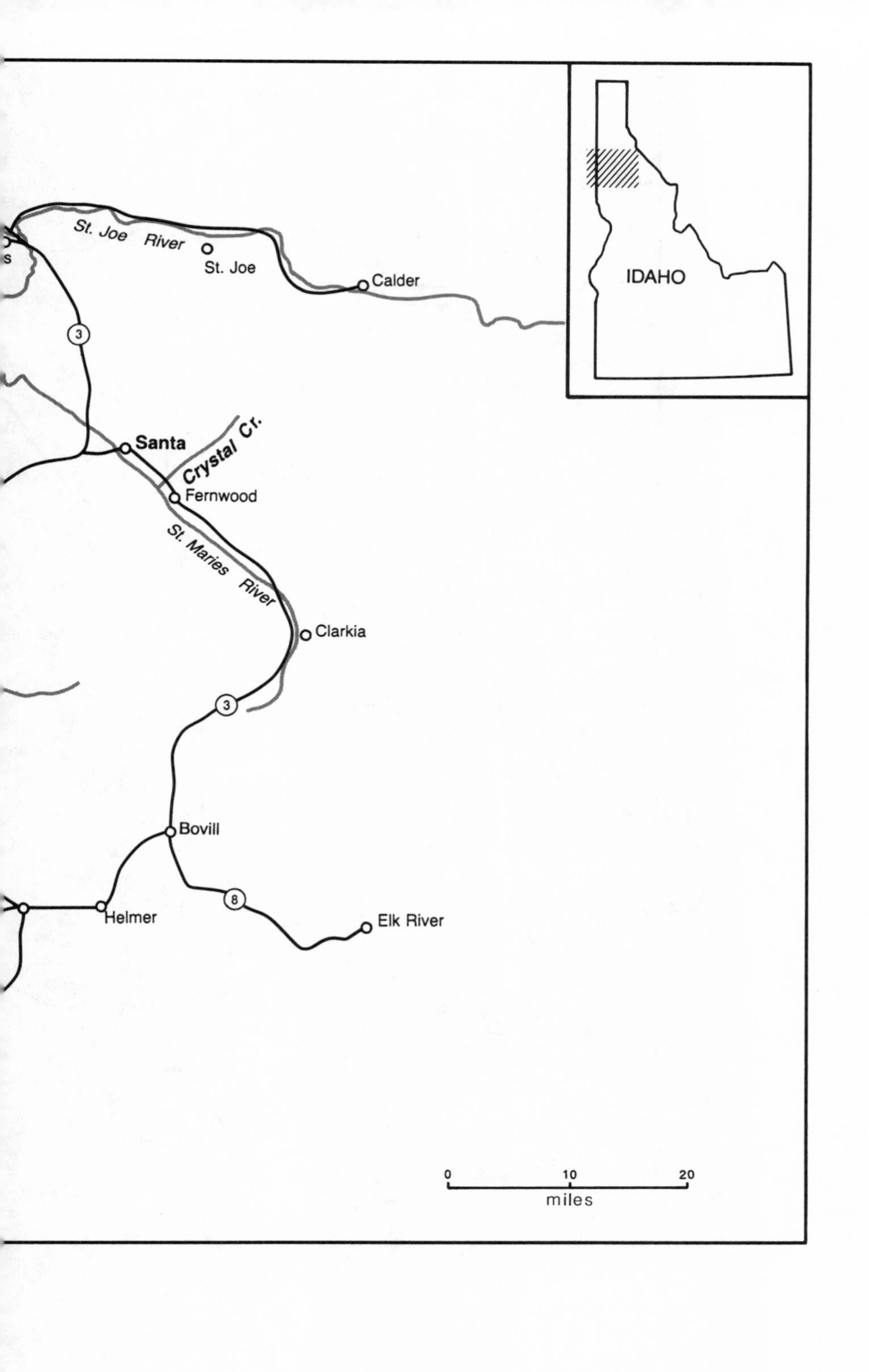

St. Joe River
St. Joe
Calder
IDAHO
3
Santa
Crystal Cr.
Fernwood
St. Maries River
Clarkia
3
Bovill
Helmer
8
Elk River
0
10
20
miles

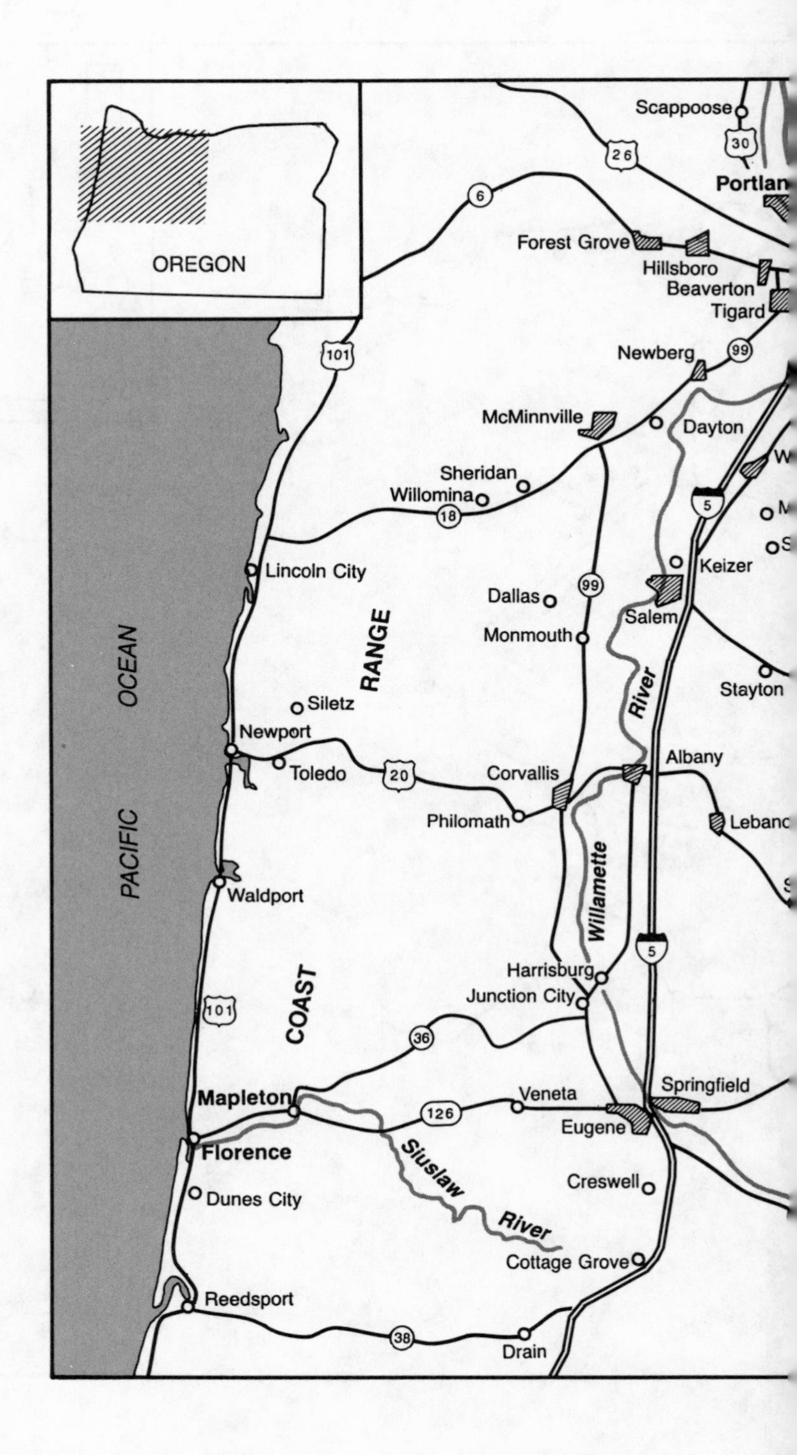
OREGON
Scappoose
30
26
6
Forest Grove
Hillsboro
Beaverton
Tigard
101
Newberg
99
McMinnville
Dayton
Sheridan
Willomina
18
5
Lincoln City
Keizer
Dallas
99
Salem
Monmouth
RANGE
OCEAN
River
Stayton
Siletz
Newport
Toledo
20
Corvallis
Albany
Philomath
PACIFIC
Waldport
Willamette
5
Harrisburg
Junction City
101
COAST
36
Mapleton
Veneta
126
Springfield
Eugene
Florence
Siuslaw
Creswell
Dunes City
River
Cottage Grove
Reedsport
38
Drain

Map 5

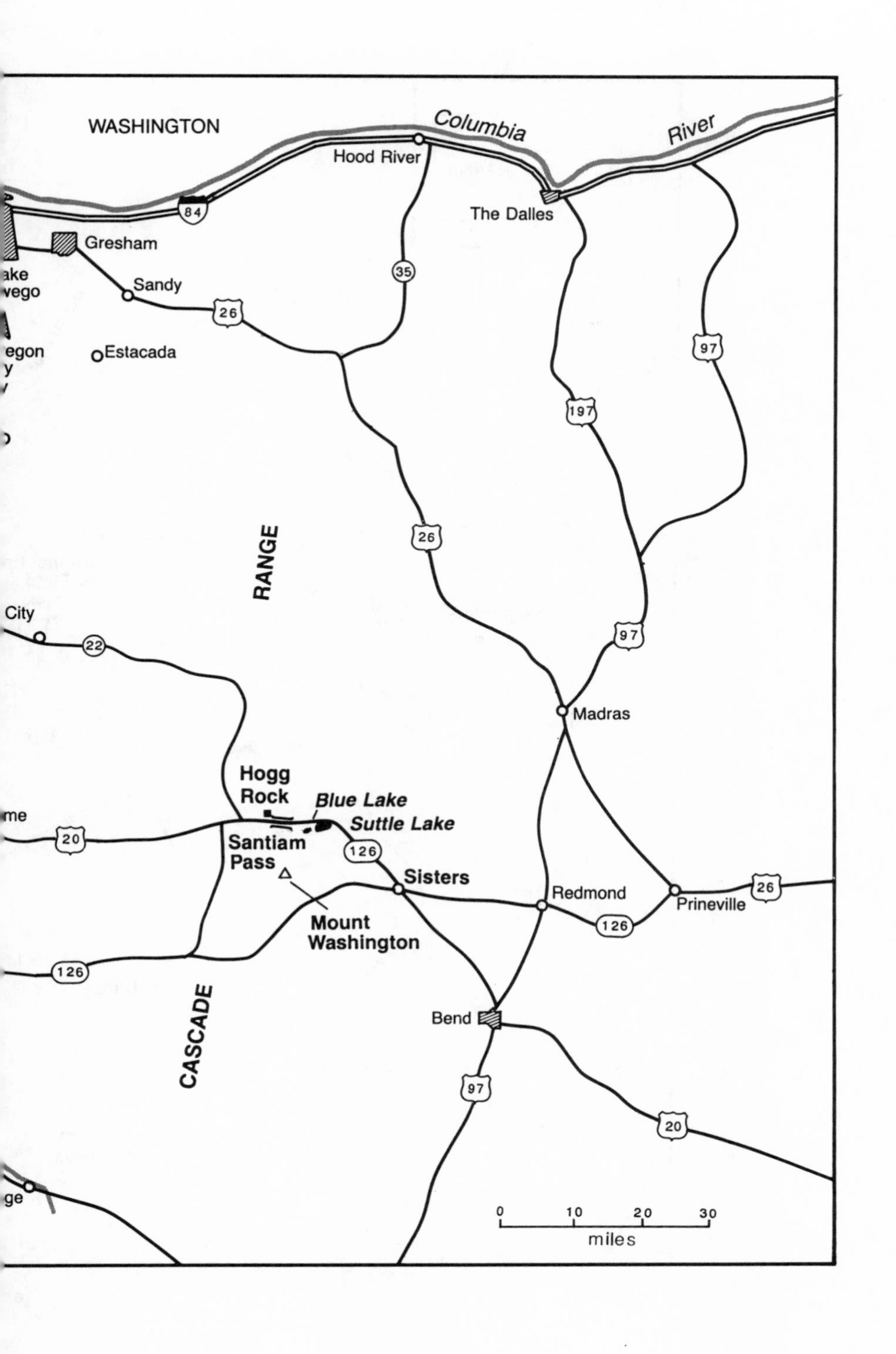

WASHINGTON
Columbia
River
Hood River
The Dalles
84
Gresham
Sandy
26
35
Estacada
97
197
RANGE
26
City
22
97
Madras
Hogg
Rock
Blue Lake
Suttle Lake
20
Santiam
Pass
126
Sisters
Redmond
Prineville
26
Mount
Washington
126
126
CASCADE
Bend
97
20
0
10
20
30
miles

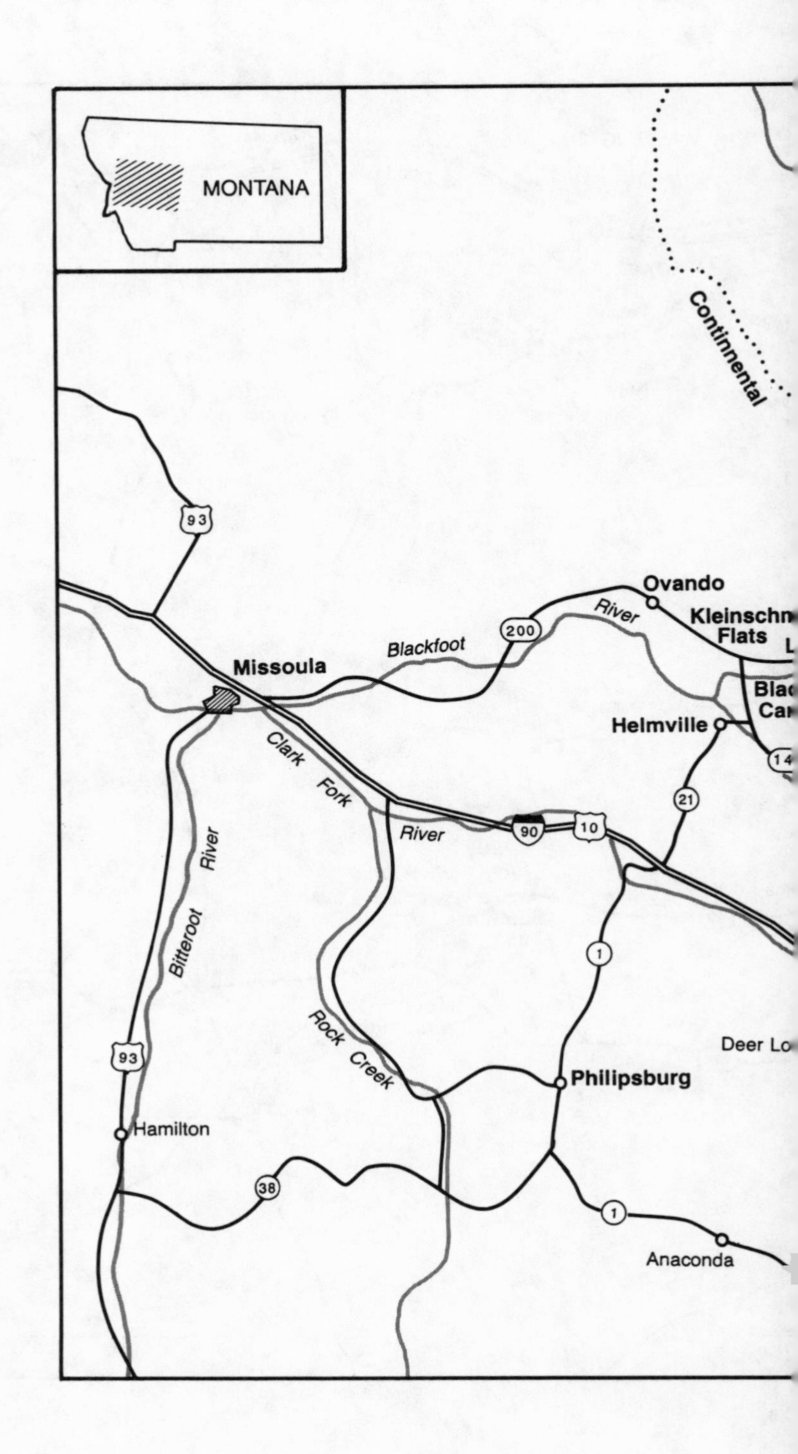

MONTANA
Continental
93
Ovando
River
Flats
200
Blackfoot
Missoula
Helmville
Clark
Fork
21
River
90
10
River
Bitteroot
1
Rock
Creek
93
Philipsburg
Hamilton
38
1
Anaconda

Map 6

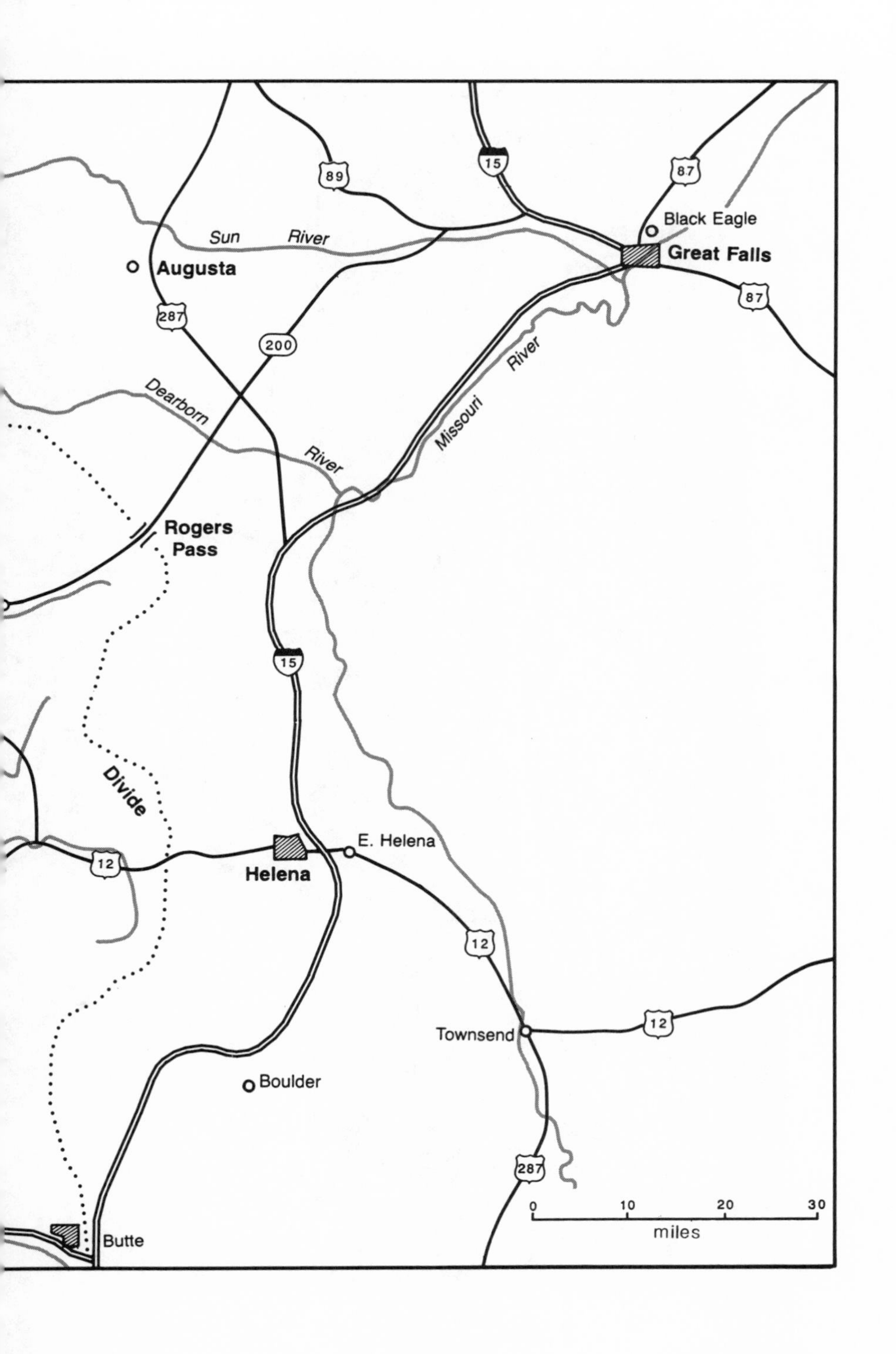
Black Eagle
Great Falls
Sun River
Augusta
Dearborn River
Missouri River
Rogers Pass
Divide
Helena
E. Helena
Townsend
Boulder
Butte
0 10 20 30
miles
89
15
87
287
200
12

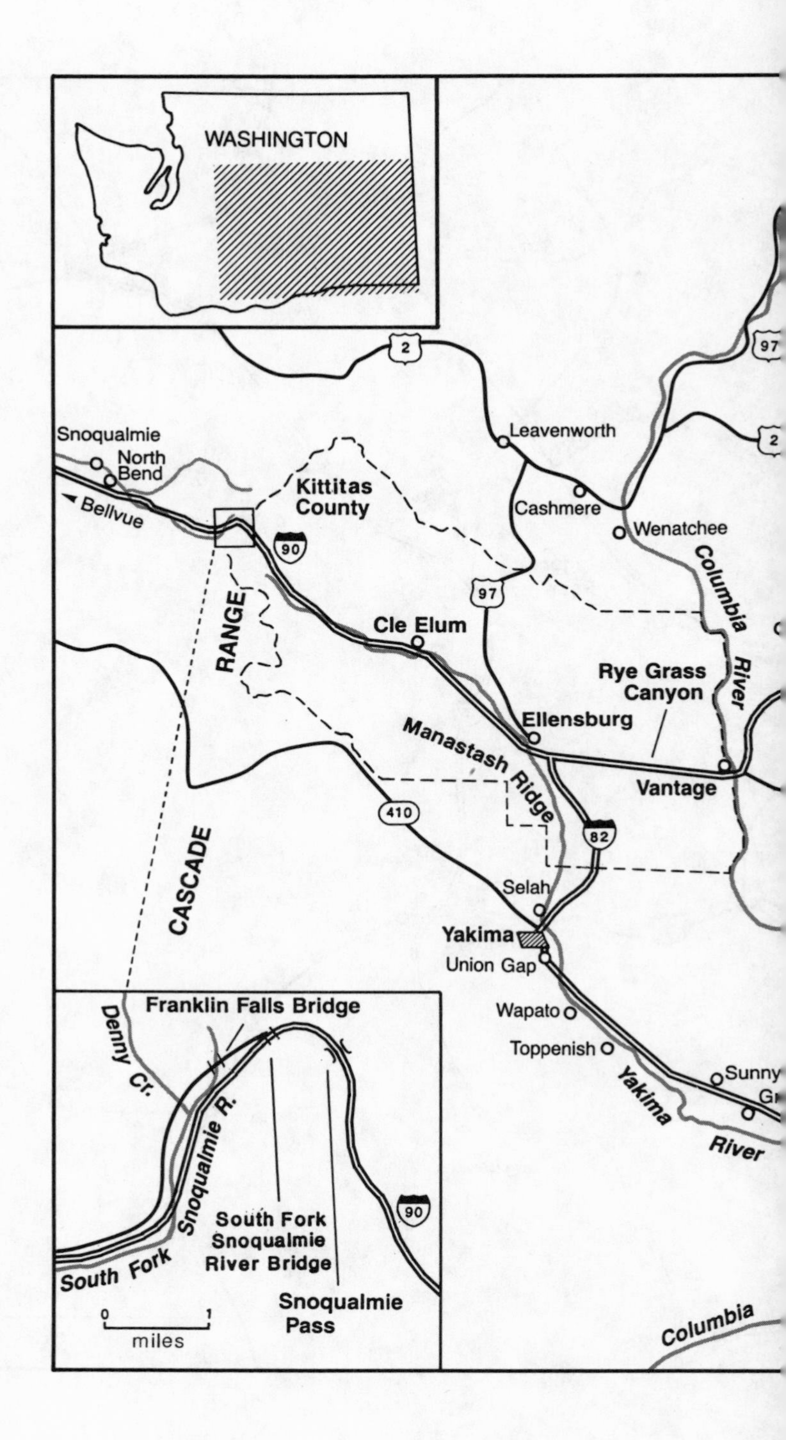

WASHINGTON
2
97
2
Snoqualmie
North Bend
Bellvue
Leavenworth
Kittitas County
Cashmere
Wenatchee
90
97
RANGE
Cle Elum
Columbia River
Rye Grass Canyon
Ellensburg
Manastash Ridge
Vantage
410
82
CASCADE
Selah
Yakima
Union Gap
Franklin Falls Bridge
Denny Cr.
Wapato
Toppenish
Yakima River
Snoqualmie R.
South Fork
90
South Fork Snoqualmie River Bridge
Snoqualmie Pass
0
1
miles
Columbia

Map 7

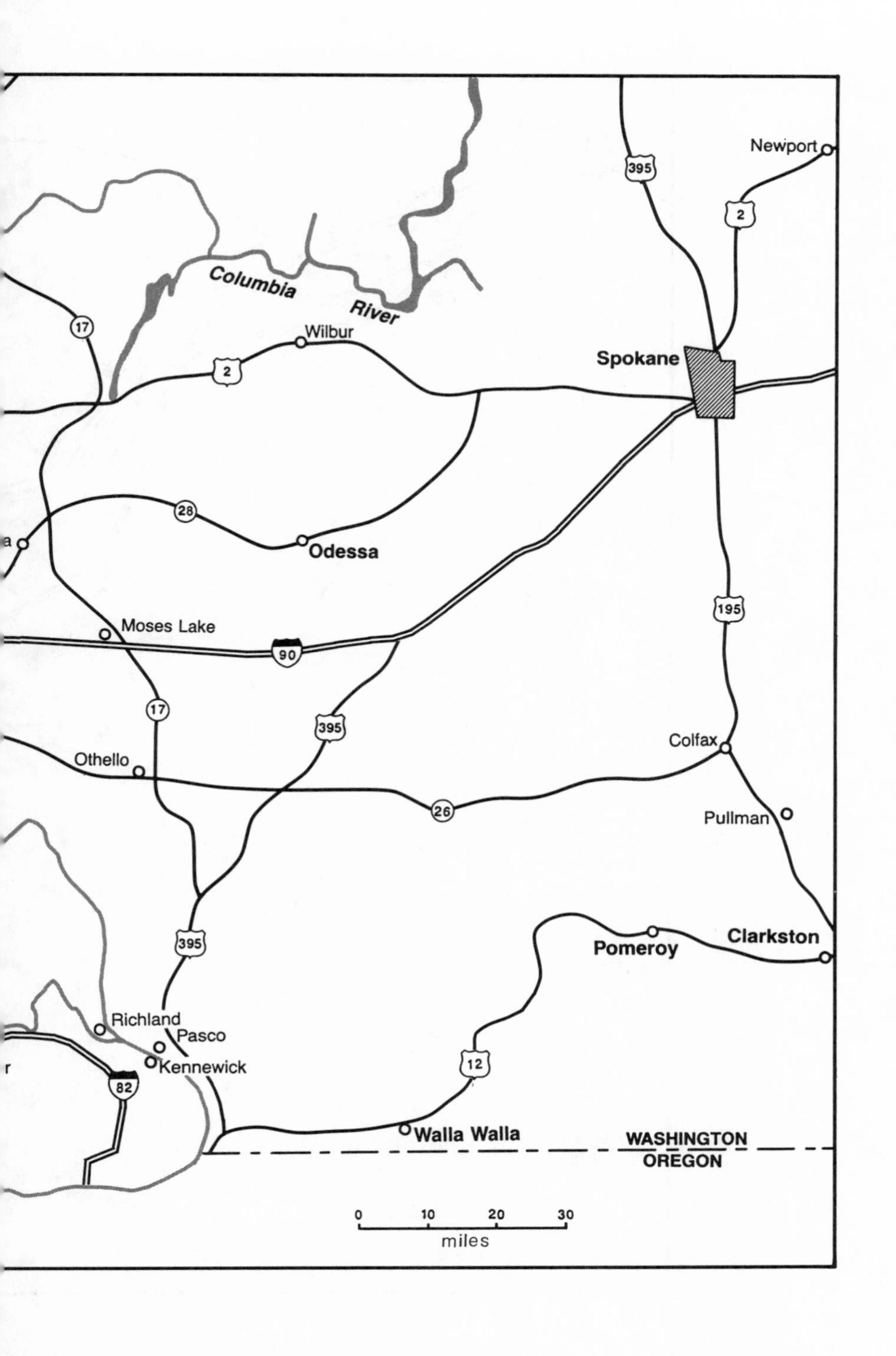
Newport
395
2
Columbia
River
17
Wilbur
Spokane
2
28
Odessa
195
Moses Lake
90
17
395
Colfax
Othello
26
Pullman
395
Pomeroy
Clarkston
Richland
Pasco
Kennewick
12
82
Walla Walla
WASHINGTON
OREGON
0
10
20
30
miles

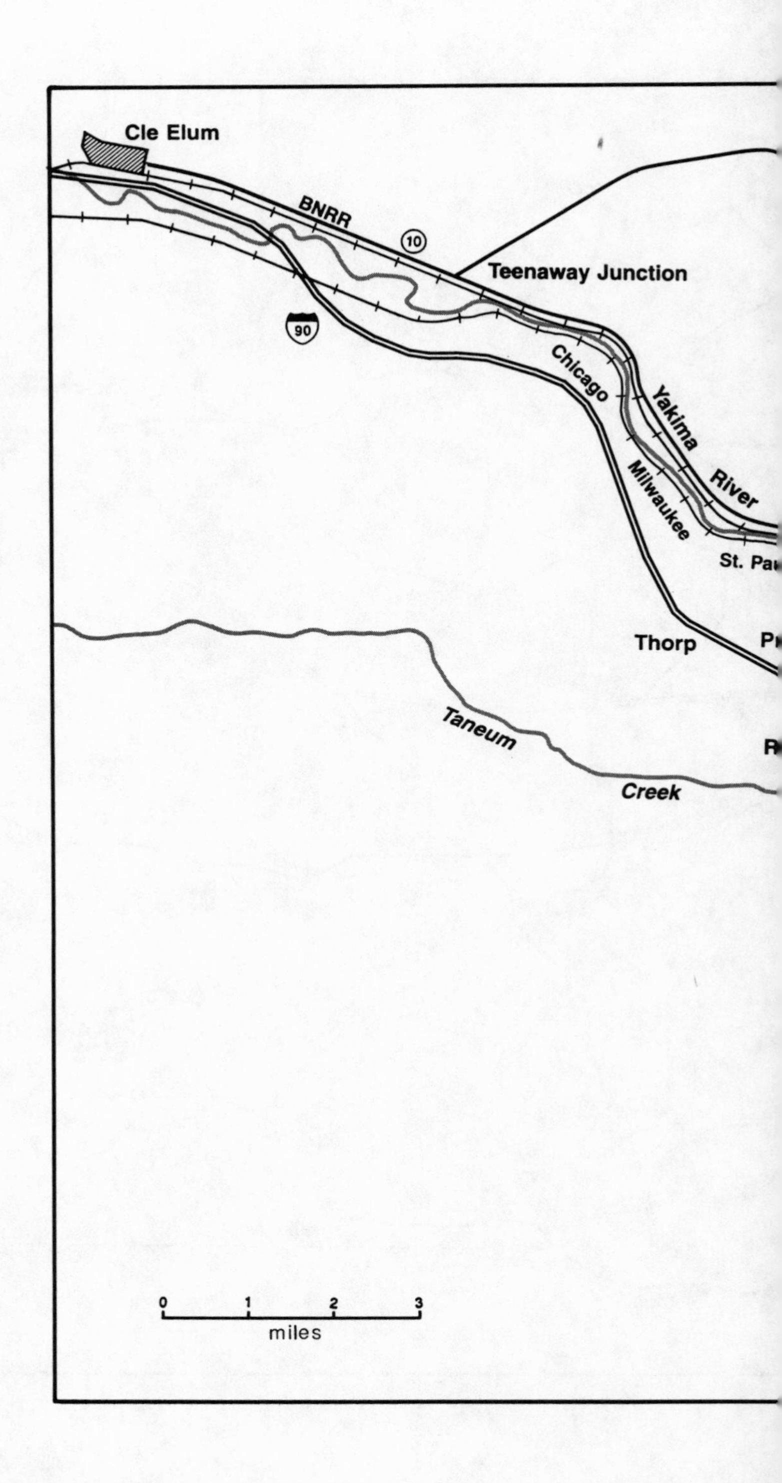
Cle Elum
BNRR
10
Teenaway Junction
90
Chicago
Yakima
River
Milwaukee
Thorp
Taneum
Creek
0
1
2
3
miles

Map 8

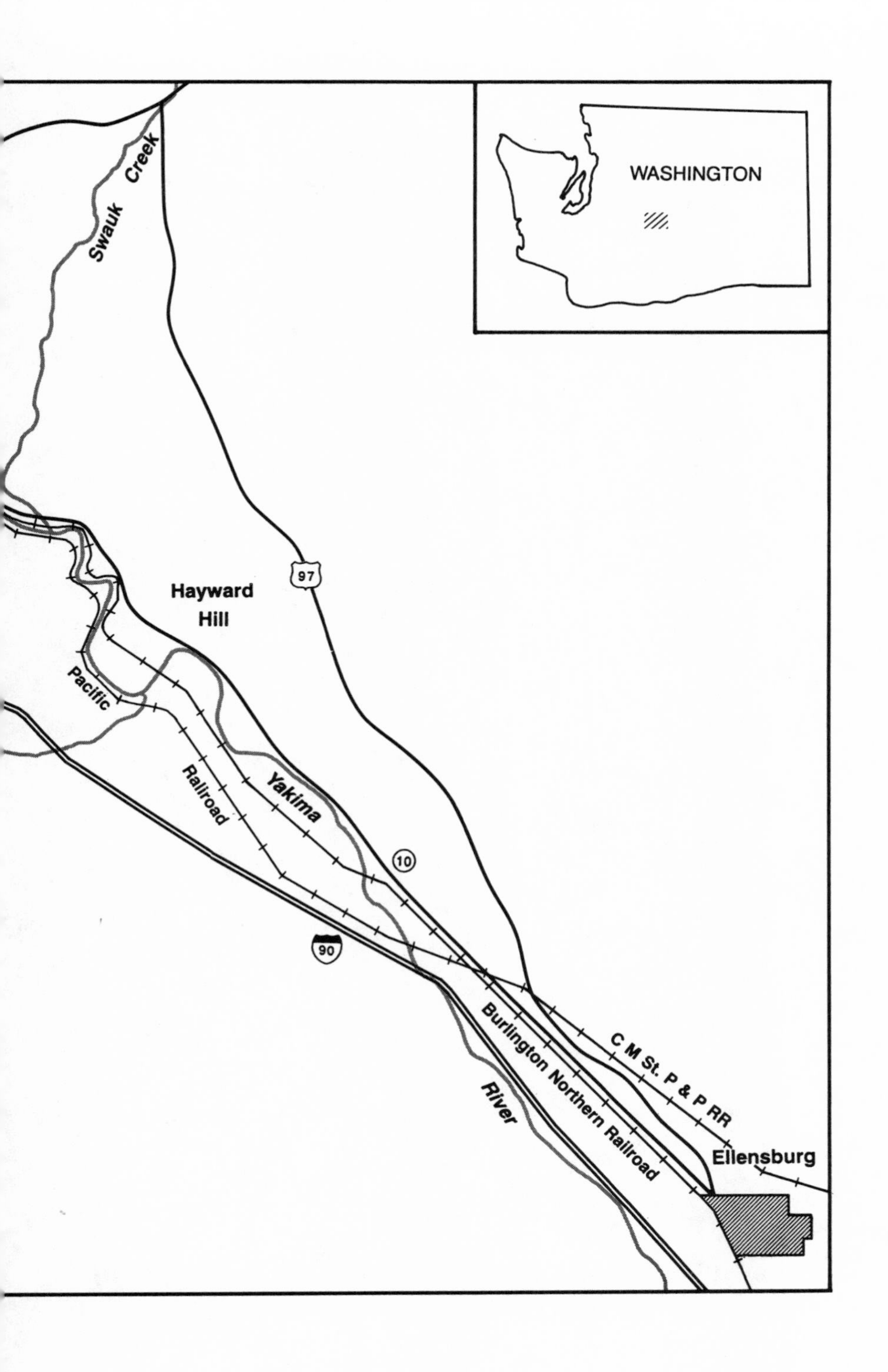
WASHINGTON
Swauk Creek
Hayward Hill
97
Pacific
Railroad
Yakima
10
90
River
Burlington Northern Railroad
C M St. P & P RR
Ellensburg